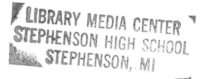

HITLER

THE MISSING YEARS

By Ernst Hanfstaengl

Introduction by John Toland

Afterword by Egon Hanfstaengl

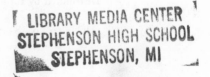

Arcade Publishing • New York

FIRST ARCADE EDITION 1994

First published in England in 1957

Library of Congress Cataloging-in-Publication Data

Hanfstaengl, Ernst, 1887–1975
Hitler : the missing years / Ernst Hanfstaengl ; introduction by John
Toland ; afterword by Egon Hanfstaengl. – 1st Arcade pbk. ed.
p.   cm.
Originally published: London : Eyre & Spottiswoode, 1957.
ISBN 1-55970-278-8 (hc.)
ISBN 1-55970-272-9 (pb.)
1. Hitler, Adolf, 1889–1945.   2. Heads of state – Germany – Biography.
3. Germany – Politics and government – 1918–1933.
I. Title.
DD247.H5H312   1994
943.086'092 – dc20
[B]   94-17042

Published in the United States by Arcade Publishing, Inc., New York
Distributed by Little, Brown and Company

HC: 10 9 8 7 6 5 4 3 2 1
PB: 10 9 8 7 6 5 4 3 2 1

BP

PRINTED IN THE U.S.A.

To the Memory
of
OSWALD SPENGLER
(1880–1936)
Historian, Philosopher, Patriot and Friend
whose unheeded warnings and prophecies
about Hitler became such grim reality

CONTENTS

INTRODUCTION BY JOHN TOLAND   5

FOREWORD TO THE ORIGINAL EDITION   9

INTRODUCTION TO THE ORIGINAL EDITION   11

LETTER TO THE AUTHOR FROM HERMANN GOERING   17

I Harvard's Gift to Hitler   21

The dozen years that made Hitler – My schooldays
with Himmler's father – Sedgwick, Heine and
Hanfstaengl forbears – Harvard and Theodore
Roosevelt – Conflict on Fifth Avenue – The predictions of a German Jew – The American military
attaché speaks of Hitler – Introduction to an
agitator.

II Tristan in the Thierschstrasse   38

Sugar in the wine – Rosenberg – The infantryman's
guide – Fitting Hitler for society – The *Stammitsch*
at the Café Neumaier – Cranks and intimates – The
basic reading of a dictator – Wagner on an upright
piano – From *Falarah* to *Sieg Heil* – A woman's
reaction – A pamphlet becomes a newspaper.

III One Side to a Statue   55

Begging expeditions – Hitler escapes a Communist
patrol – From bombs to women boxers – Hitler's
fixation with Leda and the Swan – His *faux pas* as
an art expert – Diamonds and a fedora hat – The
plans for Czechoslovakia – Hitler's gifts as a mimic –
Poison on his birthday – Orator in excelsis – Goering,
Hess and Haushofer.

IV *Particular Generals* 75

Ferment in Bavaria – Hitler and Roehm – Pyromania in the Rhineland – Jewish anti-Semites –
Dietrich Eckart loses faith – Rhinoceros whips in the
courtyard – Rosenberg insults the Catholics – An
offer from Mathilde Ludendorff – Hitler tempts
General von Seeckt – Compromising reluctant
allies.

V *Fiasco at the Feldherrnhalle* 91

Plan for a Putsch – Cracks in the *Kampfbund* –
Double-cross at the Bürgerbräu – Kahrfreitag – Red
wine for Ludendorff – Fusillade in the Residenzstrasse – My escape to Austria – Hitler's attempted
suicide.

VI *Twilight at Landsberg* 110

Goering in exile – A first sight of Geli Raubal –
Hitler's hunger strike – The acrobat of the cells –
Duel for the leadership – Welcome with *Liebestod*
– The narrowing of a mind – Operatic eroticism –
The man on the tight-rope.

VII *Hitler and Henry VIII* 126

A revision of *Mein Kampf* – No waltzes for the
Führer – Ludendorff for President – The return of
Rosenberg – A world tour rejected – The scaffold
block at the Tower – Hitler on his knees – Forced
repayment of a debt.

VIII *The Bohemian at the Brown House* 140

Art versus politics – The return of Goering – A red
ground for the Swastika – The radicalism of
Goebbels – Appearance of a Hohenzollern – An
electoral triumph – Picking the first team – Interlude with the press – A letter from the Kaiser –
Committed to the Nazis.

IX   *Geli Raubal*   *161*

Hitler takes a luxury flat – The amours of his niece – Pornographic drawings and blackmail – Soprano without talent – The unwilling sub-tenant – Suicide – Corpse without inquest – Hara-kiri and a pregnancy – The impotent Herostratus.

X   *Lohengrin Prevails*   *170*

Poacher and gamekeeper – Prejudices strengthened – The Prussians of Asia – Peripatetic boredom – The court minstrel – Assertion at arm's length – Encounter with Churchill – A message from Roosevelt – Split with Strasser – Buskers in the Kaiserhof – Two organized disappointments – No mate for the glow-worm.

XI   *Disillusionment at Nuremberg*   *196*

Neurath versus Rosenberg – First brush with Goering – Reichstag fire fever – Goebbels at Potsdam – The one-man revolution – Interventions with Himmler – Hostages for a policy – No make-up for the Mitfords – The shape of things to come.

XII   *Circus at the Chancellery*   *216*

Metternichs in shirt-sleeves – Three lunches a day – Rings around a dictator – King Kong and Ludwig II – America from a chair – The schizopedic radical – The wine merchant who deserted – The loyalties of a Fouché – A flag without a pole – Intercession with Mussolini.

XIII   *A Murderer's Welcome*   *240*

Palm court interlude – Disguised departure – Shock on the high seas – Harvard, class of '09 – The liquidation of Roehm – Assassin at bay – The mad hatter's lunch party – The Flying Dutchman.

XIV   The Last Chord   254

Aftermath of a purge – What happened at Wiessee
– Austrian misadventure – Short shrift at Neudeck
– A wheel comes full circle – Funeral March fare-
well – Analysis of a medium – The prophet and the
caliph – The militant revivalist – Pinchbeck Pericles
– The tragedy of an orator.

XV   Wilderness and Flight   271

Unacknowledged banishment – The warning of
Rosalind von Schirach – No bed of my own – The
Chancellery on the telephone – A mission to Spain –
The intrusive cameraman – Goering's plot frus-
trated – A race with the Gestapo – Fiftieth birthday
of a fugitive – Unity Mitford repeats a remark –
No joke on a parachute.

XVI   The Catoctin Conversation   287

Bodenschatz as emissary – Egon abstracted –
Bribes, blandishments and threats – The warning
of Reichenau – The non-enemy alien – Eels in a
bathing hut – Cramped quarters in Canada –
Haushofer *triunfans* – An offer to Roosevelt – State
prisoner at Bush Hill – Reports for a President – No
inducement to revolt – A black-list ignored –
Return to the ruins – No world for Hitlers.

AFTERWORD BY EGON HANFSTAENGL   303

INTRODUCTION

ERNST HANFSTAENGL was a man with two countries. His mother came from a well-known New England family, the Sedgwicks, and two of his ancestors were Civil War generals, one of whom helped carry Lincoln's coffin. In Germany two generations of Hanfstaengls had served as privy counsellors to the dukes of Saxe-Coburg-Gotha and were connoisseurs and patrons of the arts. The family owned an art-publishing house in Munich well known for its excellent reproductions.

Hanfstaengl had been brought up in an atmosphere of art and music and was himself an accomplished pianist. I have spent many hours in his Munich home listening to him play the piano with verve, his six-foot-four frame hunched over the piano, making him look like an impish bear. His nickname was Putzi (little fellow).

Adolf Hitler too had been enthralled by Putzi's music, and made him one of his closest associates in 1922. After hearing Hitler speak at a beer hall, Hanfstaengl had been fascinated by his control of the audience. "People," he wrote, "were sitting breathlessly, who had long since forgotten to reach for their beer mugs and instead were drinking in the speaker's every word." Nearby a young woman was staring at Hitler: "As though in some devotional ecstasy, she had ceased to be herself and was completely under the spell of Hitler's despotic faith in Germany's future greatness."

On the spur of the moment Putzi introduced himself. "About ninety-five percent of what you said I can set my name to, and five percent – we will have to talk about that." What he particularly objected to was Hitler's blatant anti-Semitism.

Like so many others in Germany, Hanfstaengl imagined he could control Hitler. He loaned the Führer a thousand dollars, interest free, which enabled Hitler to purchase two American rotary presses and turn his weekly Nazi newspaper into a daily. Putzi also became his foreign Press secretary.

Hitler soon became a fixture in the Hanfstaengl apartment. He fell in love with Helene Hanfstaengl and played games with her two-year-old son, Egon. He also became fascinated with Hanfstaengl's music. "Hitler dragged me around from house to house as his resident musician, and had me sit down at the piano to perform." On one occasion

5

Putzi began playing Harvard's football marches and explained how cheerleaders and marching bands would stir up the crowd to almost hysterical mass shouting. When Hitler's interest quickened, he demonstrated on the piano how the buoyant American beat could be injected into German marches, and Hitler started parading up and down like a drum major. "This is what I need for the movement!" he exclaimed. Hanfstaengl wrote several marches in this style for the S.A. band, but his most significant contribution was the transference of Harvard's "Fight! Fight! Fight!" to "Sieg Heil! Sieg Heil! Sieg Heil!"

Hitler became even closer to the Hanfstaengls after he fled from the disastrous Beer Hall Putsch and sought refuge in their country home. Here he was captured and sent to prison; and one of the first places he visited after his release was the Hanfstaengls' new home across the Isar River. It was here the Führer came on Christmas Eve to regain his composure. First he asked Putzi to play the *Liebestod* and then he romped with Egon, marching up and down like a soldier, showing the child how to carry his little sabre and imitating the sound of an artillery barrage. Later, when alone with Helene, he put his head in her lap and said, "If only I had someone to take care of me!" But he could never marry, he told her, because his life was dedicated to his country. "I thought he was acting like a little boy – not a lover – and perhaps he was," recalled Helene. "It would have been awful if someone had come in. He was taking a chance, he really was. That was the end of it and I passed it off as if it had simply not happened."

Hanfstaengl remained as Hitler's Press secretary for years. Like many of those who had helped put Hitler in power, he thought he could stem Hitler's excesses. But by 1936 Martin Bormann's influence over the Führer had gained dominance, and Putzi was reduced to a minor role. For some time the Führer had been annoyed because Hanfstaengl called him "Herr Hitler" instead of "Mein Führer" and talked to him like an equal.

Hanfstaengl knew he was in danger and told Egon, now fifteen, "Things are not well. We all believed in the movement, didn't we? I am still trying to believe in it." But he had found corruption everywhere, and war was coming with England and America. "The country is in a foul state internally. I ascribe that mainly to the blackguards who are sitting firmly entrenched behind official desks in Berlin and elsewhere. But Hitler refuses to hear me." And it looked as though the Führer himself had become corrupt.

Hanfstaengl warned his son that his enemies were almost sure to get around to liquidating him sooner or later. Several months later, on February 11, 1937 – Putzi's birthday – Hitler ordered him to fly to Spain and protect the interests of German correspondents in Franco's country. Soon after takeoff the pilot revealed that once over the area between Barcelona and Madrid, Hanfstaengl would be forced to parachute into the Red lines. That would mean death. The sympathetic pilot said nothing more, but soon one of the motors began spluttering. With a meaningful look he told Hanfstaengl that they would have to land at a small airfield.

Once on the ground, Putzi said he was going to call Berlin for instructions. Instead he phoned his secretary in Berlin, telling her that his orders had been suddenly changed and he was going to spend his fiftieth birthday with his family in Bavaria. Then he informed the pilot that the Führer had ordered him to return to Uffing. Instead he took a night train to Munich and a morning train that took him to freedom in Zurich.

The revelations in this reprint of Hanfstaengl's classic memoir will enrich the reader's understanding of Hitler, the twentieth-century Napoleon. Some historians have dismissed Hanfstaengl as a mountebank, but, with all his quirks, he was one of the few who ever stood up to the Führer and then lived to write about it in fascinating detail.

JOHN TOLAND

FOREWORD TO THE ORIGINAL EDITION

THE FINAL impulse that led to the compilation and publication of these memoirs I owe to Mr. Brian Connell. We met some years ago and he, while writing his own books, never lost sight of the story he thought I could tell. He came to Germany again in 1956 and discussed in detail a scheme of collaboration, to which I agreed. Our method was this: Mr. Connell spent two months in Bavaria and every day, for hours on end, took tape recordings of my discourse. His imagination and enthusiasm as an interrogator succeeded in overcoming my reluctance to dive into the sour memory of those desperate years. From these recordings and from previously compiled material of my own, he then prepared a draft manuscript, which resulted, after joint revision, in the present text. The burden of transcribing my roving reminiscences fell upon poor Mrs. Connell, to whom I therefore owe a large measure of gratitude.

I am no less indebted to my own wife, Renata, for her active help with the secretarial chores and for patiently putting up with the unending domestic upheavals that always go together with literary labours.

The story, of course, and the responsibility for it are mine, but full credit must go to Mr. Connell for having devised a relatively painless method of reducing speech to print and for having filtered out unnecessary detail.

Finally I want to pay tribute to those without whom there would have been no story: to my friends and comrades of those years – many of them no longer alive – who stuck by me, who hoped, worked and took risks, only to be cruelly disillusioned just as I was.

ERNST HANFSTAENGL
Munich
March 1957

INTRODUCTION TO THE ORIGINAL EDITION

IN THE YEARS following World War Two, as key figures of the Nazi era dropped out of the picture, firsthand accounts of that period were lost to history. It quickly became impossible to reconstruct from eye-witnesses the astonishing story of the twenty years between the two wars that brought Hitler to power and the Western world very nearly to its knees.

Those seeking to analyse the motive force of these two decades would be surprised to discover how many members of Hitler's immediate entourage survived the war years. Most of them were seedy relics, uncomfortable ghosts in dirty raincoats, haunting this or that Munich suburb: Emil Maurice, an early intimate and his first chauffeur; Hermann Esser, one of the few Party orators who could hold his own with his master; Heinrich Hoffmann, crony-photographer; Sepp Dietrich, bodyguard and later S.S. general – even one-armed Max Amann, who published *Mein Kampf* and the *Völkischer Beobachter*. In retrospect, they were all minor figures, with neither the insight nor the perception to give a coherent account of the political genius and monster in whose wake they had their being. But one survivor of the years that brought Hitler from obscurity to power was of a very different calibre – Dr. Ernst F. Sedgwick ("Putzi") Hanfstaengl.

Hanfstaengl was a representative of that dwindling human species – a character. His appearance alone singled him out in any crowd. He was a towering six-foot-four, the thick hair on his enormous head barely specked with grey even into his seventies. The twinkling eyes above the bold nose and prognathous jaw reflected the endless stream of humorous comment and brazen *boutades* that composed his conversational fireworks. His huge hands could rend a piano in the direct tradition of the Lisztian romantics, and there were few men who dared question his judgement in matters of pictorial art. Of mixed German-American parentage and upbringing, what somehow came through was pure Celt. As he looked back on the bitterness of a life that had included nearly ten years of exile, the mobile face could assume the air of an avenging Druid.

In the little group of provincial plotters who gravitated to Hitler during the inchoate years after World War One, Hanfstaengl must have stood out like a sore thumb. He had left Germany at the height of her imperial glory to work in the United States and came back to find his country crushed and desolate. His romantic nature was fired by the incandescent promise of this almost unknown agitator, his disillusionment only completed by the triumph he had intuitively foreseen. He became the only literate member of Hitler's inner circle, and brought to this relationship far more than he ever received. When he progressed from being Hitler's window on the outside world and artistic mentor to the role of unwelcome conscience, he found himself frozen out. The process took a dozen years, but then he had to run for his life.

With his American wife, Hanfstaengl represented a new factor in Hitler's existence. The family name was one to conjure with in Munich. His father and grandfather had been welcome counsellors at the Wittelsbach and Coburg courts. They were respected pioneers in the field of art reproduction and prominent members of the Romantic movement represented by Richard Wagner and Ludwig II, the last, mad, royal Maecenas of Bavaria. Hanfstaengl himself provided the aura of Harvard, a genuine acquaintance with past, actual, and future presidents of the United States, *entrée* not only to the best Munich and German society, but attachment to the intangible net of international social intercourse, and an artistic accomplishment which went straight to the heart of Hitler's tortured soul – the ability to play Wagner's music superbly on the piano.

To hear Hanfstaengl thunder through the crescendos of the *Meistersinger* prelude or of the *Liebestod* was an experience. The powerful fingers had, after the war, lost some of their cunning, and the associations of mood served anecdotal reminiscence rather than musical memory, but it was still possible to perceive the hold this talent had on the immature mind that Hanfstaengl had once tried to influence. For this was the impossible task that Hanfstaengl set himself in those embryonic years – to mould into some statesmanlike form the spellbinding oratorical gifts and immanent potential of Adolf Hitler.

In contrast to such provincial academicians as Dietrich Eckart and Gottfried Feder, and pseudointellectual fanatics like Rudolf Hess and Alfred Rosenberg, Hanfstaengl was the only educated man of good family and cultural background at Hitler's elbow. Hanfstaengl had lived fifteen years in the United States, remaining at liberty on parole even when America entered the war. He was deeply imbued with the latent strength of the maritime powers, and tried to wean Hitler away from the Balts who wanted revenge against Russia and the military fanatics who wanted revenge against France. His thesis was that Germany would never find equilibrium and greatness again without a rapprochement with Britain and particularly the United States, of whose incredible industrial and military potential he had been a witness. The basic premise he tried to lodge firmly in Hitler's mind was that all thoughts of settling old scores on the Continent would prove illusory if the two saltwater nations were ranged on the wrong side.

A Protestant himself, Hanfstaengl tried to restrain Hitler and his chief theorist, Rosenberg, from their campaign against the Church in predominantly Catholic Bavaria. He fought political radicalism in all its forms and, while supporting the basic objective of a national renaissance, tried to attract Hitler to the traditional values he himself represented. With countless other people of his class and type, Hanfstaengl thought Hitler could be normalized, both personally and ideologically. They were all to be disillusioned and betrayed in their turn, for failing to recognize that the basic drive of Hitler's character was not reformist but nihilist.

The Hanfstaengl household was the first to try to make Hitler socially acceptable. They introduced him to the world of art and culture, and in those early years theirs was almost the only private circle in which he found himself at ease. After the Ludendorff Putsch it was to their villa in the Bavarian alps that he fled for succor. During his prison term the Hanfstaengls provided one of the few centres of loyalty and after his release made a final attempt to inculcate in him their standards. Then there was a hiatus until, with ultimate power looming ever more certain, Hanfstaengl attempted (unsuccessfully) to apply the social and musical gifts that still attracted Hitler to divert the revolution into respectable channels before it was too late.

Hanfstaengl was a merry and amusing companion, full of charm and vitality. He had a mocking, teasing way about him, an inextinguishable capacity for anecdotal embroidery and a total lack of inhibition in his remarks and comments. He enjoyed the licence of a Shakespearean jester, punctuating his rodomontade with tart and telling observations. Moreover, he possessed one channel to Hitler with which no one else could compete. In the exhausted pauses of the final political campaigns, often late at night, Hitler would turn to the form of relaxation that only Hanfstaengl could provide, the hour-long session on the piano that would ease Hitler's overwrought nerves and often make him receptive to Hanfstaengl's counsels of moderation.

With power in his hands, Hitler would start to dispense with the respectable front that Hanfstaengl, with his international connections, provided for the Party's heterogeneous hierarchy. Even after his personal break with Hitler at the end of 1934, and until his flight from Germany in February 1937, Hanfstaengl retained the nominal post of foreign Press chief of the N.S.D.A.P. His open opposition to the methods of the revolution and his unbridled criticisms of those responsible for them soon made him intolerable to those in power. Should he appear to protest unduly in his memoirs about his personal resistance and attitudes to the Nazi regime, there were plenty of witnesses, German and foreign, who could testify to every word and more. One story he does not tell is how at a crowded reception he called Goebbels a swine to his face. Ten further years of exile, internment, and frustration were the price he had to pay for his early idealism.

He ended his days modestly in the same house in Munich that once echoed with the voices of Hitler, Goering, Goebbels, Eva Braun and others long dead. By association and temperament he could place himself for hours in a state of total recall. Not only was he one of the best raconteurs of his time, but a superb mimic who could remember the atmosphere and tone of voice of conversations held twenty-five and thirty-five years earlier. To close one's eyes and hear Hitler thundering, Goering expostulating, and early leaders like Dietrich Eckart and Christian Weber declaiming was to undergo an experiment in time. Like his erstwhile intimate, Hanfstaengl was a master of the spoken word. Somewhere in the memoirs I have reconstituted with him, he talks of the marches and musical compositions for which he had provided the melody, relying on others to complete the orchestration. I have had the exhilarating task of orchestrating his flood of reminiscence.

As a man of true artistic temperament, he had a psychological insight into Hitler's personal character and repressions not remotely matched by anyone in constant contact with him during the formative years they were together. To the incomplete if extensive patchwork of Hitlerian biography and Nazi history he brings a conclusive picture of Hitler, the man in the making. He was able to evaluate as an intelligent intimate the neuroses that determined Hitler's megalomania. There is no record like it because no other man is or has ever been equipped to tell the story. If the question is asked what political influence Hanfstaengl had on this unbalanced demon, then the answer, ultimately, must be none. It was to Hanfstaengl's credit that he remained untainted by the regime's excesses. In the end Hitler only listened to those who pandered to his prejudices and wholly destructive passions. But as a chronicler of the process that made him what he became, Ernst Hanfstaengl was unique.

BRIAN CONNELL

Hermann Goering's letter to the author following the latter's flight to avoid assassination at the hands of the Nazi regime. See overleaf for translation.

Berlin W 8, den 19. März 1937
Leipziger Str. 8.
Fernspr.: A 2 Flora 6341, 7071.

Lieber Hanfstaengl!

Wie mir heute mitgeteilt worden ist, befindest Du Dich
seit einiger Zeit in Zürich und hast die Absicht, vorläufig
nicht nach Deutschland zurückzukehren.

Jch nehme an, dass die Gründe hierfür auf Deinen letzten
Flug von Staaken nach Wurzen i.Sa. zurückzuführen sind. Jch
versichere Dir, dass die ganze Angelegenheit nur einen harmlo-
sen Scherz darstellen sollte. Man wollte Dir wegen einiger
allzu kühner Behauptungen, die Du aufgestellt hast, Gelegen-
heit zum Nachdenken geben. Etwas Anderes war wirklich nicht
beabsichtigt.

Jch habe Oberst Bodenschatz zu Dir geschickt, der Dir
persönlich noch einige Aufklärungen geben wird. Jch halte es
aus verschiedenen Gründen für dringend notwendig, dass Du
mit Bodenschatz sofort nach Deutschland zurückkehrst. Jch
erkläre Dir ehrenwörtlich, dass Du Dich hier bei uns wie
immer in aller Freiheit bewegen kannst. Lass also allen Arg-
wohn fallen und handele vernünftig.

Mit kameradschaftlichen Grüssen

Heil Hitler!

*Jch erwarte, dass
Du meinem Wort
Glauben schenkst!*

Dear Hanfstaengl,

According to what I have been told today, you* are now in Zürich and do not intend for the time being to return to Germany.

I presume that the reason for this is your recent flight from Staaken to Wurzen in Saxony. I assure you that the whole affair was only intended as a harmless joke. We wanted to give you an opportunity of thinking over some rather over-audacious utterances you have made. Nothing more than that was intended.

I have sent Colonel Bodenschatz to you, who will give you further explanations in person. I consider it vitally necessary for various reasons that you come back to Germany straight away with Bodenschatz. I assure you on my word of honour that you can remain here amongst us as you always have done in complete freedom. Forget your suspicions and act reasonably.

With friendly greetings,

Heil Hitler!

HERMANN GOERING

PS. I expect you to accept my word.

* The German uses the familiar, second person singular, form.

HITLER: THE MISSING YEARS

CHAPTER I

HARVARD'S GIFT TO HITLER

The dozen years that made Hitler – My schooldays with Himmler's father – Sedgwick, Heine and Hanfstaengl forbears – Harvard and Theodore Roosevelt – Conflict on Fifth Avenue – The predictions of a German Jew – The American military attaché speaks of Hitler – Introduction to an agitator.

THE LOG-CHEST in the corner of the fireplace in my library is still covered with the travelling-rug I lent to Hitler when he was a prisoner in Landsberg. It is not a particularly hallowed memento, but a constant reminder of the dozen years of his rise to power. During that formative period I was an intimate member of his inner circle, of which I am probably the only articulate survivor. It was to my house in Munich, now laboriously regained after painful years of exile, that he came for his first meal after release from jail and where, nearly a decade later, he celebrated with Eva Braun the year of his triumph. Mine was the first Munich family of standing into which he was introduced when he was still unknown. Throughout our long association I tried to imbue him with some of the norms and ideas of civilized existence, only to be thwarted by the ignorant fanatics who were his closest cronies. I fought a running and losing battle against Rosenberg and his hazy race mystique, against Hess and Haushofer with their narrow foot-slogging misconceptions of global politics and strategy, and against the sinister and finally determining radicalism of Goebbels.

People have said I was Hitler's court jester. Certainly I used to tell him my jokes, but only to get him into the sort of mood when I hoped he would see reason. I was the only man who could hammer out *Tristan* and the *Meistersinger* to his satisfaction on the piano, and when this put him in the right frame of mind I could often enter a caveat against some more outrageous piece of behaviour on the part of one of his associates. For years he used me to give an air of respectability to his Nazi Party and when he could no longer stand my public criticism of the excesses of his new Germany he hounded me out of the country with the Gestapo on my heels.

There have been scores of books about Hitler and his era. The public records of his régime were produced at the Nuremberg trial or have appeared since in official American and British publications. I cannot hope and would not even try to compete with this massive documentation of his public career. What seems to me to be still missing is an account of the man, particularly of the development of his character during precisely those years that I knew him so well. When I met him in the early 'twenties he was a minor provincial political agitator, a frustrated ex-serviceman, awkward in a blue serge suit. He looked like a suburban hairdresser on his day off. His chief claim to notice was his golden voice and transcendent powers as an orator on the platform of one of his Party meetings. Even then, he was so little regarded that the sparse reports in the press did not even spell his name aright.

By the time of the Roehm Putsch in 1934, not long before I broke with him, he had become a murderer, the power-hungry daemonic monster the world knew and rued. Doubtless the facets of his character which permitted this development were always present. A man's temperament does not change. But the final product was the result of a combination of circumstances, environment, too many bad and ignorant advisers and, above all, personal, intimate frustrations of the most abysmal sort. The story I have to tell, from close association and observation, is of a man who was impotent, in the medical sense of the term. The abounding nervous energy which found no normal release sought compensation first in the subjection of his entourage, then of his country, then of Europe and would have imposed itself on the world if he had not been stopped. In the sexual no-man's-land in which he lived, he only once nearly found the woman, and never even the man, who might have brought him relief.

It took me many years to plumb the depths of his personal problem. The normal human being reacts only slowly to the abnormal, and even then tries to convince himself that a return to normality is possible. Hitler was all of a piece. His political conceptions were warped and foolhardy. Again the normal person assumes that argument, example and evidence will produce an approximation to orthodox thinking. These were my twin misconceptions. I remained in Hitler's vicinity because I was convinced that his natural genius must bring him to the top. In that, at least, I was right. But when he got there his faults were magnified, not diminished. It was the experience of power which finally corrupted him. What happened thereafter was only the natural consequence of what had gone before, and that is the story I propose to tell.

*   *   *

One vicarious connexion with the Nazi hierarchy goes back to my schooldays. My form master at the Royal Bavarian *Wilhelmsgymnasium* before the turn of the century was none other than Heinrich Himmler's father. The grandfather had been a gendarme in some village on Lake Constance, but the father had risen in the world and had been at one time tutor to Prince Heinrich of Bavaria. As a result he became a terrible snob, favouring the young titled members of his class and bearing down contemptuously on the commoners, although many of us came from well-to-do and prominent families. The son was much younger than I was and I remember him only as a pallid, moon-faced brat whom I used to see occasionally when delivering extra work at his father's house in the Sternstrasse. He went to the same school in the end and I remember hearing from other old boys that he had a particularly unpleasant reputation as a sneak, always running to his father and other teachers with tales about his fellows. But by that time I was far away studying at Harvard.

I am in fact half American. My mother was born a Sedgwick-Heine. My maternal grandmother came from the well-known New England family and was a cousin of the General John Sedgwick who fell at Spotsylvania Court House in the Civil War and whose statue stands at West Point. My grandfather was another Civil War general, William Heine, who was on General Dix's staff in the Army of the Potomac. Trained as an architect, he had fled his native Dresden after the Liberal revolution of 1848, helped to decorate the Opéra in Paris and then emigrated to the States. There he became a well-known illustrator and accompanied Admiral Perry as official artist on the expedition to Japan. In the funeral cortège of Abraham Lincoln, he was one of the generals who carried the coffin.

My mother, who died in 1945 at the age of eighty-six, could still remember the scene clearly, and had equally vivid recollections of seeing Wagner and Liszt at her father's family home back in Dresden, where she first met Edgar Hanfstaengl, my father. He was one of the most spectacularly handsome men of his age and had been, I fear, the direct cause of the broken engagement between King Ludwig II of Bavaria and his beautiful cousin Sophie Charlotte, Duchess of Bavaria, who later became Duchess of Alençon by her marriage to a grandson of Louis-Philippe.

I do not want to insist unduly on these personal details, but my family background played a determining part in my relations with Hitler. The Hanfstaengls were substantial folk. For three generations they were privy councillors to the Dukes of Saxe-Coburg-Gotha and well known as connoisseurs and patrons of the arts. The family enterprise my grandfather founded was, and remains to this day, one of the pioneers in the art reproduction field. My Hanfstaengl grandfather's photographs of three German Kaisers, Moltke and Roon, Ibsen, Liszt, Wagner and Clara Schumann set the standards of their time. My father kept open house at the villa he built in the Liebigstrasse, at that time on the outskirts of Munich. Few names in the artistic world failed to grace the guest book over the years, Lilli Lehmann and Arthur Nikisch, Wilhelm Busch, Sarasate, Richard Strauss, Felix Weingartner and Wilhelm Backhaus. My parents were friends of Fritjof Nansen and Mark Twain. The atmosphere was almost ostentatiously international. My mother had decorated part of the house in shades of green because it was the favourite colour of Queen Victoria, whose signed portrait, dedicated to my father on some occasion, looked at us from its heavy silver frame. Conversation was heavily interlarded with French expressions. Guests sat on the *chaise-longue* behind the *paravent,* with closed *rouleaux* and the ladies suffered from *migraine.* The *teint* was treated with *parfum* and friends had a *rendez-vous* for a *tête-à-tête* in the *foyer* of the opera. My family was Bismarckian monarchist, needless to say with a personal aversion to Wilhelm II.

At the same time, there was great enthusiasm for social and technical progress. The Liberal tradition of 1848 was strong. We even had our own bathroom, at a time when the Prince Regent went to the newly renovated Four Seasons Hotel once a week for his scrub. The great argument of capitalism versus socialism already waxed hot and the great prophet of a new relationship between employer and worker was Friedrich Naumann with his national-social ideas. I can remember when I was no older than thirteen becoming a regular reader of his weekly magazine *Die Hilfe* and his advocacy of a social monarchy on a Christian Socialist basis remained my strongest political trait. As I was to learn from bitter experience, it was not the sort of National-Socialism Hitler had in mind.

That was the atmosphere into which I was born in 1887, which these days is at least three worlds away. It also saw the inception of my infant nickname of 'Putzi' which I have had to suffer in impotent annoyance ever since. At the age of two I caught diphtheria, at a time when serums and child surgery were little trusted. My life was only saved by an old retainer, a peasant woman who fed me untiringly from a spoon, crooning: 'Putzi, eat this now Putzi.' In Bavarian country speech 'Putzi' means little fellow, and although I am now seventy and still six-foot-four the name has stuck.

I had three governesses, of whom my favourite was Bella Farmer, a roses and cream English beauty who came from Hartlepools and had been found for my father during one of his visits to England by the wife of the great Victorian painter Alma-Tadema. She had gone through a list of applicants for my mother and picked out the prettiest one. Even so the most lasting influence of my boyhood was Sergeant-Major Streit. He was a splendid man, the son of a forester in Kissingen. He had grown his impressive moustachios in the Bavarian Royal Guard and my father employed him on the recommendation of a friend, General von Euler, to put a bit of stuffing into a quartet of sons in danger of getting spoilt by too many artistically-minded adults. He came in every Sunday afternoon to teach us military drill and had us marching up and down the lawn like Frederick the Great's *Lange Kerls*. I believe my unfortunate sister, Erna, was even included in these manœuvres.

Streit used to put on an act of bawling us out like a lot of clumsy recruits and we adored him. He was an imposing figure, and held us spellbound with his stories of military prowess, although where he picked them up I do not know, as I do not think the Bavarian army ever won a battle in the memory of man. It all had a special effect on me, as I was marooned in America from 1911 to 1921, missing the whole of the First World War and was never able to suppress a yearning and an inferiority complex at the thought of the service I had missed, which decimated my generation and killed two of my brothers.

It was decided that my share of the family enterprise would be to take over in due course the branch which my father had set up in the 1880's on Fifth Avenue in New York. The first step was for me to get to know my mother's country, so in 1905 I was sent to Harvard. It was quite a vintage period, and I made friends with such outstanding future figures as T. S. Eliot, Walter Lippman, Hendrik von Loon, Hans von Kaltenborn, Robert Benchley, and John Reed. A near accident also led to my becoming a welcome young guest at the White House. I was a husky young fellow in those days and was trying to make the crew. We were out training on the Charles River one cold spring morning in 1906 when some fool of a canoeist got into difficulties in the swift current and tipped himself out. Everyone else seemed to consider it a joke, but I did not like the look of it, jumped into a boat and rowed to where he was floundering. He was pretty well all in and I had to dive in fully clothed and push him up into the boat, changing out of my soaking things to go out with the crew.

The next day the Boston *Herald and Globe* came out with a great story about 'Hanfstaengl, Harvard's Hero' and how the fellow, who apparently was a theological student, would have drowned without me, and so on, the cheapest rubbish. It had my name spelt in some unbelievable fashion, but at least it became known all over the college and that is how I got to know young Theodore Roosevelt, eldest son of the President.

I had acquired something of a reputation at Harvard as a piano player. There was some reason for this, after all. My teachers in Munich had been August Schmid-Lindner and Bernhard Stavenhagen, the last pupil of Liszt, and my big hands gave me a very fair mastery of the Romantic school. However, they were chiefly in demand for spirited renderings of the stirring American football marches. I even composed one myself, called *Falarah*, based on an old German tune. The Harvard football team used to take me along to pep them up on the piano before their games. President Theodore Roosevelt, a fellow extrovert, had heard of my prowess through his son and invited me to Washington in the winter of 1908. I was to see him again frequently in later years, but my chief memory of this occasion, a stag party in the small hours in the White House basement, is of breaking seven bass strings on his magnificent Steinway Grand.

I returned to Germany from Harvard in 1909 for a year's military service in the Royal Bavarian Foot Guards. We might as well have been back in the eighteenth century for all the military instruction we got. We shouldered arms, trooped the colour, stood guard outside the royal palace, and my only experience of anything resembling hostilities was when some Harvard friends, led by Hamilton Fish, later the isolationist U.S. Congressman, saw me standing sentry and threatened to knock off my *Pickelhaube* and use it for a football game in front of the Feldherrnhalle. However, when I threatened to call out the guard they left me in peace. Then, after another year of study in Grenoble, Vienna, and Rome, I returned to the States and took over the Hanfstaengl branch on Fifth Avenue.

I took most of my meals at the Harvard Club, where I made friends with the young Franklin D. Roosevelt, at that time a rising New York State Senator, and received several invitations to visit his cousin Teddy, the former President, who had retired to his estate at Sagamore Hill. He gave me a boisterous welcome and two pieces of advice which were by no means without influence on my way of thinking. "Well, Hanfstaengl," he said, "how did your military service go? I bet it did you no harm. I saw something of your army at Doeberitz as the Kaiser's guest, and discipline like that never hurt anybody. No nation can degenerate which maintains those standards." I must say I found them surprising words, as Wilhelm II was not exactly making Germany popular at the time, but it was an additional prop to the idealized picture of the army inculcated by Sergeant-Major Streit. Later we got to talking about art, literature, and politics, and the ex-President came out with the phrase which has stuck with me ever since: "Hanfstaengl, your business is to pick out the best pictures, but remember that in politics the choice is that of the lesser evil."

The Hanfstaengl representation was a delightful combination of business and pleasure. The famous names who visited me were legion: Pierpont Morgan, Toscanini, Henry Ford, Caruso, Santos Dumont, Charlie Chaplin, Paderewski, and the daughter of President Wilson. When war broke out, I cannot say that I was surprised. Years before, an old Harvard friend of mine from New Orleans named Freddie Moore, who had lived much of his life in Constantinople, had told me: "Mind you, Hanfy, the next war will not start on the Franco-German frontier but in the Balkans", and now, with the shots at Sarajevo, his prophecy had come true.

There was little doubt where American sympathies would fall in the long run, but I tried to keep the German flag flying as best I could. I used to get the bands from the German ships blockaded in New York harbour to come and play for our colony in the Hanfstaengl establishment. When a hostile crowd gathered as they were playing the *Wacht am Rhein*, I switched them quickly to the *Blue Danube*. But in a population which came to regard dachshund dogs as fifth columnists this was only short-term evasive action. I had my shop-windows stove in once and thereafter found discretion the better part of valour. When America finally joined the Allied side I was fortunate in having Senator Elihu Root, who had been Theodore Roosevelt's Secretary of State, as my lawyer. In exchange for my promise to indulge in no anti-American activities, I was not interned. "I would blow you all up if I could, but one measly little bridge is not enough to change the fortunes of war," I told him. And so they let me be, although my freedom of movement was eventually restricted to Central Park. This did not prevent the Custodian of Enemy Property from taking over the assets of the Hanfstaengl firm in the final months of the war. They were worth half a million dollars and were sold at auction for about $8,000. However, immediately after the Armistice, I was permitted to set up a little business of my own which I called The Academy Art Shop, just opposite Carnegie Hall, and this kept me going for the next three years.

News from Germany was sparse. I heard that the Bolsheviks had seized power in Munich, but at that time the word did not have the meaning it has today, and I rather had the impression that it was some form of popular resistance movement against the victors and was by no means displeased. I was detained in the States as a result of the dissolution of our diplomatic representation and in 1920 I was married. My wife's name was Helene Niemeyer, and she was the only daughter of a German-American business man who had emigrated from Bremen. The following year our son Egon was born. I really felt it was time to return home, and, after making arrangements to sell out to my partner, an apostle-like character named Friedrich Denks, the son of a Lutheran minister, we embarked in July 1921 on the s.s *America* for Bremen. I had been away from Germany for ten years, and was travelling on an imposing document issued by the Swiss Consul in New York as the representative of German interests. It was not to be very long before it saved Adolf Hitler's life.

I found a Germany riven by faction and near destitution. The city workers, followers of the Centre Party and capitalists supported the new republic, the Junkers, upper middle class and peasants yearned for the old monarchy. Even the bracing, malt-laden air of Munich could not compensate for the unpainted look of the houses and the peeling façade of the great Court theatre. My family was at the station to meet us, reduced to my mother, Erna, and my eldest brother, Edgar, and the first difficulty which greeted us at the Four Seasons Hotel was to find milk for little Egon. It was rationed and there was none to be had, except by ordering wild quantities of coffee to qualify for the minute jugs of cream which accompanied each pot. Fortunately, my mother, true to her Connecticut past, had bought a small farm near Uffing on the Staffel Lake at the foot of the Alps, so that unlike most Germans we were not short of food. Even so, Mother was shamefully cheated by the farm servants, who took advantage of the rocketing prices of inflation to sell the produce on the black market and pocket the difference.

Almost the first political event which greeted my return was the murder of Matthias Erzberger, who had signed the 1918 Armistice, by a couple of young Right Wing radicals. Counter-threats, reports of separatism, Putschism, and terrorism filled the columns of the newspapers. The tone of the press increased daily in violence and abuse. It became evident to me that Germany, politically speaking, was a madhouse, with a thousand opinions and no saving idea. I was by habit of thought Conservative, or at least a monarchist, looking back to the happier days of Ludwig II and Richard Wagner. Like most expatriates, the clock had stopped for me at the point where I left Germany and I felt that everything which was old and reminded me of the old days was good and the new things which did not fit into that conception were bad. I felt resentful at the contempt shown to the Army and distressed at the poverty of the honest artisan. I had been spared so much of the misery of the previous decade and wanted in a confused way to help, but could find no outlet.

To get my bearings I decided to study German history. We rented an apartment which belonged to the stepdaughter of the painter Franz von Stuck at No. 1 Gentzstrasse in Schwabing, the Montparnasse of Munich, and I got down to my books in the hope that previous events might provide some clue to the dilemma of the times. I discovered in the person of the American loyalist, Benjamin Thompson, Count Rumford, the ideal figure round which to group my researches. In the last decade of the eighteenth century he had reorganized the administration and public life of Bavaria for the Elector Karl Theodor. I found so many apt parallels in his work of social reform that I decided to write a book about him.

One of the people to whom I talked of my plan was Rudolf Kommer, a brilliant Austrian writer I had known in New York. He immediately saw in the project a superb idea for a film, and during most of the summer of 1922 I worked with him on the script at a villa in Garmisch-Partenkirchen. We finally ended up with something that had the dimensions of Tolstoy's *War and Peace*, so it is hardly surprising that the film was never made. However, there was much good intellectual company to compensate, including many of his Jewish friends like Max Pallenberg, the well-known actor, and his even more famous wife, Fritzi Massary. In their cynical disparagement of the old régime we stood poles apart politically, but we became firm friends.

One prophecy of Kommer's remained burned in my memory over

the years. I met him walking on the Partnachklamm the day the
papers carried the news of another political assassination, that of the
Jewish Minister for Foreign Affairs, Walter Rathenau. It happened
at a time when the anti-Semitic campaign in Germany was assuming
serious proportions and there had recently been a rash of red
swastikas daubed on walls and rocks round Garmisch with insulting
anti-Jewish inscriptions.

"That is a dirty business your monarchist friends have organized,"
Kommer said. (He said monarchist, as the term National-Socialist
was hardly known yet.) "This race romanticism of theirs will get
them nowhere. There is only one danger. If any political party
emerges with an anti-Semitic programme directed by Jewish or half-
Jewish fanatics we shall have to watch out. They would be the only
people who could put it over." How right he was time was to show.

*   *   *

It is a far cry from Harvard to Hitler, but in my case the connexion is direct. In 1908 I took part in a show called *Fate Fakirs* at
the Hasty Pudding Club in which I was dressed up in arch-student
fashion as a Dutch girl called Gretchen Spootsfeiffer. Another
member of the cast was Warren Robbins. By 1922 he had become
a senior official in the American Embassy in Berlin, at which time
I had been living back in Munich for a year. I had been up to see
him not long previously and during the second week of November
received a telephone call from him:

"Listen, Hanfy," he said. "What are you Bavarians up to?" I had
to tell him that in all conscience I did not know. The whole country
was a hotbed of political agitation in those troubled post-war years
and I had not really been trying to keep the thread of events in my
head. "Well, we are sending our young military attaché, Captain
Truman-Smith, down to have a look round," Robbins went on.
"Look after him and introduce him to a few people, will you?"

He turned out to be a very pleasant young officer of about thirty,
a Yale man, but in spite of that I was nice to him. I gave him a letter
to Paul Nikolaus Cossmann, editor of the *Münchener Neueste Nachrichten*, and told him to drop in to lunch at my flat whenever he felt

like it. I must say he worked like a beaver. Within a few days he had seen Crown Prince Rupprecht, Ludendorff, Herr von Kahr, and Count Lerchenfeld, who were senior figures in Government circles, and others. He soon knew much more about Bavarian politics than I did. We were having lunch on the last day of his visit, which was November 22, when he told me that he had more or less finished his round of visits. The Embassy wanted him back and he was leaving by the night train. "I tell you one thing, though," he said, "I met the most remarkable fellow I've ever come across this morning."

"Really," I replied. "What's his name?"

"Adolf Hitler."

"You must have the name wrong," I said. "Don't you mean Hilpert, the German nationalist fellow, although I can't say I see anything particularly remarkable in him."

"No, no," Truman-Smith insisted. "Hitler. There are quite a lot of placards up announcing a meeting this evening. They say he puts signs up saying 'No entry for Jews', but he has a most persuasive line about German honour and rights for the workers and a new society. . . . I have the impression he's going to play a big part, and whether you like him or not he certainly knows what he wants. He says the people in Berlin will never unite the nation the way they are going on at the moment. The first thing is to get the red rabble off the streets and the youngsters away from the street corners, instil some sort of order and discipline into them again and restore a measure of self-respect into the Army and the people who fought in the war. He really seems to have a sense of direction which none of the others have. They gave me a Press ticket for his meeting this evening, and now I shall not be able to go. Could you possibly have a look at him for me and let me know your impressions?"

And that is how I met Hitler.

I saw Truman-Smith off at the station, where we met a singularly ill-favoured individual who was waiting on the platform, a sallow, untidy fellow, who looked half-Jewish in an unpleasant sort of way. Truman-Smith introduced us: "This is Herr Rosenberg. He's Hitler's Press chief and gave me the ticket for this evening." I was far from impressed, but we saw the train off and then my new acquaintance asked if he could accompany me to the meeting. So we went out and took a tram to the Kindlkeller beer-hall, where it was taking place. I could get little out of Rosenberg beyond the fact that he was a Balt and totally ignorant of the world outside Central Europe.

The Kindlkeller, which was a big L-shaped hall, was crammed full with a very mixed audience. There seemed to be a lot of people of the concierge or small shopkeeper class, a sprinkling of the former officer and minor civil servant type, a tremendous number of young people, and the rest artisans, with a high proportion of the spectators in Bavarian national costume. Rosenberg and I pushed our way through to the press table, which was on the right side of the platform.

I looked round the hall and could see no one in the audience or on the platform I knew. "Where is Hitler?" I asked a middle-aged journalist next to me. "See those three over there? The short man is Max Amann, the one with the spectacles is Anton Drexler, and the other is Hitler." In his heavy boots, dark suit and leather waistcoat, semi-stiff white collar and odd little moustache, he really did not look very impressive – like a waiter in a railway-station restaurant. However, when Drexler introduced him to a roar of applause, Hitler straightened up and walked past the press table with a swift, controlled step, the unmistakable soldier in mufti.

The atmosphere in the hall was electric. Apparently this was his first public appearance after serving a short prison-sentence for breaking up a meeting addressed by a Bavarian separatist named Ballerstedt, so he had to be reasonably careful what he said in case the police should arrest him again as a disturber of the peace. Perhaps this is what gave such a brilliant quality to his speech, which for innuendo and irony I have never heard matched, even by him. No one who judges his capacity as a speaker from the performances of his later years can have any true insight into his gifts. As time went on he became drunk with his own oratory before vast crowds and his voice lost its former character through the intervention of microphone and loud-speaker. In his early years he had a command of voice, phrase and effect which has never been equalled, and on this evening he was at his best.

I cannot have been more than eight feet away and watched him carefully. For the first ten minutes he stood at attention, while he gave a very well-argued résumé of the historical events of the previous three or four years. In a quiet, reserved voice, he drew a picture of what had happened in Germany since November 1918: the collapse of the monarchy and the surrender at Versailles; the founding of the Republic on the ignominy of war guilt; the fallacy of international Marxism and Pacifism; the eternal class war *leitmotif* and the resulting hopeless stalemate between employers and employees, between Nationalists and Socialists.

There was almost a note of Viennese coffee-house conversation in the grace of some of his phrases and the sly malice of his insinuations. There was no doubt of his Austrian origin. Although he spoke most of the time in a good High-German accent, occasional words would give him away. I remember him pronouncing the first syllable of the word Europe or European in the Latin fashion, *ayoo,* which is typical of Vienna, instead of the North German *oy,* and there were other examples difficult to render into English. As he felt the audience becoming interested in what he had to say, he gently moved his left foot to one side, like a soldier standing at ease in slow motion, and started to use his hands and arms in gesture, of which he had an expressive and extensive repertoire. There was none of the barking and braying he later developed and he had an ingenious, mocking humour which was telling without being offensive.

He scored his points all round the compass. First he would criticize the Kaiser as a weakling and then he rounded on the Weimar Republicans for conforming with the victors' demands, which were stripping Germany of everything but the graves of her war dead. There was a strong note of appeal to the ex-serviceman in his audience. He compared the separatist movement and religious particularity of the Bavarian Catholics with the comradeship of the front-line soldier who never asked a wounded comrade his religion before he sprang to help him. He dwelt at length on patriotism and national pride and quoted approvingly the rôle of Kemal Ataturk in Turkey and the example of Mussolini, who had marched on Rome three weeks earlier.

He stormed at war profiteers, and I remember him getting a roar of applause when he criticized them for spending valuable foreign currency on importing oranges from Italy for the rich, when gathering inflation was facing half the population with starvation. He attacked the Jews, not so much on a racial basis, as accusing them of black marketeering and waxing fat on the misery round them, a charge which it was only too easy to make stick. Then he thundered at the Communists and Socialists for desiring the disruption of German traditions. All these enemies of the people, he declared, would one day be *beseitigt*, literally removed or done away with. It was a perfectly proper word to use in the circumstances, and I read no sinister connotation into it. I doubt even whether it had the meaning in Hitler's mind that it later acquired, but then that was to be a long story.

As he warmed to his subject he started to speak more rapidly, his hands tellingly suggesting the highlights of thesis and antithesis, symbolizing the rise and fall of his cadences, emphasizing the magnitude of problems and the fleeting pizzicato of his ideas. Occasionally there were interjections. Then Hitler would slightly raise his right hand, as if catching a ball, or would fold his arms, and with one or two words bring the audience over to his side. His technique resembled the thrusts and parries of a fencer, or the perfect balance of a tightrope-walker. Sometimes he reminded me of a skilled violinist, who, never coming to the end of his bow, always left just the faint anticipation of a tone – a thought spared the indelicacy of utterance.

I looked round at the audience. Where was the nondescript crowd I had seen only an hour before? What was suddenly holding these people, who, on the hopeless incline of the falling mark, were engaged in a daily struggle to keep themselves within the line of decency? The hubbub and mug-clattering had stopped and they were drinking in every word. Only a few yards away was a young woman, her eyes fastened on the speaker. Transfixed as though in some devotional ecstasy, she had ceased to be herself and was completely under the spell of Hitler's despotic faith in Germany's future greatness.

Hitler paused to wipe the perspiration from his forehead and take a deep gulp from a mug of beer passed up to him by a middle-aged man with a dark moustache. It supplied the finishing touch, the local, personal note, acting as a further impetus to the enthusiasm of the malt-minded Munichers. It was hard to decide whether Hitler drank to give the audience a chance to applaud, or whether they applauded to give him a chance to drink.

"That was Ulrich Graf who handed up the beer," my neighbour said. "He's Hitler's bodyguard and follows him wherever he goes. There is a price on Hitler's head in some of the other States, you know." I looked at Graf and saw that after taking the mug back, his right hand returned to the bulging pocket of his coat. From the firm way in which he kept his hand there, his eyes fixed on the front rows, I knew he was holding a revolver.

The audience responded with a final outburst of frenzied cheering, hand-clapping, and a cannonade of table-pounding. It sounded like the demoniacal rattle of thousands of hailstones rebounding on the surface of a gigantic drum. It had been a masterly performance. I had really been impressed beyond measure by Hitler. In spite of his provincial manner, he had seemed to have a much wider horizon than the normal German politician one met. With his incredible gifts as an orator he was clearly going to go far, and from what I had seen of his entourage there seemed no one likely to bring home to him the picture of the outside world he manifestly lacked, and in this I felt I might be able to help. He seemed to have no conception of the part America had played in winning the war and viewed European problems from a narrow, continental standpoint. Here, at least, I felt I could put him right.

That was for the future. He was standing on the platform recovering from his bravura exhibition. I walked over to introduce myself. Naïve and yet forceful, obliging and yet uncompromising, he stood, face and hair soaked in perspiration, his semi-stiff collar, fastened with a square imitation-gold safety-pin, melted to nothing. While talking he dabbed his face with what had once been a handkerchief, glancing worriedly at the many open exits through which came the draughts of a cold November night.

"Herr Hitler, my name is Hanfstaengl," I said. "Captain Truman-Smith asked me to give you his best wishes." "Ah, yes, the big American," he answered. "He begged me to come here and listen to you, and I can only say I have been most impressed," I went on. "I agree with 95 per cent of what you said and would very much like to talk to you about the rest some time."

"Why, yes, of course," Hitler said. "I am sure we shall not have to quarrel about the odd five per cent." He made a very pleasant impression, modest and friendly. So we shook hands again and I went home. That night I could not go to sleep for a long time. My mind still raced with the impressions of the evening. Where all our conservative politicians and speakers were failing abysmally to establish any contact with the ordinary people, this self-made man, Hitler, was clearly succeeding in presenting a non-Communist programme to exactly those people whose support we needed. On the other hand, I had not liked the look of those immediate supporters I had seen. Rosenberg and the people round him seemed to me distinctly dubious types. Then an aphorism of Nietzsche floated into my mind and provided consolation: "The first followers of a movement do not prove anything against it."

CHAPTER II

TRISTAN IN THE THIERSCHSTRASSE

Sugar in the wine – Rosenberg – The infantryman's guide –
Fitting Hitler for society – The Stammtisch *at the Café*
Neumaier – Cranks and intimates – The basic reading of a
dictator – Wagner on an upright piano – From Falarah *to*
Sieg Heil – *A woman's reaction – A pamphlet becomes a*
newspaper.

IF I HAD fallen under Hitler's oratorical spell, it was with reservations. The second time I heard him speak I was less impressed. I was
late and, not wishing to create a disturbance, remained near the
door. The distance reduced the strength and magnetic appeal of
Hitler's voice and made the whole thing more impersonal, more like
reading a newspaper. He was threatening a monster campaign of
incitement to violence against the French in the event of their
occupying the Rhur. If the government would not stand up for the
nation, the nation must act for itself, he was saying. In veiled words
he hinted at a plan of insurrection for resisting a French incursion
on the Rhine by guerrilla warfare. This sounded to me like the
language of a desperado. Overpopulated Germany would never lend
itself to the carrying on of a war by irregular bands of *francs-tireurs*.
Whenever Hitler touched on foreign politics he expressed alarming
views, disproportionate and extravagant. It was clear that he did
not realize how Germany looked as seen from the outside. Yet there
was still something which reconciled me to him – a certain cosmopolitan ingredient, the flair of the Danube – that richer German
political horizon which I had encountered when a student in
polyglot Vienna. What was at the back of this curious man's brain?
I felt the impulse to meet him in a smaller circle and talk to him
alone.

Not long after, there was another meeting in the Zirkus Krone,
and I took my wife and one or two other friends along to hear him

from one of the boxes. As far as I remember, the first wife of Olaf
Gulbransson, the famous artist and *Simplicissimus* cartoonist, and
Frau von Kaulbach, the widow of the well-known painter, were in
the party. Afterwards we went up and I introduced the ladies to
Hitler. He was delighted with my wife, who was blonde and beautiful and American. He accepted very readily when she said how
pleased we would be if he would come to coffee or dinner at the flat.
Soon he was visiting us frequently, pleasant and unassuming in his
little blue serge suit. He was respectful, even diffident and very careful to adhere to the forms of address still *de rigueur* in Germany
between people of lower rank when speaking to those of better
education, title, or academic attainment. The only striking things
about him were an extraordinary luminous quality in his blue eyes
and his sensitive hands, plus, of course, very definite gifts of expression in conversation.

He had a winning way with him, the sort of spontaneity that
attracts children, and Egon became devoted to him. I remember just
before one visit the child had knocked his knee against the leg of
a hideous pseudo-Renaissance chair which formed part of the furniture. It was carved in the form of a lion, with its tongue sticking
out, rather like one of the gargoyles on Notre-Dame. It was a
sharp crack and Egon began to bawl. Hitler was announced and
came into the room just as I was trying to pacify the boy by slapping the lion and saying, "There, we'll teach him to bite you," or
something to that effect. Hitler came right over and slapped the
lion on the other leg just to keep it in order as well. And, of course,
Egon beamed. It became a regular play between them. Every time
Hitler came he would slap the lion and say to the boy, "Now, has he
been behaving himself?"

Stories are sometimes told that we were the people who taught
Hitler table-manners. That is not so. He was not as uncouth as that.
But he did have some curious tastes. He had the most incredible
sweet tooth of any man I have ever met and could never be given
enough of his favourite Austrian cakes heaped with whipped cream.
At one meal I thought I would treat him to a bottle of Prince
Metternich's best Gewürztraminer. I was called out of the room to
the telephone and as I came back caught him putting a heaping

spoonful of castor-sugar in the glass. I pretended I had not seen and he drank the concoction with evident relish.

He was a voracious reader and positively stormed the historical library I was building up. He could not read enough about Frederick the Great and the French Revolution, historical parallels out of which he was trying to distil a policy for Germany's difficulties. For years the great Frederick was his hero and he never tired of quoting examples of the king's success in building up Prussia in the face of overwhelming odds. This did not seem to me a particularly pernicious obsession, as Frederick had always been a man who knew where to stop. The trouble was that when Hitler came to power he transferred his historical allegiance to Napoleon, who did not know where to stop, a fault which eventually involved Hitler in equal disaster.

His other politico-military master was Clausewitz, whom he could quote by the yard, and this was another source of his undoing. Neither he nor any of his entourage—and it must be remembered that substantially the same fellow-conspirators of the 1920's took over the leadership of Germany in the 1930's—acquired any conception of the strength of the salt-water powers. They thought on purely continental lines. To them international power politics were based on the limitations inherent in land warfare, and in my decade of struggle to influence the workings of Hitler's mind I never really succeeded in bringing home the importance of America as an integral factor in European politics.

My first attempt to wean him away from his dangerous harping on the need for a *revanche* against France as a means of restoring Germany's position in the world, came during one of his very early visits. We were sitting together after lunch when he asked quite modestly, "Well, Herr Hanfstaengl, and how do you see the world situation and its effect on Germany?" And then he let me talk for seven or eight minutes, listening with great attention and never attemping to interrupt. It was, I fear, an attitude he was gradually to lose over the course of his rise to power.

"Well, now," I said, "you have just fought in the war. We very nearly won in 1917 when Russia collapsed. Why, then, did we finally lose it?" "Because the Americans came in," he said. "If you recognize that, we are agreed and that is all you need to know," I went on. "I was over there during the war and I can tell you that this is an absolutely new factor in European politics. Where did we stand in 1917? The French were mutinying, the British had nearly had enough, and then what happened? The Americans mobilized two and a half million soldiers out of nowhere and sent over 150,000 a month to hold the front. If there is another war it must inevitably be won by the side which America joins. They have the money, they have developed this tremendous industrial power, and you will ignore them at your peril. The only proper policy for you to advocate is friendship with the United States. That is the only way to maintain peace in Europe and build up again a position for our country."

He seemed to take all this in and muttered, "Yes, yes, you must be right," but the idea was so new to him he never digested it. His other cronies had the same infantryman's mentality that he did, and whenever I thought I had driven a point home, one of them would always produce an argument to counteract it, and back we were in the days of Clausewitz, Moltke, and the Kaiser. In his questions Hitler revealed to me that his ideas about America were wildly superficial. He wanted to hear all about the skyscrapers and was fascinated by details of technical progress, but failed utterly to draw logical conclusions from the information. The only American figure for whom he had time was Henry Ford, and then not so much as an industrial wonder-worker but rather as a reputed anti-Semite and a possible source of funds. Hitler was also passionately interested in the Ku Klux Klan, then at the height of its questionable reputation. He seemed to think it was a political movement similar to his own, with which it might be possible to make some pact, and I was never able to put its relative importance in proper perspective for him.

I soon found that he was deeply under the spell of Rosenberg, who was far more the Party theoretician than the mere press-agent to whom Truman-Smith had introduced me. He was the anti-Semitic, anti-Bolshevist, anti-religious trouble-maker, and Hitler seemed to have a very high opinion of his abilities as a philosopher and writer. Until Goebbels appeared on the scene, which was some years later, Rosenberg was the principal antagonist in my attempts to make Hitler see reason. At a very early stage, probably during the same talk, I warned Hitler of the dangers of Rosenberg's racial and religious diatribes. I am a Protestant myself, but I knew the deeply ingrained Catholic sense of Bavaria and told Hitler he would make no headway as long as he continued to offend it. He always professed to see the strength of my arguments, but there was never any way of telling whether he was going to act on them or not.

I was so convinced that the extraordinary force of Hitler's oratory must make him a political power to be reckoned with, that I considered it even more necessary to bring him into contact with people of some position and standing. I introduced him to William Bayard Hale, who had been a classmate of President Wilson at Princeton and for years the chief European correspondent of the Hearst newspapers. He had more or less retired and had chosen to live the rest of his life in Munich. He was a very wise and intelligent observer of affairs and I often brought him together with Hitler in the Hotel Bayrischer Hof, where he was living. There was also a German-American artist of considerable talents, Wilhelm Funk, who had a lavishly equipped studio furnished with exquisite Renaissance furniture and tapestries and something of a *salon* which included people like Prince Henckel-Donnersmarck and a number of national-minded wealthier business men. But when they made veiled suggestions about a political alliance, Hitler shied away. "I know these people," he told me, "their own meetings are empty and they want me to come along and fill the hall for them and then split the proceeds. We National-Socialists have our own programme and they can join up with us if they like, but I will not come in as a subordinate ally."

I also brought him together with the family of Fritz-August von Kaulbach, who had been a member of a very distinguished family of artists in Bavaria, hoping that their civilized minds and manners might have some influence on Hitler through their common interest in the arts. At some period Hitler had also come to know the Bruckmanns, who were big publishers in Munich, and included Houston Stewart Chamberlain among their authors. Our two families knew each other well, and Elsa Bruckmann, a former Princess Cantacuzène, who was a considerably older woman, made something of a protégé of Hitler. Significantly he was impressed by her family title and they shared a passion for Wagner and Bayreuth. However, when I found that she had also extended her patronage to Rosenberg I made a point of never going to her *salon*. For a family which had entertained Nietzsche, Rainer Maria Rilke and Spengler I could never understand their being taken in by such a charlatan.

This civilized society was quite new to Hitler and his reactions had a touch of *naïveté*. He had also been introduced to the Bechstein family, who made their famous pianos in Berlin, but visited Munich frequently. They invited him to dinner at their *de luxe* hotel in a private suite and he reported on it to me wide-eyed. Frau Bechstein had been *en grande toilette* and her husband had worn a dinner jacket. "I felt quite embarrassed in my blue suit," Hitler told me. "The servants were all in livery and we drank nothing but champagne before the meal. And you should have seen the bathroom, you can even regulate the heat of the water." Frau Bechstein was a dominating woman who developed a motherly interest in Hitler. For a long time she was convinced that she was going to be able to marry her daughter Lotte to him and tried first to adapt his clothes to the requirements of society. Apparently during that evening she convinced him of the necessity of acquiring a dinner jacket and starched shirts and patent leather shoes. I was appalled at this and warned him that no leader of a working-class movement could dare in the circumstances of the time in Germany to be seen around in such things. So he hardly ever appeared in it, but did take a fancy to the patent leather shoes which for a time he wore on every occasion.

By this time I had decided that I would in a quiet way support the National Socialist Party. As a member of the family firm my hands were to some extent bound and I felt that any assistance I gave should be kept as much in the background as possible. Not long after I had started going to Hitler's meetings I called on Max Amann, who at that time was the business manager of the Party's weekly newspaper, the *Völkische Beobachter,* in his shabby offices in the Thierschstrasse. The first person I saw there, to my discomfiture, was a flashy figure I had noticed at the first meeting, who put on a great show of trying to persuade me of the necessity of openly joining the Party and starting a campaign among the leading Munich families. He whipped out a gold pencil and, pushing a membership application form before me, began to force matters. He urged me to subscribe a dollar a month, a small fortune in Germany at the inflated rate of exchange, out of the proceeds of the art shop I had liquidated in New York. I felt I was being forced into a position which he planned to exploit and managed to stall him off until Amann came out from his inner office.

He was a rough fellow who had been Hitler's sergeant-major during the war, but he saw my point immediately and further endeared himself to me by voicing the gravest suspicions about the fellow who had accosted me when I entered. The affairs of the Party seemed surrounded by this air of conspiracy and intrigue. Hitler himself lived a shadowy existence and it was very difficult to keep track of his movements. He had the Bohemian habits of a man who had grown up with no real roots. He was hopelessly unpunctual and incapable of keeping to any sort of schedule. He walked around leading a fierce Alsatian named 'Wolf' and always carried a whip with a loaded handle. Ulrich Graf, his bodyguard, followed him everywhere. He would drop in after breakfast at Amann's office and then usually call in at the *Beobachter* office round the corner in the Schellingstrasse, and talk away with anyone who was fortunate enough to find him there.

He never stopped talking all day, committed nothing to paper, issued no directives and was the despair of his staff. He would make appointments and never be there, or would be discovered somewhere looking at second-hand motor-cars. Cars were an obsession with him. He had great plans, by no means so ill-conceived, for motorizing the embryo S.A., which kept order at his meetings and marched in demonstrations. He felt this would give them a head start on the police, who still went round on foot. But first he needed a car for himself to get round to meetings more quickly. He picked up one vehicle which looked like a dismantled horse-cab without a top, but soon exchanged this for a Selve car, with funds he had drummed up in a mysterious way from someone. It was a rattling monster and each end looked as if it was going different ways, but he seemed to think it conferred additional dignity on him and from that time on I do not think I ever saw him take a tram or bus again.

Once or twice a week he used to call in on a little stationer named

Quirin Diestl, who had a shop near the Regina Hotel. Frau Diestl was a great admirer of his and always served particularly good black coffee and cakes. Diestl himself was a little rowdy with red hair and a red moustache, cut à la Hitler. He looked rather like a chipmunk. He knew all the latest local gossip and slanderous stories and was always ready to start a brawl with hecklers at the Party meetings.

Hitler's intimates were nearly all modest people. As I got to know him I started attending the Monday evening *Stammtisch* at the Café Neumaier, an old-fashioned coffee-house on the corner of the Petersplatz and the Viktualien Markt. The long, irregular room, with built-in benches and panelled walls, had space for a hundred people or so. Here he was in the habit of meeting his oldest adherents, many of them middle-aged married couples, who came to have their frugal supper, part of which they brought with them. Hitler would speak *en famille* and try out the technique and effect of his newest ideas.

Gradually I got to know quite a number of the inner circle. Anton Drexler, the original founder of the Party, was there most evenings, but by this time he was only its honorary president and had been pushed more or less to one side. A blacksmith by trade, he had a trade union background and although it was he who had thought up the original idea of appealing to the workers with a patriotic pro-gramme, he disapproved strongly of the street fighting and violence which was slowly becoming a factor in the Party's activities and wanted it built up as a working-class movement in an orderly fashion. Another old hand was Christian Weber; he was a horse-dealer, a big, burly fellow who also went round with a whip and enjoyed knocking Communists about. At that time he was by no means the brute he later became and was terribly flattered when I had him to the flat for coffee. He had an oddly intuitive sense of the bottomless pit of Hitler's mind and foresaw many of the things people like myself fought to avoid. All he really wanted out of life was a secured position of some small dignity. The third most prominent member was Dietrich Eckart, to whom I took a distinct liking. He was a man of education, a poet, whose German version of *Peer Gynt* remains the standard translation. He was very Bavarian and looked like an old walrus, and his handsome income from book royalties helped fill the Party coffers. He it was who had first taken Hitler under his wing in the Party, although he was already beginning to regret it.

Other regulars included Hermann Esser, the ex-Communist and *enfant terrible* of the Party, its best speaker after Hitler; Gottfried Feder, an unsuccessful engineer, who had become a financial crank and was advocating the liquidation of Germany's war debts by national bankruptcy; he was also a man of some education and his family had acted as advisers to the Otto of Bavaria who had become the first king of Greece. Then there was a slightly mysterious man named Lieutenant Klintzsch, who was one of the stormtrooper leaders and had been and probably still was a member of the Organization Consul, which had been associated with Captain Ehrhardt in the abortive Kapp Putsch in Berlin in 1920 and had a hand in the murders of Erzberger and Rathenau. The minor characters included Haugg, Hitler's driver for a short period and Emil Maurice, the former clock-maker who succeeded him and, of course, Amann and Ulrich Graf. Other faithful but not particularly effective supporters included a couple named Lauböck – the man was quite a high railway official at the East Station; Oskar Koerner, a merchant, and a fur merchant named Wutz whose wife had been trained as a soprano.

None of these people knew me and at first felt it incumbent on them to be somewhat distant. Was this tall man with his slight German-American accent really a Hanfstaengl of Munich or was he an impostor like so many others who sought Hitler's company? But when some of my former comrades in the *Wilhelmsgymnasium*, the University and the Foot Guards greeted me, confidence grew. This slow process rather pleased me. It proved their caution as well as a certain dignity. The first person to evince any real cordiality was Ulrich Graf, whose exquisite sturdy head had all the quality of a Hans Memling portrait. He was a minor employee in the city council and an honest, decent fellow.

I also gained the confidence of old Singer, who was the Party treasurer and turned up at the coffee-house sometimes. He used to organize the collections at the meetings and stuff the takings in a small tin trunk, which he then used to hump home under his arm.

I went back with him once and watched him empty the pile of dirty, almost valueless, bank-notes on to his dining-room table and start carefully counting and sorting them. There was no supervision and his wife had long since retired to the warmth of the bedroom. As in most Munich houses during this desperate winter, only one room was warmed by a small stove. I can still feel the damp chill of the other rooms in my bones today. Out of such modest beginnings did the Party grow.

After these coffee-house sessions Hitler would put on his long black coat and black slouch hat, which made him look like an absolute desperado, and with Weber, Amann, Klintzsch and Graf, all well armed, walk back to the Thierschstrasse, where he had a tiny flat at number 41. I took to joining the group and as confidence in me grew, Hitler allowed me to call at his flat during the day.

He lived there like a down-at-heels clerk. He had one room and the use of a quite large entrance-hall as a sub-tenant of a woman named Reichert. It was all modest in the extreme and he remained there for years, although it became part of an act to show how he identified himself with the workers and have-nots of this world. The room itself was tiny. I doubt if it was nine feet wide. The bed was too wide for its corner and the head of it projected over the single narrow window. The floor was covered with cheap, worn linoleum with a couple of threadbare rugs, and on the wall opposite the bed there was a makeshift bookshelf, apart from a chair and rough table the only other piece of furniture in the room. The building is still standing and the flat intact, more or less as I remember it. On the outside wall, incongruously enough, in a little alcove in the stucco, there is still a weather-beaten china Madonna.

Hitler used to walk around in carpet slippers, frequently with no collar to his shirt and wearing braces. There were quite a lot of illustrations and drawings hanging on the wall, and the books were an indicative mixture. I made a list of them at the time which I still have. The upper shelves were those he liked to refer to in front of visitors. They included a history of the Great War by Hermann Stegemann, and Ludendorff's book on the same subject; German histories by Einhardt and Treitschke; Spamer's illustrated encyclopaedia, a work dating from the nineteenth century; Clausewitz'

Vom Kriege and the history of Frederick the Great by Kugler, a biography of Wagner by Houston Stewart Chamberlain and a potted world history by Maximilian Yorck von Wartenburg. The respectable volumes also included a tome called *Geographical Character Pictures* by Grube, a collection of heroic myths by Schwab and the war memoirs of Sven Hedin.

These were the books which formed Hitler's opinions and knowledge for the years to come. But perhaps more interesting was the bottom shelf, where in an abrupt descent from Mars to Venus, editions of a semi-pornographic nature lay discreetly shrouded in Edgar Wallace thrillers. Three of these well-thumbed volumes consisted of the curious studies of Eduard Fuchs—the *History of Erotic Art* and an *Illustrated History of Morals*.

Frau Reichert found him an ideal tenant. "He is such a nice man," she used to say, "but he has the most extraordinary moods. Sometimes weeks go by when he seems to be sulking and does not say a word to us. He looks through us as if we were not there. He always pays his rent punctually in advance, but he is a real Bohemian type." She said this sort of thing to other people and malicious opponents later suggested that Hitler came from Bohemia and that the Braunau where he was born was in fact the one near Sadowa. In later years, when this came to Hindenburg's ears, it was the reason for the old Field Marshal coining his contemptuous phrase about 'this Bohemian corporal'. He even talked about it to Hitler who said 'but no, I was born at Braunau on the Inn' and the old man thought he had been tricked by Hitler's detractors and became more friendly to him as a result.

No one could get Hitler to talk about his early years. I used to try to lead him on by saying how much I had enjoyed Vienna and drinking wine in the Grinzing hills and so on, but he would shut up like a clam. One morning when I came in rather unexpectedly, a big lump of a boy stood at the open kitchen door. He turned out to be Hitler's nephew, the son of his half-sister who had married a man named Raubal and still lived in Vienna. He was an ill-favoured lad and Hitler was somewhat displeased that I had seen him.

The Thierschstrasse flat was also where I first played the piano for Hitler. There was no room for a piano in my own place in the

Gentzstrasse, but in his hall there was a rickety little upright model standing up against the wall. This was at a time when Hitler was having a certain amount of trouble with the police, in fact there were very few times when he was not. There was a special branch man in the police headquarters who was a secret Nazi and used to come along and tell him whether there were any warrants being issued in connexion with his political activities or what cases were coming up that might affect him. There was also a suggestion at the time that the Party was getting funds from the French occupation authorities, although this is impossible to believe in view of the violent campaign they carried on after the occupation of the Ruhr at the beginning of 1923.

Be that as it may, Hitler had to appear from time to time as a witness in the frequent political trials and he was always strung up before these sessions. He knew I was a pianist and asked me to play something to calm him. I was a bit out of practice and the piano was terribly out of tune; but I played a Bach fugue, to which he sat listening in a chair, nodding his head in vague disinterest. Then I started the prelude to the *Meistersinger*. This was it. This was Hitler's meat. He knew the thing absolutely by heart and could whistle every note of it in a curious penetrating vibrato, but completely in tune. He started to march up and down the hall, waving his arms as if he was conducting an orchestra. He really had an excellent feel for the spirit of music, certainly as good as many a conductor. This music affected him physically and by the time I had crashed through the finale he was in splendid spirits, all his worries gone, and raring to get to grips with the public prosecutor.

I am a very fair pianist and I had good teachers, but being of a somewhat vehement turn of mind, I play with what a number of people would consider over-elaborate emphasis, with plenty of Lisztian *fiorituri* and a fine romantic swing. This was just what Hitler liked. Probably one of the main reasons why he kept me near him for so many years, even when we began to differ radically over policies, was this particular gift I apparently possessed of playing the music he liked in exactly the orchestral style he preferred. The effect with the little upright piano and the linoleum floor was to produce the ringing tones of a Steinway in Carnegie Hall.

After that we had innumerable sessions together. He had no time for Bach and not much more for Mozart. There were not enough climaxes in the music for his turbulent nature. He would listen to Schumann and Chopin and liked certain pieces of Richard Strauss. Over the course of time I taught him to appreciate the Italian operas, but in the end it always had to be Wagner, *Meistersinger, Tristan and Isolde* and *Lohengrin*. I must have played them hundreds of times and he never grew tired of them. He had a genuine knowledge and appreciation of Wagner's music, and this he had picked up somewhere, probably in his Vienna days, long before I knew him. The seed may even have been sown in Linz, where at the beginning of the century there was a pupil of Liszt named Göllerich, who was the local orchestral conductor and a Wagner enthusiast, but wherever it was, it had become part of Hitler's being. I came to see that there was a direct parallel between the construction of the *Meistersinger* prelude and that of his speeches. The whole interweaving of *leitmotifs,* of embellishments, of counter-point and musical contrasts and argument, were exactly mirrored in the pattern of his speeches, which were symphonic in construction and ended in a great climax, like the blare of Wagner's trombones.

I was almost the only person who crossed the lines of his groups of acquaintances. Normally he kept them all in watertight compartments and never told them where he had been or where he was going or took any of them with him. Sometimes he asked me to accompany him to the Lauböcks for tea and had me sit down at their piano. I think it rather tickled his fancy to be able to produce someone with this accomplishment. Laubök was a very loyal follower and as nationalist fervour in Bavaria increased kept a quantity of arms and ammunition hidden in his railway yards for the Nazis. He was always perfectly polite to me, but belonged to a sober group in the Party which resented the manner in which Hitler had taken to a person so different from themselves and considered it positively dangerous to the cause to have him frequenting the houses of my friends. Gottfried Feder even brought out a pamphlet which accused Hitler of preferring 'the company of beautiful women' to his obligations as the head of a working-class Party. This was a direct reference to my sister Erna, and particularly to my wife, for whom Hitler had developed one of his theoretical passions, a tendency which will loom large and tragic in this story.

It was on another occasion, at the house of Heinrich Hoffmann, his photographer friend, that I started playing some of the football marches I had picked up at Harvard. I explained to Hitler all the business about cheer leaders and marches, counter-marches and deliberate whipping up of hysterical enthusiasm. I told him about the thousands of spectators being made to roar 'Harvard, Harvard, Harvard, rah, rah, rah!' in unison and of the hypnotic effect of this sort of thing. I played him some of the Sousa marches and then my own *Falarah,* to show how it could be done by adapting German tunes, and gave them all that buoyant beat so characteristic of American brass-band music. I had Hitler fairly shouting with enthusiasm. "That is it, Hanfstaengl, that is what we need for the movement, marvellous," and he pranced up and down the room like a drum majorette. After that he had the S.A. band practising the same thing. I even wrote a dozen marches or so myself over the course of the years, including the one that was played by the brown-shirt columns as they marched through the Brandenburger Tor on the day he took over power. Rah, rah, rah! became *Sieg Heil, Sieg Heil!* but that is the origin of it and I suppose I must take my share of the blame.

One thing that became borne in on me very early was the absence of a vital factor in Hitler's existence. He had no normal sex life. I have said that he developed an infatuation for my wife, which expressed itself in flowers and hand-kissings and an adoring look in his eyes. She was probably the first good-looking woman of good family he had ever met, but somehow one never felt with him that the attraction was physical. It was part of his extraordinary gift for self-dramatization, part of hidden complexes and a constitutional insufficiency which may have been congenital and may have resulted from a syphilitic infection during his youth in Vienna.

At this early period the details were unknown to me and one could only sense that something was wrong. Here was this man with a volcanic store of nervous energy, with no apparent outlet except his almost medium-like performances on a speaker's platform. Most of his women friends and acquaintances were the mother-type, Frau

Bruckmann and Frau Bechstein. There was another woman in her sixties I met, named Carola Hoffmann, who was a retired school-teacher and had a little house in the Munich suburb of Solln, which he and his cronies used to use as a sort of sub-headquarters, where the good lady mothered Hitler and fed him with cakes.

We used to think at one time that Jenny Haugg, his driver's sister, was his girl friend. She had a nice figure and big eyes and looked like a shopgirl, which indeed she was. She was a niece, or at least a relation, of Oskar Koerner and was an employee in his toy shop near the Viktualien Markt. Frau Anna Drexler, to whom I used to talk about it, said that Jenny and Adolf met at the house of a little jeweller named Joseph Fuess in the Corneliusstrasse, but that the girl had a youthful crush on Hitler which he in no way recipro-cated. She even used to carry around a little pistol in an armpit holster as his voluntary extra bodyguard. When he had dinner with us in the Gentzstrasse he would go out on the balcony as the evening drew on and watch for his car to arrive. Jenny would often be sitting in the back seat waiting for him. They would drive off together, but I knew he was only going to a café to stay up talking half the night. A bit of petting may have gone on, but that, it became clear to me over the course of time, was all Hitler was capable of. My wife summed him up very quickly: "Putzi," she said, "I tell you he is a neuter."

One evening as we were walking home from the Café Neumaier, Hitler signalled to the others that he wanted to go ahead with me alone. I had been feeding him with ideas and items of news culled from the foreign press and had been agreeably surprised to find them cropping up in his speeches. The man was open to influence and I felt encouraged to continue exerting all I could. "Herr Hanfstaengl," he said, "you must not feel disappointed if I limit myself in these evening talks to comparatively simple subjects. Political agitation must be primitive. That is the trouble with all the other parties. They have become too professorial, too academic. The ordinary man in the street cannot follow and, sooner or later, falls a victim to the slap-bang methods of Communist propaganda."

I agreed wholeheartedly and told him that one of the things which had most impressed me with the conviction of his eventual success was his ability to speak in homely terms, with a real punch behind his words. I told him, and it was not all that far-fetched a comparison, given the totally different conditions in the two countries, that he reminded me of Theodore Roosevelt. The former President had a vigour and courage, a vitality and familiarity with all manner of men, with a style of action and utterance which, being so direct, had endeared him to the plain folks. "People in Munich say that all you and your Party stand for is tumult and shouting, brutality and violence," I went on. "It may console you to know that all those things were said about Roosevelt, but he did not listen and carried the country with him." I told him of the effective use in American political life of telling catch-phrases and explained how this was buttressed by snappy headlines in the newspapers, putting ideas over with a phonetic, alliterative impact.

"You are absolutely right," Hitler replied. "But how can I hammer my ideas into the German people without a Press. The newspapers ignore me utterly. How can I follow up my successes as a speaker with our miserable four-page *Völkische Beobachter* once a week? We'll get nowhere until it appears as a daily." He told me of the great plans they had for this if only they could find the funds.

It must have been that evening that I decided to render more substantial help. About this time I received one of the instalments due to me for surrendering my share in the Academy Art Shop in New York to my partner. It was about $1,500, but that represented an absolute fortune when converted into depreciated marks. Apparently there were two American rotary presses for sale, and if their purchase could be financed it meant that the *Beobachter* could come out as a daily in a full size format. I learnt that a thousand of my dollars would make up the required sum, incredible as it may seem, and one morning I went down and handed it over to Amann in greenbacks, on the understanding that it should be an interest-free loan. He and Hitler were beside themselves. "Such generosity. Hanfstaengl, we shall never forget this. Wonderful." I was as pleased as they, as I felt that with its transformation from a shrill pamphlet to a daily, my influence might serve to increase its appeal and broaden its outlook. I got a *Simplicissimus* cartoonist named

Schwarzer to design the new masthead and suggested the slogan *Arbeit und Brot* – work and bread – myself.

The *Beobachter* came out as a small format daily in February 1923. The purchase and installation of the rotary presses and internal reorganization took some time and the first issue in the large size was in fact dated August 29, 1923. In the meantime I had been given my first taste of the divide and rule tactics by which Hitler maintained his position in the Party. As successor to Dietrich Eckart, whose health was beginning to fail, he appointed Alfred Rosenberg as editor.

CHAPTER III

ONE SIDE TO A STATUE

*Begging expeditions – Hitler escapes a Communist patrol –
From bombs to women boxers – Hitler's fixation with Leda
and the Swan – His* faux pas *as an art expert – Diamonds and
a fedora hat – The plans for Czechoslovakia – Hitler's gifts as a
mimic – Poison on his birthday – Orator in excelsis – Goering,
Hess and Haushofer.*

THE PARTY was permanently short of funds. In fact the conversion
of the *Beobachter* into a daily, for all its propaganda value, had only
made the financial situation worse in other respects and Hitler was
always on the look-out for other sources to tap. He seemed to think
that I would be useful with my connexions, but however interested
and encouraging my friends were, they did not choose to dip into
their pockets. I simply have no clear idea where the Party revenues
came from. There is little doubt that, in its early stages, the German
army command in Bavaria had provided subsidies for an organization which gave every promise of fighting the Communists, but by
1923 I suspect this source was drying up, as the Nazis were becoming
too independent. Most of the subscriptions were private. There was
a Frau von Seidlitz who had helped over the printing presses and
two Finnish ladies living in Munich who subsidized what they
assumed was an anti-Bolshevist crusade, probably under the
influence of Rosenberg. Dietrich Eckart picked up a lot of the bills
himself. He had a substantial income from his book royalties. Some
of the national-minded Bavarian industrialists were doubtless
prodded into giving a cheque from time to time, but it was all hand-
to-mouth stuff and there were always debts awaiting payment and
nothing to meet them with.

Hitler seemed to think that I would give an air of respectability to
his begging expeditions and we went on several trips round Munich
and its environs visiting prominent citizens. One journey I recall was

to Bernried, on the Starnberg Lake, to see a retired consul-general of private means named Scharrer, who was married to a member of the Busch family from St. Louis. They had a colossal *nouveau-riche* establishment full of white peacocks, borzois and tame swans, but we got no change out of them, at least not on that occasion. As the situation was getting serious Hitler determined to try his luck in Berlin. There was a business man there named Emil Gansser, of the firm of Siemens & Halske. He was often in Munich and was an admirer of Hitler, and a friend, I think, of Dietrich Eckart. He was an imposing figure, in spite of his broad Swabian dialect; he wore stiff white collars and starched shirts, was always dressed in a black coat and striped trousers and was an educated man of some substance. He had promised to try and interest his acquaintances in Berlin and Hitler had determined to see if the personal touch would produce results.

Rather to my surprise he asked me to accompany him and we drove off one morning, it must have been about the beginning of April, with Emil Maurice at the wheel of the ramshackle Selve. Fritz Lauböck, a callow youth of about eighteen, made up the party. At that time Hitler had some idea of making him his secretary. We took the Leipzig road, which leads through Saxony, where the Government at that time was more or less in the hands of the Communists. Hitler was taking a considerable risk in travelling this way, as an order was out for his arrest there as a nationalist agitator and there was even a price on his head. A few months before they had arrested Ehrhardt, the Organization Consul leader, who had been down on the Tegern Lake to see his former Kapp Putsch conspirator General Lüttwitz and had also been in touch with Hitler over plans for the campaign against the French in the Ruhr.

We were just coming up to Delitzsch, travelling fairly fast round a curve, when we saw the road was blocked by a unit of Communist militia. I don't think any of us said anything, there was no time. But I saw Hitler tense and his hand take a firm grip on his heavy whip, as we came to a stop. I had a sudden inspiration. "Leave it to me," I muttered as the militia came up and asked to see our identity documents. I got out of the car and produced the impressive Swiss passport on which I had travelled back from the States. "I am Mr.

Hanfstaengl," I said, in the most atrocious German-American accent I could muster. "I am a paper manufacturer and printer and I am visiting the Leipzig Fair. This is my valet," pointing to Hitler, "my chauffeur and the other gentleman is the son of a German business associate." It worked. My papers were written in English and they made no attempt to look at the documents of the others, but waved us on in surly fashion. I jumped in and we tore off.

Hitler fairly babbled his thanks: "Hanfstaengl, you really carried that off well. They would have had my head. You have saved my life." How true this was I do not know. He would certainly have faced a stiff prison sentence and had he been in gaol the events of 1923 which culminated in the Feldherrnhalle Putsch might have turned out quite differently. He might never have acquired the notoriety on which his future rise to power was based. But he never forgot the incident. In later years whenever we drove within miles of the spot he would turn round and say: "Hanfstaengl, do you remember? That was a nasty situation you got me out of." Even so, I think he resented having been called my valet, even as a ruse, and when garbled accounts of this incident were given in the later Nazi biographies, my name was never mentioned in connexion with it.

We got to Berlin and drove through the Brandenburger Tor past the Adlon Hotel. I suddenly thought, heavens what happens if any of my friends see me in this company, especially Kommer or Pallenberg – it was one of their haunts. I was still keeping my support for the Nazis as secret as possible and could not afford any social uproar on the subject. I said that I would spend the night at an Evangelical hospice behind the State Theatre in the Unter den Linden, so I was dropped off after making arrangements to meet the next day. I had not the faintest idea where Hitler was staying and in fact I do not think he even told Maurice until the last moment. It was typical of the extraordinary personal security arrangements he took all his life. It was only later that I learnt that accommodation had been arranged for him by Ohnesorge, a senior post office official whom he knew and in the fullness of time appointed Postmaster-General in the Nazi Government.

Gansser lived somewhere out in the suburb of Steglitz and we had some difficulty finding the house. He came and opened the door very carefully himself and, to my astonishment, I found that behind his staid exterior he was a crackpot inventor. There were tubes and retorts and presses all over the place and the bathroom looked like a scene out of *Faust*. He was apparently making some new form of bomb no bigger than a tennis ball which would blow up a house. He was an engaging and in fact harmless character and took a great fancy to me. I found out later that he was always telling Hitler what a good influence I was. He and Hitler disappeared together for a while and then we set off in another vehicle, which our host had organized, although he did not accompany us. It was a closed van, again part of Hitler's mania for secrecy. We drove all over Berlin and Hitler would get out leaving my six-foot-four curled up inside like a grasshopper. What on earth use to him I was I do not know, as he never told me who he had seen or what the result was. Perhaps I just kept up his spirits.

I did not get the impression that the canvassing was very successful and Hitler had plenty of time to spare. On the Sunday morning after we arrived, we arranged to meet at the war museum. Hitler had promised to show young Lauböck round Berlin and this is where he probably felt most at home. We foregathered, not at the entrance, but somewhat secretly up on the first floor, by the glass cabinet which contained the last uniform of Frederick the Great, who was, with Marshal Blücher, Hitler's historical idol at the time.

Hitler must have been in the museum before, as he knew all the guide-book facts by heart and this mute evidence of past Prussian military glory was clearly balm to his nostalgia. He spouted endless facts and details about the guns and uniforms, maps and impedimenta with which the place was filled, but I remember chiefly his morbid fascination with the sculptured embellishments on the cornices and keystones in the courtyard. These were a series of heads of dying warriors by Schlüter: "I can tell you, Hanfstaengl, when you have seen war from the front lines as long as I did, you are lost in admiration for Schlüter's genius. He was unquestionably the greatest artist of his time. Even Michelangelo did nothing better or more true to life." I could not help being impressed by what Hitler said. I had this sense of insufficiency at not being able to take part in the war myself. There was still a very strong tinge of the ex-servicemen's association in the Nazi Party and in this I found some compensation.

Looking back at the visit now, some of Hitler's reactions provided an interesting insight into his character. There was this idealization of death in the Schlüter masks, his Frederick the Great and Blücher cult and the satisfaction he found in the more than life-sized statues of warriors – the élite, like the giant grenadiers of Frederick William I, destined to sacrifice themselves on the battlefield. As we walked out to the Unter den Linden again, we went past the two monuments by Rauch of Frederick the Great, on horseback and Blücher, on foot. I remarked how strange it was that the old Marshal had not been depicted at his most typical – mounted at the head of a cavalry charge. This did not appeal to Hitler's infantry mind at all. "*Ach*, Hanfstaengl," he said, "what difference would a horse make? They all look at same and only spoil concentration on the figure of the rider." Hitler was allergic to horses, and when he came to power abolished all the cavalry divisions in the German Army, an act which his generals in the Russian campaign were bitterly to regret.

I tried to get Hitler to fall in with a trick I had learnt from the well-known artist and etcher Luigi Kasimir, whom I had met as a student in Vienna and then accompanied on a tour through Italy. Kasimir always maintained that you could only appreciate the success of a sculptor's work if you walked right round a statue, viewing it from all angles. Although I was now talking on my own subject, Hitler preferred not to comply. He declared that the best effect could only be gained by standing within the range of vision of the figure depicted in the statue, and when I insisted, said that the traffic on the Unter den Linden made my circular tour impossible. He repeated his first argument when we went over to look at the monument to William I by Begas, which is, from the artistic point of view, one of the best equestrian statues in the world. I realize now that in this, as in so many other circumstances, Hitler only recognized or was interested in one aspect of a problem. He would never admit that there were two sides to a question – or to a statue.

Our next stop was the national gallery. This at least was my home ground and I was about to lead him to a dozen of the best pictures and talk about their style and place in history when Hitler took charge again. He simply could not bear not to dominate any situation in which he found himself, but in this case his mania for always being right led him astray. "The first thing is for young Fritzl to get a general impression," he said – *einen Ueberblick* – it was a favourite word of his and highly indicative of his mental processes. He liked to get a superficial view of a whole situation in his mind before dealing with the details of its parts. We swept past the Dutch and Italian primitives like a patrol of Bersaglieri. There was a slight slowing of the pace in front of Leonardo da Vinci's *Flora*, but we only came to a stop opposite Rembrandt's *Man in a Golden Helmet*:

"There you have something unique," Hitler pontificated. "Look at that heroic, soldier-like expression. It proves that Rembrandt, in spite of the many pictures he painted in Amsterdam's Jewish quarter, was at heart a true Aryan and German!" Here was just the way not to teach young Lauböck about art, but worse was to come. With barely a glance at the superb Berlin Vermeers, we galloped in search of Hitler's other artistic hero, Michelangelo. The Berlin museum had no originals of this master, only a marble statue of the young John the Baptist which is ascribed to him, probably erroneously. Hitler came to a halt in front of this lightly poised, almost feminine figure and proclaimed, for Lauböck's benefit: "Michelangelo – that is the most monumental, the most eternal figure in the history of human art," all the time looking round somewhat desperately for better examples of his work. "What have they done with the casts they used to have in this room? Stay here a moment and I will go and find them."

With this he disappeared, leaving me to put young Lauböck right about the one example in front of us, telling him that Michelangelo could only really be studied in Florence and Rome. Hitler did not come back, so we went after him. We found him lost in concentration in front of Correggio's *Leda and the Swan*. He pulled himself together as we arrived, and although it was the sensuous portrayal of the two central figures which had fascinated him, read us a hasty lecture about the wonderful play of light on the bathing nymphs in the background. Over the course of time I discovered that the subject of this picture was almost an obsession with him. In later years this, almost the most obscene of classical subjects, was sure to obtain a gold medal for any modern German artist who used it as his subject at one of the Nazi exhibitions.

We quick-marched again and were just passing through the Italian Baroque room on the way to the exit when Hitler came to a sudden halt in front of Caravaggio's *Matthew the Apostle*, a somewhat florid and not particularly successful composition. I was thunderstruck, especially as it was the first Christian subject at which Hitler had cast a glance. Then I understood. With his hunger for Michelangelo still unsatisfied, Hitler had misread the plaque. The name of the artist started with Michelangelo all right, but he had overlooked the other two words, which read Amerighi – Caravaggio. "There you are, Fritzl," said Hitler triumphantly. "There was no end to his genius. There is no time now but we shall have to come back and look at it again." I often wondered whether he did and whether he ever found out his mistake.

That afternoon, as there seemed nothing better to do, I suggested to Hitler that we go and spend a couple of hours at the fun fair in Luna Park. We looked around the side-shows and found that one of the main attractions was a group of women boxers. This seemed to appeal to him, so in we went and watched several matches. It was, I suppose, quite daring stuff for its day, with the women in abbreviated trunks and vests, mincing around and landing the occasional tap. It was all pure circus, but Hitler was rivetted. He managed to keep his face expressionless and made a few superior comments about boxing being a very fine thing, that this was only a put-up job and not the right thing for women and so on. But we had to stay until the show was over. "Well, at least it was better than this duelling with sabres that goes on in Germany," Hitler remarked, but I could see he was keeping a very tight rein on himself. After all women boxers are not the highest form of aesthetic spectacle and Hitler was taking good care not to show how much he had enjoyed it.

We had a couple of beers and were admiring the sunset from the top of a long terrace of steps, more or less on our way out, when someone with a camera recognized Hitler and tried to take a photograph of him. Who it was I do not know to this day, as the Nazis had practically no organization in Berlin at all. It may have been

someone who had seen him in Munich. Hitler was horrified.
Perhaps he had a bad conscience about the women boxers. He
went straight up to the man and said he must surrender his film,
that he could not possibly allow a picture of himself taken in Luna
Park to appear, that he would be ruined, that it would cause a
tremendous scandal and more in the same vein. The argument went
on for an hour and more, with Hitler reaching ever greater heights
of hyperbole, how this would be the final blow to the German
Freedom Movement, like a man possessed. In the end the other poor
fellow, who had really meant no harm, but merely wanted a good
picture as a souvenir, gave in and promised that he would not
develop the film, to which indeed he kept, as it certainly never
appeared anywhere. If it had become known that Hitler was in
Berlin it might have had quite serious results, as Karl Severing, the
Prussian Minister of the Interior, was a declared enemy of the
N.S.D.A.P. and had, I believe, also issued an order for Hitler's
arrest.

During the second or third evening in Berlin Hitler took me along
to dinner with the Bechsteins. They had one of those hideous great
houses built in the 1870's, somewhere in the centre of the city. It was
all very pretentious in the manner of the Berlin *haute bourgeoisie,*
but fortunately the daughter Lotte was not there, so I was spared
being involved in Frau Bechstein's domestic plot. We talked about
politics, the Party and the future, but our hosts shied away whenever the question of money came up. No, times were difficult, there
were so many obligations and Herr Hitler must understand. This
did not prevent Frau Bechstein sitting there with diamonds as big as
cherries strung round her neck and wrist, so I ventured a social
solecism and suggested that if only she could raise money on them it
would keep the Party going for months. I was to learn later that she
did just that with some of her jewellery, although Hitler never mentioned the fact. All we got as we were ushered out was a hat. As we
came into the cloakroom he could not find the broad-brimmed black
gangster affair in which he normally went round. In its place there
hung a very expensive greyish-yellow fedora. "It is one of my husband's," said Frau Bechstein, "and he would like you to accept it as
a present." Hitler took it and thanked his hostess profusely. At least

it looked better than the other one and did not emphasize the pallor of his face to the same extent.

It had been a fruitless enough trip and Hitler was pleased to leave again the next morning for Munich. We took a long detour to avoid Saxony and finally spent the night at the Post Hotel opposite the station in Bayreuth, where Hitler signed himself in as an author. He had been introduced to Siegfried and Winifred Wagner, I think by Dietrich Eckart, but they were not at their home on this occasion, so I suggested the next morning that we should go and look at the festival theatre, which he had never seen.

The place was all locked up, but I managed to find a caretaker who let us in, and there, lo and behold, in the dim light the stage was set for the *Flying Dutchman*. It was the same scenery which had been left standing when war broke out in August 1914. The theatre had never been used since and nothing had been touched. It was an ideal moment for a little family history, as the original stage setting had been devised by my great-grandfather, Ferdinand Heine, who did much work at the Dresden Opera House, where it was first produced. He had designed the scenery for the first performance of Weber's *Freischütz* and later became an older friend and patron of Wagner. There is quite a collection of Wagner letters to him and they produced *Rienzi* together as well as the *Flying Dutchman*. Hitler drank in all these details and was impressed and moved. We walked all round the theatre, finally stopping in the room which Wagner had used as a study, where his instructions to the artists and staff still hung on the wall. Hitler was entranced and I was pleased to have impressed him, as I felt it gave me a broader base from which to try and influence his political ideas.

I had been increasingly uneasy since our first serious talk in the Gentzstrasse flat, as although he had seemed to take in quite a lot of my information about America, the subsequent weeks had found him again returning to his old ideas of political strategy in purely Continental terms. On the last lap to Munich we stopped for a picnic lunch. I can remember the spot exactly. We drove up into a wood just before crossing the Danube and sat watching the river sweep by. We had ham and cheese sandwiches and bottles of beer. He talked about the journey and then mentioned the monument outside Leipzig

we had seen on the way up, which commemorates the Battle of the
Nations against Napoleon in 1813.

"The most important thing in the next war will be to make sure
that we control the grain and food supplies of western Russia,"
Hitler said. I was appalled. Rosenberg and company had been at
him again. Rosenberg, who spoke Russian better than he did
German, wielded tremendous influence on Hitler and his associates
when it came to propagating this anti-Bolshevist, anti-Russian line.
Anyone who could claim to be a Russian expert was able to sing this
sort of song in the Party all day long and Rosenberg was the most
adept at it. Behind their arguments lay the desire to return to their
lost lands in the Baltic countries.

I tried to turn Hitler's thoughts into less fanciful channels. "It is
no good," I told him. "Even if you overrun western Russia it will
not help in the long run. You can have all the wheat in the world,
but you need more than that to fight wars. The country to reckon
with is America, and not only do they have more wheat than you can
ever capture, but more iron and more steel and more coal and more
clear blue sky and more people. If you have them on the other side
you will lose any future war before you start it." He half grunted and
stopped short, but I could sense that the argument had not really
sunk in.

Soon he was off on another tack, complaining about the roads
over which we had just travelled. In all conscience they had been
bad enough, most of them dirt and flint tracks, with the Bavarian
highways even worse than the Prussian. "Look at the way we have
to travel round Czechoslovakia to get to eastern Germany," he said.
"The whole thing is a nonsense. Half the people on the other side of
the border are Germans anyway and it is all wrong to have this alien
government placed across our lines of communication." Then dropping his voice: "What is more, we shall have to get those Skoda
works in Pilsen under German control one of these days." And this
mind you was in early 1923. I only regarded this line of thought as
a possibly curable aberration in those days, but it shows the extraordinary tenacity of his ideas. I was probably entirely wrong in sup-
posing that they could ever be influenced, but in many respects he was
still malleable and I looked on his false conceptions as something that

might be successfully combated. "Mind you get hold of that Pilsen beer too," I had joked. He had come out of his reverie and laughed.

We got up and drove the last few miles home. There was nothing in the surroundings to detain him. He had little eye for, and took little pleasure in, the beauties of nature as such. Trees and streams and hills evoked no positive response. He was essentially a town dweller and only felt at home in the market place. His mind was filled with the plans of a frustrated architect. He liked to sketch new buildings or draw vast urban vistas, but the country-side had no message for him. He was already spending a certain amount of time at Berchtesgaden, which he subsequently made into his nearest approach to a home, but although he would sit brooding over the mountain scenery, it was really only the solitude that fed his thoughts. The solitude and the sense of power that came from the height, and the fact that he was able without interruption to plot and plan political moves with his cronies.

For all that he was an entertaining travelling companion. He would sit whistling or humming passages from the Wagner operas, which kept us both amused for many an hour. In all the years I knew him, however, I never heard him whistle a popular tune. He was also a gifted mimic with a sharp sense of the ridiculous. He could imitate Gansser's Swabian accent to a nicety, but his star turn was a sort of symposium of the type of patriotic orator then very common in Germany and by no means extinct since – the politically conscious, semi-professorial figure with a Wotan-like beard. Hitler's nationalism was practical and direct, but they would boom away about Siegfried's sword being drawn out of its scabbard and lightning playing round the German eagle and so forth. He could invent this mock rhodomontade *ad infinitum* and be very funny about it. He also knew by heart the greater part of a dreadful poem which some admirer had written in his honour. This poetaster had looked up in the rhyming dictionary all the German words which end in 'itler', of which there are several score, and had produced an endless series of ill-scanning couplets. When he was in a good mood Hitler would repeat this with embellishments of his own and have us in tears of laughter. His other party pieces included imitating Amann in a rage with some importunate bill collector, or that little red-haired horror

Quirin Diestl insulting a political opponent. He could also imitate market women and children superbly. Some people might say that a gift for mimicry is the sign of an undeveloped personality. In his case it was an example of the extraordinary *rapport* he could establish with the minds and emotions of others. It was a trait which Hitler kept for as long as I knew him.

A day or two after our return Hitler celebrated his birthday, on April 20. I went along during the morning to congratulate him and found him alone, although the grubby little flat was stacked from floor to ceiling with flowers and cakes. Yet Hitler was in one of his curious wary moods and had not touched a single one of them. There they were, with swastikas and eagles in whipped cream all over them, looking like the bakers' pavilion at a village fair. It was not much to my taste, I am a beer and sausages man myself, but even my mouth watered. "Well, Herr Hitler," I said, "now you can really have a feast." – "I am not at all sure they are not all poisoned," he replied. "But they are all from your friends and admirers," I told him. "Yes, I know," he replied. "But this house belongs to a Jew and these days you can drip slow poison down the walls and kill your enemies. I never eat here normally."

"Herr Hitler, you've been reading too many of those Edgar Wallace thrillers," I answered, but nothing would persuade him, and I literally had to take a taste myself before he would touch them. Then he started to brighten up, as I had come along to pander to another of his superstitions – astrology. I had looked up the dates and found out that he not only shared the same birthday with such redoubtable Putsch-makers as the Pole, Albert Korfanty, who had led the third insurrection in Upper Silesia in 1921, and Napoleon III, but that it was the same date on which Cromwell had dissolved Parliament. Hitler had always had a romantic obsession with Cromwell and this delighted him. "Ah, Cromwell," he said, "that's my man. He and Henry VIII are the only two positive figures in English history."

It seemed a good moment to bring up something which had been worrying me ever since I had met him, and that was his stupid little moustache. There had been a time during the war when he let it grow, but the first time I saw him it was already clipped back to the ridiculous little smudge which made it look as if he had not cleaned his nose. I called on the evidence of Van Dyck, Holbein and Rembrandt to bear witness that a moustache should either grow out full or at most be clipped to the end of the lips. I said I felt it would be much more dignified if he followed one of these patterns. He took it quite unmoved. "Don't worry," he said, "I am setting a fashion. As time goes on people will be pleased to copy it." And in due course it was to become as much a Nazi trade mark as the brown shirt.

In fact he was not vain about his appearance. He was always decently, soberly and unostentatiously dressed and did not expect to impress on his exterior alone. His appeal lay in his power as an orator, and this he knew and played on for all he was worth. He was a *Sprachmensch* and believed in the power of the spoken word to overcome all obstacles. He even judged others by the same standards, and he never really had confidence in the ability of anyone who could not talk forcibly, reserving his special approval for those who could hold a large audience. This is one of the basic reasons for the final rise in his confidence of Goebbels, although the diabolical little doctor had not at this time appeared on the scene. Not that any of the Nazis were national figures in 1923. The spring edition of the Brockhaus encyclopaedia referred to Hitler vaguely as Georg Hitler and a *Times* newspaper dispatch in which he had been referred to in connexion with Ehrhardt spelt his name as Hintler.

I had by this time been to a number of his public speeches and was beginning to understand the pattern of their appeal. The first secret lay in his choice of words. Every generation develops its own vocabulary of catchwords and phrases, and these date their thoughts and utterances. My own father talked like a contemporary of Bismarck, the people of my own age bore the stamp of Wilhelm II, but Hitler had caught the casual camaraderie of the trenches, and without stooping to slang, except for special effects, managed to talk like a neighbour of his audience. In describing the difficulties of the housewife without enough money to buy the food her family needed in the Viktualien Markt he would produce just the phrases she would have used herself to describe her difficulties, if she had been able to formulate them. Where other national orators gave the painful impression of talking down to their audience, he had this priceless gift of expressing exactly their own thoughts. He also had the good sense, or instinct, to appeal to the women in his audience, who were after all the new political factor in the 1920's. Many a time I have seen him face a hall plentifully sprinkled with opponents ready to heckle and interject, and in his search for the first body of support, make a remark about food shortages or domestic difficulties or the sound instinct of his women listeners which would produce the first bravos. And time and again these came from women. That would break the ice.

By now I was numbered among his immediate supporters, sitting behind him on the platform. Time and again I noticed that during the first part of his speeches he stood with his knees braced back, rigid and immobile, until he provided the first sounding shot which brought a response. Every speech he gave had a past, a present and a future. Each appeared to be a complete historical survey of the situation and although his gift of phrase and argument was infinite in its variety, one sentence always reoccurred at an early stage: "When we ask ourselves today what is happening in the world, we are obliged to cast our minds back to. . . ." That was the sign that he had his audience under control and, taking the events leading up to the collapse of the Kaiser's Germany, he would build up the whole pyramid of the current situation according to his own lights.

The gestures which had so impressed me the first evening I saw him were as varied and flexible as his arguments. They were not, as in other speakers, stereotyped movements to find some employment for his hands, but an integral part of his method of exposition. The most striking, in contrast to the dull slamming of the fist into the palm of the other hand of so many orators, was a soaring upward movement of the arm, which seemed to leave infinite possibilities piercing the air. It had something of the quality of a really great orchestral conductor who instead of just hammering out the downward beat, suggests the existence of hidden rhythms and meaning with the upward flick of his baton.

To continue the musical metaphor, the first two-thirds of Hitler's speeches were in march time, growing increasingly quicker and leading up to the last third which was primarily rhapsodic. Knowing that a continuous presentation by one speaker would be boring, he would impersonate in a masterful way an imaginary opponent, often interrupting himself with a counter-argument and then returning to his original line of thought after completely annihilating his supposed adversary. There was a curious tinge to the finale. It was gradually being borne in on me that Hitler was a narcissus type for whom the crowd represented a substitute medium for the woman he did not seem able to find. Speaking for him represented the satisfaction of some depletion urge, and to me this made the phenomenon of his oratory more intelligible. The last eight to ten minutes of a speech resembled an orgasm of words.

I hope it will not appear too blasphemous when I say that he had learnt a lot from the Bible. He was to all intents and purposes an atheist by the time I got to know him, although he still paid lip-service to religious beliefs and certainly acknowledged them as the basis for the thinking of others. His pattern of looking into the past and then repeating the basis of his beliefs four times over derived directly from the New Testament, and no one can say it was not a proven method. His political arguments were based on what I came to call the system of the horizontal figure of eight. He would move out to the right, expend his criticism and curve round to the left for approval. He would continue on to reverse the process and come back dead centre to end up with *Deutschland über alles* to a roar of joint applause. He would attack the former ruling classes for their surrender of the nation, their class prejudices and feudal economic system to applause from the Left-Wingers, and then riddle those who were prepared to decry the true traditions of German greatness to the applause of the Right-Wingers. By the time he had finished he had everyone agreeing with everything that he had said. It was an art no one else in Germany possessed and my absolute conviction that it must in due course lead him to the top of the political pile only confirmed my intention of staying as near to him as I could.

Hitler suffered no one in the room when he was working on his speeches. In the early years he did not dictate them as he did later. It took him between four and six hours to block one out on large foolscap sheets, about ten or twelve in number, with, in the end, only fifteen or twenty words on each as a cue. When the hour of the meeting approached he used to walk up and down the room as though rehearsing in his mind the various phrases of his argument. During this time the telephone would keep ringing, with Christian Weber, Amann or Hermann Esser on the line, to tell Hitler how things were going in the hall. He would ask how many people there were, what their mood was or whether much opposition was to be expected. He would give continuous directions concerning the handling of the audience while they were waiting for him and, half an hour after the meeting had started, would call for his overcoat, whip and hat and go out to the car preceded by his bodyguard and chauffeur. On the platform he used to place his sheets of notes on a table at his left and, as he had finished with each one, pass it over to a table on his right. Each page would suffice for ten or fifteen minutes of his speech.

When he had finished the band used to play the national anthem. Hitler would salute to right and left and leave while the music was being played. He had usually reached his car before the singing was over. This sudden withdrawal had a number of advantages. In addition to facilitating his exit unmolested to the car, it prevented the exultation of the crowd from petering out, saved him from unwelcome interviews and left intact the apotheosis picture the public had received from the end of his speech. He once said to me: "Most speakers make the great mistake of hanging around after their speech is over. This only leads to anticlimax, as argument and discussion can completely undo hours of oratorical labour."

Where he had me, and in the course of time millions of others, completely confused is that he did not give vital words the same meaning as we did. When I talked of National-Socialism I meant it in the old Friedrich Naumann sense, a fusion of all that was best in the traditional and socialist elements of the community. Hitler was not thinking along the lines of a patriotic confederation of this sort at all. We all knew, but overlooked the deeper implications of the fact, that the first flowering of his personality had been as a soldier. The man speaking up on the platform was not only a superb orator, but also a former army instructor who had succeeded in winning the minds of fellow-servicemen tainted by the November revolution. When he talked of National-Socialism what he really meant was military-Socialism, Socialism within a framework of military discipline or, in civilian terms, police-Socialism. At what point along the line his mind took the final shape it did I do not know, but the germ was always there. He was not only a great orator, but taciturn and secretive to a degree, and he seemed to have an instinctive sense of what not to say in order to mislead people concerning his true intentions. But there again I am speaking with the hindsight of thirty years.

I had by this time taken to dropping in frequently at the *Völkische Beobachter* offices, usually with a clip of foreign newspapers excerpts in the hope of getting them to pay some attention to events in the outside world. I had little success. Instead of making an effort to deal constructively with the affairs of the League of Nations, for example, all Rosenberg wanted were articles and news items dealing with his particular anti-Bolshevist, anti-clerical or anti-Semitic prejudices. However, I did get to know two more Hitler lieutenants, Hess and Goering. I soon found the latter more entertaining company than anyone else in the entourage. He had made his way to Bavaria after the post-war collapse of Germany, as the safest haven for those with nationalist sentiments. Goering was not the intellectual type, but he had entered Munich University and attended a series of lectures by the well-known historian Karl Alexander von Müller, on the subject of the German war of liberation against Napoleon. Hess had attended the same course and they had both gravitated to Hitler for the same reason which had attracted me, after hearing one of his speeches.

Hess was installed as a sort of administrative aide-de-camp to Hitler, and Goering was engaged in building up and endeavouring to bring under his control the embryo S.A. Hess was a moody introvert, jealously suspicious of anyone who approached Hitler too closely. He came of quite a decent family and his uncle had done his military service in the same guard artillery regiment, under the Prince Regent Luitpold, in which my brother had been killed as an officer in the war. But even this did not provide a point of contact and he was as morose and aloof with me as with everybody else. In later years, he endeared himself to me slightly more by asking me to play Beethoven during one of my piano sessions. He had been to school in Bad Godesberg, near Bonn, Beethoven's birthplace, and had developed a liking for the master's music.

Goering was a complete *condottiere*, the pure soldier of fortune, who saw in the Nazi Party a possible outlet for his vitality and vanity. Nevertheless, he had a jovial, extrovert manner and I found myself very much at home with him. Before long we were on 'thou' terms and that was probably as much due to our wives as anything. Karin Goering, who had an Irish mother, came of a substantial Swedish family and was at least a lady, a woman of charm and education, and she and my wife Helene saw a lot of each other. Goering had a certain humorous contempt for the little squad of Bavarians round Hitler, whom he regarded as a bunch of beer-swillers and rucksack-carriers with a limited, provincial horizon. In his over-loud way he at least brought a whiff of the great outside world with him, and his war record with its *pour le mérite* had given him a much wider set of contacts.

He and Karin lived extremely well, although most of the money was hers, and they had a house out at Obermenzing, near the Nymphenburg Palace, where he had fitted up a sort of plotters' corner in the cellar, all very Gothic and Germanic, with great pewter tankards. My wife and I used to go out there sometimes, but not very often, as we had no car and had to rely on the Goerings to get us there and back. In fact, my only form of transport was a gigantic, elderly Swift bicycle which had belonged to my father, who was the same size as I am. This I kept by me right up into the 'thirties, by which time I was without any question the only unmotorized member of the Nazi hierarchy. But then I took an idealistic view of the Party's duty to the working classes. I remember rebuking Goering once at one of the Munich cafés for screwing a monocle into his eye and then looking round with the stupid air of superiority that the wearers of such objects usually affect. *"Mein lieber Hermann,"* I told him, "this is supposed to be a working-class party and if you go round looking like a Junker we shall never attract their support." Whereupon he looked rather deflated and sheepish and stuffed it in his pocket.

Hitler found Goering useful, but was a little cynical about the *ménage*. He called on us late one evening after he had been out there and mimicked the pair of them for my wife. "It is a real love-nest," he told her. "It is darling Hermann this and darling Hermann that" – imitating Karin's slightly too-fond voice. "I have never had such a home and I will never have one" – continuing with a sort of mock-sentimentality, "I have only one love and that is Germany." (An echo of Wagner's *Rienzi*, I might add.)

The Goerings also had an unpleasant-looking gardener named Greinz, to whom I took an immediate dislike and who was to play a highly dubious rôle before the year was out. He was always out-wardly full of the true Party spirit, barking slogans and flashing his eyes, but I never trusted him. "Hermann," I said one day, "I will bet any money that fellow Greinz is a police spy." "Now really, Putzi," Karin broke in, "he's such a nice fellow and he's a wonder-ful gardener." "He's doing exactly what a spy ought to do," I told her; "he has made himself indispensable."

Goering and Hess could not stand each other and provided one of the many personal rivalries in the party which endured through the years and enabled Hitler to play one off against the other. Apart from their differences in temperament, they had both been fliers during the war, but instead of this bringing them together it only seemed to exacerbate their relationship. Moreover, Goering was a man of action and had little time for the theoreticians of the Party. In his confused way this was the capacity in which Hess fancied himself. He had a common background with Rosenberg when, as members of the racial Thule Society, they had narrowly escaped with their lives at the time of the Munich Soviet Republic in 1919. He had also come greatly under the influence of the Bavarian General Haushofer, who had spent a period of duty in the Far East and had come back a rabid Japanophile.

Haushofer had a chair at Munich University and his geo-political nonsense helped to provide a number of the mental barriers which I had to try and surmount in order to influence Hitler's mind. The only foreign ally of which the Rosenberg-Hess group could conceive was Japan, the Prussians of the East, as they called them, and I tried over the years in vain to make them see that such an alliance would inevitably bring Germany into conflict with the United States. But the trouble was that there were many of them and only one of me.

Every time I tried to bring Hitler to his senses, one of them would always start him on the wrong track again.

As often as I tried to pump some salt water into Hitler's veins the others blinded him with the dust of the infantry. Up he would come with the old catch-phrases of *Ostpolitik* and stab-in-the-back, the brave German Army betrayed, treachery on the home front, the coming day of reckoning with the November criminals in Berlin and the final passage of arms with France. There he would be back with Clausewitz, and this led to the identification of these crazy longings with the military figure who was lending his prestige to the nationalist ferment – the man who was regarded as a tragic figure who had been betrayed by Freemasons and Socialists and Communists, the great hope and the galleon figure of German militarism and the unbeaten Army – General Ludendorff. On him they pinned their hopes, and the result was nearly to prove Hitler's undoing.

CHAPTER IV

PARTICULAR GENERALS

*Ferment in Bavaria – Hitler and Roehm – Pyromania in the
Rhineland – Jewish Anti-Semites – Dietrich Eckart loses faith
– Rhinoceros whips in the courtyard – Rosenberg insults
the Catholics – An offer from Mathilde Ludendorff – Hitler
tempts General von Seeckt – Compromising reluctant allies.*

THE NAZIS were only one of the numerous Right Wing radical
organizations flourishing in Bavaria at the time. In fact, apart from
the trump card they held in Hitler, they were by no means the most
numerous or important. Bavaria had become the refuge of a whole
rag-bag collection of militant nationalists, some of whom were unemployed members of the former *Freikorps*, which had helped the
Army to beat down the soldiers' Soviets that had sprung up all over
Germany after the war. The reason why they were left free to plot
and agitate in Bavaria was twofold. First, there was the historical
antipathy of Catholic, separatist-minded Bavaria towards Protestant
Berlin and its Central Government. Secondly, the Bavarians had had
a sharp dose of Communism under the régimes of Kurt Eisner and
Ernst Toller after the war, and after their ejection the Government
had remained firmly in the hands of the *Reichswehr* and a succession
of Conservative State cabinets. With the Central Government in
Berlin predominantly Socialist, the Bavarian authorities sought
actively to thwart it and encouraged for their nuisance value all the
disgruntled Right Wing elements who flocked south for safety.

To describe the situation as confused is an understatement. Most
Bavarians wanted to restore the Wittelsbach monarchy. But some of
them wanted the King to rule again over an independent Bavaria,
some wanted him to become the head of a new Danubian confederation, and others wanted the family installed as German Kaisers. The
acknowledged leader of the Right Wing refugees from the rest of
Germany was Ludendorff, but he was anathema to the Bavarian

nationalists, due to his crack-pot attacks on the Roman Catholic Church, and his followers were distrusted as Prussians. The French occupation of the Ruhr in January 1923 provided a final seasoning to this brew, and the whole year was spent in a rage of nationalistic agitation, with most of the intransigence emanating from Bavaria. The chief part played by Hitler was to try to unite the various patriotic organizations and secure the co-operation of the Bavarian Government, and particularly of the local *Reichswehr*, for a march on Berlin to overthrow the Socialist Government and repudiate the terms of the Versailles Treaty. That he got as far as he did is an astonishing example of what one determined man can accomplish in times of such confusion.

He worked more or less openly with the Ehrhardt Brigade people, although there was much mutual distrust between them, and it was in the fight to maintain the S.A. as a separate organization that Goering won his spurs. When I first started going to the *Beobachter* offices, which was the headquarters of the plot, the two men on guard outside Hitler's door were not S.A. men at all, but members of the Organization Consul, that section of the Ehrhardt group which had been behind the murders of Erzberger and Rathenau, although there is no reason to suppose that Hitler was in any way involved with these assassinations. In any case, how any work ever got done in the office is beyond me. Hitler was a man who thought everything could be accomplished by speeches and that underlings could be left to look after the paper work.

He drove everyone to exasperation, as he could never be relied upon to turn up for an appointment and it was impossible to get a decision out of him. One unfortunate collaborator, who will have a part to play later in this story, was Captain Hans Streck, who was a close confidant of Ludendorff. He was a former artillery officer who had been on the Bavarian General Staff and wanted to organize the office along efficient lines. When he tried to bring some order into the motor pool by sacking drivers who turned up late for duty, he found Hitler insisting that they should be reinstated because they were old Party members. In the end he just gave up. Lt.-Col. Hoffmann, who was in fact an Ehrhardt man and Goering's adjutant, complained of the same thing. Hermann was bone-lazy. His car would arrive at the door hours late for an appointment, with Karin sitting in the back with some titled woman friend. Before he could be pinned down, they were off again to have lunch at one of the expensive restaurants.

With all this, Hitler kept up a drum-fire of exhortation. *"Meine Herren,"* he would say, when they managed to pin him down in conclave, "don't bother me with details. There will be time enough for them. Within a fortnight we act, come what may" – so that in the midst of disorganization everyone was kept at white heat. There were endless marches and demonstrations, reviews and speeches and sabre-rattling, but nothing decisive ever occurred. One ghastly fiasco was a great review of the semi-militarized formations out on the Fröttmaninger Heide, which was supposed to end with their marching into the town and occupying the Government buildings. The only trouble was that it was pelting with rain and Goering, who was riding up and down on a white horse with his *pour le mérite* strung round his neck, was soaked to the skin. Some were for marching, but most were not, and in the end all that happened was that the leaders came back to my Gentzstrasse flat for some much-needed hot coffee.

At about the same time, May 1, a similar demonstration was held on the Oberwiesenfeld, for which some of the S.A. men had raided an Army depot and got hold of some machine-guns. The *Reichswehr* had been allowing them to train with them for weeks and they probably thought they had a right to them. However, Army headquarters thought this was going too far and made them hand them all back. It was all a distinct blow to Hitler's prestige.

The whole movement was much more military in its style in those days. There were not so many swastikas and the processions were always headed by the German war standard. The S.A. usually marched together with the *Viking Bund*, who were Ehrhardt's militarized formations. The music was Bavarian, but the colours were the black, white and red of the Kaiser's Reich. In fact the Imperial flag gave its name to another organization, the *Reichskriegsflagge*, which was headed by Captain Roehm, and that is where I first came across him. He had been the political adviser on the staff of General von Epp, who had liberated Munich from the Communists in 1919, and he was still a serving officer in Munich on the staff of the local

Army Commander, General von Lossow. He was a man of considerable influence and Hitler's chief link with the *Reichswehr.*

Whether by then he had developed the proclivities for which he
became notorious is an open question. Certainly during the war his
interest in women had been normal and some say he only returned
as a homosexual from two years of exile in Bolivia in the later
'twenties. But even if he was not yet an active pervert there were
plenty of others around who were. Heines and one or two other
patriotic organization leaders became notorious for their tastes in
this direction. And when I thought of my earliest contact with a
Nazi recruiting agent, it occurred to me that there were far too many
men of this type around Hitler.

Part of the curious half-light of his sexual make-up which was
only slowly beginning to preoccupy me, was that, to say the least, he
had no apparent aversion to homosexuals. I suppose it is true to say
that in any male movement of this sort, with one man at its head,
you are bound to have a lunatic fringe of sexual perverts. Such men-
admirers will always gravitate into a group which, through its very
cohesion, manages to take over some of the leading posts. But the
Balts and Prussians, who formed such a large proportion of the
membership of these organizations, did not seem to share my misgivings. "Do not worry, these people will fight like lions against
Bolshevism. It will be like the Sparta of old," they used to say. "It
becomes a sort of *Liebestod* for them when they fall in front of the
enemy." Hitler had a circumlocution for it. "My most enthusiastic
followers must not be married men with wives and children," he
would proclaim. "No one with family responsibilities is any good for
street fighting."

It was also in Roehm's company that I saw Heinrich Himmler
again, although the connexion was not what you might think. The
school sneak had become a sort of adjutant, who ran the administrative side of the *Reichskriegsflagge*, while Roehm attended to his
Army duties. He had a pale, round, expressionless face, almost
Mongolian, and a completely inoffensive air. Nor in his early years
did I ever hear him advocate the race theories of which he was to
become the most notorious executive. Somewhere, in the meantime,
I think it was in Weihenstephan, he had studied to become a

veterinary surgeon, although I doubt if he had ever become fully qualified. It was probably only part of the course he had taken as an agricultural administrator, but, for all I know, treating defenceless animals may have tended to develop that indifference to suffering which was to become his most frightening characteristic. We had, however, a common Bavarian background and that and my having studied under his father added a little warmth to our acquaintance. He was never anything but polite and forthcoming and even friendly with me. After the Nazis assumed power this was to have its uses.

I used to think back to Himmler's father sometimes, when the Rosenberg clique expounded their ideas of a crusade against Russia. At some time or other Himmler *père* had undertaken a remarkable journey by sledge right across Russia as far as Novaya Semlya and he had never been able to get the impression of these vast spaces out of his mind. At school he used to chalk a map on the blackboard and point out the impossibility of ever conquering Russia from the west. "Russia is an open triangle," he used to say. "Whoever marches in from the west can only capture ever larger wastes of snow and must suffer the fate of Napoleon." I remembered his arguments and drawings with absolute clarity and sometimes quoted him in an attempt to confound Rosenberg and company. But his son's friends thought they knew better!

As light relief from this constant atmosphere of revolt, Hitler would often go to the cinema in the evening, a form of relaxation which continued right through the years when he was Chancellor. In fact I have known him put off serious conferences in order to see a film. One of the great successes of the time was the *Fredericus Rex* film, which came out in two parts, with Otto Gebühr playing the rôle of Frederick the Great. I had seen the first part the previous year at Garmisch with Rudolf Kommer and the second part ran for weeks in the spring of 1923 at the Sendlinger Tor Platz cinema. My wife and I took Hitler to see it. He was most impressed, but it was typical of him that the scene which had pleased him most was that in which the old king, played by Albert Steinrück, had threatened to have the crown prince beheaded. "That is the best part of the film," Hitler ranted as we came out, "what a classic example of discipline when a father is prepared to condemn his son to death. Great deeds require harsh measures." Then we got on to talking about the resistance movement in the Ruhr during the French occupation and I brought up the historical parallel of the Russian resistance to Napoleon. Suddenly Hitler thundered: "Hanfstaengl, I tell you only guerrilla tactics will be effective. If the Russians had shown any scruples in 1812, Napoleon would never have been defeated and Rostopchin would never have had the courage to set fire to Moscow. What does it matter if a couple of dozen of our Rhineland cities go up in flames. A hundred thousand dead would mean nothing providing Germany's future was assured." I was thunderstruck – we were on the open street and were just walking past the Schiller monument. I could only shrug my shoulders and say that Rostopchin provided a bad example for Germany as we were deprived of the most important strategic element, the endless space of Russia. It was still too early to see that this pyromaniac aspect of Hitler's character would end in his nihilistic readiness to see Germany reduced to dust and ashes.

I was not the only one who worried about these sudden outbursts of Hitler. Dietrich Eckart was as preoccupied as I was and in despair at the influence that Rosenberg was gaining on him. Eckart had always been one of my favourites, a big bear of a man with sparkling eyes and a genuine sense of humour. But one day when I called on him at the *Boabachter* I found him literally in tears. "Hanfstaengl," he groaned, "if only I had known what I was doing when I introduced Rosenberg into the Party and then allowed him to take over the editorship here, with his rabid anti-Bolshevism and anti-Semitism. He does not know Germany and I have a very strong suspicion that he does not know Russia either. And then that name of his on the front page. He will make a laughing-stock of us all if this goes on." I thought back to Rudolf Kommer's remark about an anti-Semitic programme directed by Jewish or half-Jewish fanatics – Rosenberg was distinctly Jewish in appearance, although he would have been the first to protest furiously if anyone had questioned his ancestry. Yet I used to see him most mornings sitting in a dingy café at the corner of the Briennerstrasse and the Augustenstrasse, with a Hungarian Jew named Holoschi, who was one of his principal assistants. The man called himself Hollander in Germany and was another of these Jewish anti-Semites. In later years Rosenberg became the intimate friend of Steffi Bernhard, who was the daughter of the editor of the *Vossische Zeitung*, but this did not prevent him from producing ceaselessly the arguments and propaganda with which the Nazis sought later to justify their worst excesses. I suspected the Aryan background of many of the others, Strasser and Streicher looked Jewish to me, as well as later figures like Ley. Frank, and even Goebbels, would have had difficulty in proving their pedigree.

Eckart made no bones about speaking his mind. A group of us were walking across the Max-Joseph Platz one day after lunch on the way to Hitler's flat and I was a couple of yards ahead with him. "I tell you I am fed up with this toy-soldier stuff of Hitler's," he growled. "Heaven knows the Jews are behaving badly enough in Berlin and the Bolshevists are an even worse lot, but you cannot build a political party on the basis of prejudices alone. I am a writer and a poet and I am too old to go along with him any more." Hitler was only just behind and must have caught the tenor of the words, but he made no sign and no comment.

I was even more worried about Rosenberg's anti-clerical diatribes, especially in Catholic Bavaria. It seemed to me suicidal to go out of the way to offend such a vast majority of the population. I took Hitler aside one day and tried to make him see the danger by explaining it in his own terms. I had come across some figures somewhere and told him that more than 50 per cent of the holders of the Iron Cross were Catholics, although they only formed a third of the total population. "These people are good soldiers and good patriots," I insisted. "Just the sort of supporters we need to get on to our side." I had also met, accidentally, a Benedictine abbot named Alban Schachleiter. I had sat next to him in a tram and brought down the point of my umbrella on his sandalled foot. He bore me no ill will and as I found that he was a fellow Bayreuth enthusiast we got on famously. He had been evicted from Czechoslovakia and, although he had a certain amount of sympathy for Hitler's general political line, deplored the Party's anti-clericalism. I met him again at the house of my sister Erna, and we arranged to lunch there together with Hitler. They got on very well and Hitler listened and nodded and appeared to be impressed by the abbot's arguments. I was delighted, convinced that I had brought a useful influence to bear, but the contact did not last long. In a way I was myself the cause of the break, which was a by-product of the shooting of Leo Schlageter.

The French had executed Schlageter in Düsseldorf on May 26 for acts of sabotage. The Nazis later claimed him as one of their own and made him one of the major figures in their Pantheon, but I doubt very much whether he was ever a member of the Party. The news reached me at Uffing on the Staffel Lake, where I had just bought a house, as it had proved impossible to find anything comfortable in Munich to substitute for our little three-roomed flat. The papers were full of the Schlageter affair and the various patriotic organizations planned to hold a mass demonstration in his memory on the Königsplatz in Munich on the following June 1, which, as I recall, was a Monday. Schlageter's parents had been devout Catholics and it seemed to me essential for Hitler to take part in the meeting, and I hoped it would be possible to give it a solemn religious flavour as well as a patriotic one.

I caught the train to Berchtesgaden but found Hitler in an unforthcoming mood. No, there was so much to do and there would be so many people speaking anyway, it was not worth his time. He perked up a little when I suggested that the thing to do was to transport the coffin in solemn procession round Germany in imitation of the passage of President Lincoln's funeral, which my mother had seen and so often described to me. This did not prove practicable, but I had also armed myself with the works of Carlyle, and pointed out the quotation to Hitler about 'any nation which fails to honour its dead can no longer call itself a nation'. This appealed to him immensely and we sat down to block out the speech together round this central idea.

By this time it had become late and I decided to stay the night at the boarding-house Hitler used to frequent at Berchtesgaden. The place was crowded and I found myself doubling up with Dietrich Eckart, who was in his most disillusioned mood and distinctly dampened my spirits. The Pension Moritz it was called, run by a former racing driver named Büchner. His wife, Elisabeth, was a towering Brünnhilde type with a flashing gold tooth, and Hitler had developed for her one of his unproductive, declamatory passions. He used to play the romantic revolutionary for her benefit, stamping round and cracking a rhinoceros-hide whip she had given him. Before we went to sleep, Eckart unburdened himself for hours about Hitler: "You know, Hanfstaengl," I remember him saying, "something has gone completely wrong with Adolf. The man is developing an incurable case of *folie de grandeur*. Last week he was striding up and down in the courtyard here with that damned whip of his and shouting, 'I must enter Berlin like Christ in the Temple of Jerusalem and scourge out the moneylenders', and more nonsense of that sort. I tell you, if he lets this Messiah complex run away with him he will ruin us all."

I had had the further idea of getting Schachleiter to bless the standards of the S.A. formations taking part in the Schlageter demonstration and had been very pleased when I got Hitler to agree to it. After the speeches – Hitler spoke last and scored one of his greatest successes – they marched in formation to the church of St. Boniface, behind the Königsplatz, where the remains of Ludwig I of Bavaria lie, and the banners were blessed with holy water after Schachleiter had preached a pretty inflammatory sermon about 'this great freedom movement', and so on. What happened a couple of days later? Rosenberg came out in the *Beobachter* with another of his really offensive anti-clerical leaders, with stupid insults about Christ and taunts against the Catholics. It was really too much. Poor Schachleiter was not only furious, but had to leave the living at St. Boniface not long after because of the storm which had been aroused. I took Hitler to task, telling him that Rosenberg was spoiling everything, but as usual he found excuses, said he would talk to Rosenberg and in the end did nothing.

All that was left of my part in the affair was the Schlageter song which I composed at the time and which became an integral part of the Nazi brass-band repertoire. I cannot write music myself, but I thumped out the melody and got an old Imperial *Kapellmeister* to orchestrate it for me. The Schlageter affair had really brought the general atmosphere to crisis pitch, and in spite of my disappointment I was determined to keep as near to Hitler as possible in the hope that more profitable occasions would present themselves for exercising a restraining influence.

I was very busy getting the Uffing house into order and arranged for a high stone wall to be built round it, with the somewhat vague idea that if we were going to be faced by a state of emergency it would prove a useful retreat. Hitler came over one day and stayed to lunch and then we went on to Murnau, where he was to address a meeting. I cannot remember quite why, but a number of people had come down from Munich to hear him and we went on afterwards to the house of Gottfried Feder, who lived near by. Feder had been one of the founder-members of the Party and was its financial expert, but a hopeless crank. I do not want to harp on the subject, but he looked so Levantine and swarthy that his nickname in the Party was 'the Nubian bath-attendant'. He was by no means an uncultivated man and was the brother-in-law of Karl Alexander von Müller, the historian. He had an attractive wife with a very pleasant soprano voice and after dinner and coffee I sat down and played the piano for her. It was a lovely August evening. The doors were open, the moon was shining and Hitler relaxed and was rather enjoying himself.

Just as we were congratulating ourselves on humanizing him, one of the guests insisted on starting a high-flown philosophical discussion. This was Mathilde von Kemnitz, who was to become the second Frau Ludendorff. She was an impressive woman of ample proportions, who, I think, was already contributing something to the inchoate ideas of founding a new Nordic religion which was later to occupy most of their time. She boomed away about the universe and Nordic blood and Hitler got pretty testy with her. "As far as I am concerned the universe only has astronomical meaning," he tried to cut her short. But this smacked too much of materialism for her. She went on about the necessity of producing a new philisophy for the age until Hitler broke in and said: "It is no business of mine to found a new philosophy. My problems are purely practical and political. Perhaps in the future some philosopher will succeed in reducing what we have done to some neat new system."

This was unfortunately just the opening his partner needed. Rising to her full height—she was wearing a sort of chiffon tent and every outline of her massive person was clearly visible – she announced: "But Herr Hitler, that philosopher already stands before you." This was too much even for Hitler, who tore his eyes away from her silhouette and stood up to go. It was now quite late, but the Feders pressed us to stay with them. So in the end we shared a bedroom, Hitler on the bed and myself on the couch at its foot. "You see," I told him, "you not only have to deal with the Communists but with the whole tribe of blue-stockings. They will get you yet. I doubt if you will sleep very well tonight." He chuckled. I often used to tease him like this, and I was almost the only person from whom he would take a certain amount of badinage.

The political situation in Bavaria had by this time reached boiling-point. The fall of the Cuno Government in Berlin on August 13 and the gradual lifting of French pressure in the Ruhr gave a new impetus to nationalist agitation. At Nuremberg, at the beginning of September, a hundred thousand men from the patriotic organizations paraded past Ludendorff and made him the head of an alliance called the *Deutscher Kampfbund*. Shortly afterwards Hitler was appointed its political chief. On September 26 the Bavarian Premier, von Knilling, declared a state of emergency and appointed General von Kahr commissioner-general with supreme administrative powers. On the same day, President Ebert in Berlin delegated the executive functions of government throughout the Reich to the Minister of Defence, Gessler, and the head of the *Reichswehr*, General von Seeckt, with instructions to maintain law and order through the local army commanders. The commanding general in Bavaria was von Lossow, a man who was still personally under the spell of Ludendorff and sufficiently contemptuous of the Berlin Government to ignore its orders. He played a waiting game, ready to use his forces to advantage depending on whether Ludendorff and Hitler on the one hand, or the Bavarian separatists, who could count on the support of von Kahr, would successfully take the initiative.

Although I only came into possession of the facts years later through a relative of my second wife, Colonel von Selchow, there had been a highly significant conference between Seeckt, Lossow and Hitler as early as March 11, 1923. Selchow had been Seeckt's adjutant at the time, and apart from Lossow's adjutant, Captain Oxner, was the only other person present.

Seeckt had come to Bavaria on a tour of inspection and shortly before he left Lossow persuaded him to meet a 'political prophet' who Lossow maintained must play a considerable part in the future. The interview took place in the Army headquarters building, where Hitler launched into a tirade lasting an hour and a half about the situation. He ranted about the French in the Ruhr, the Lithuanians in Memel, the Communist Government in Thuringia and suggested, in short, that Germany was on the brink of collapse. His plan called for a coalition of all nationally-minded people, the formation of a huge militia under the S.A. and the expansion of the army. The French were to be forced out of the Ruhr and the shackles of the Versailles Treaty broken. At the end he gazed at Seeckt and said: "Herr General, I offer you the leadership of the whole German working-class movement."

Seeckt, who had listened to this outburst without interrupting once, replied curtly: "Herr Hitler, what is your attitude to the soldier's oath of allegiance?" Hitler jumped from his chair: "Herr General, my offer was not intended to conflict with your present duty of loyalty. It is self-evident that you cannot break your oath to the Weimar Government. We National-Socialists will see to it that the members of the present Marxist régime in Berlin will hang from the lamp-posts. We will send the Reichstag up in flames and when all is in flux we will turn to you, Herr General, to assume the leadership of all the German workers."

Now it was General von Seeckt's turn to rise: "In that case you and I, Herr Hitler, have nothing more to say to each other." As Hitler was ushered out Oxner went over to Selchow and whispered: "From now on Seeckt is a dead man." In the train on the way back to Berlin Seeckt talked to his adjutant for hours about this episode: "Come what may," he commented, "General von Lossow has assured me that Hitler cannot make a Putsch without the *Reichswehr*, and that suffices for the time being. I simply do not believe that the *Reichswehr* could be brought to fire on other *Reichswehr* units."

Hitler had never at any time referred to this conversation when talking to me. Selchow wrote down the details that night in his diary and his evidence is absolutely incontrovertible. The most astonishing aspect is the fact that Hitler had Lossow and his staff under his spell to such a degree that Oxner could commit such a flagrant breach of military discipline.

Such a situation of conflicting loyalties was made to order for Hitler. The *Reichswehr* had in the past regarded the Nazis with a benevolent eye and although their support had waned they might yet be won over again. The separatists were rivals but in their detestation of the Berlin Government possible allies. Definite action might yet weld every faction into a common front. The Nazis were growing in favour with many sections of the public and Hitler felt it only needed a major demonstration of some sort to make the position crystallize. He had powerful allies and could permit himself dangerous liberties. Franz Gürtner, the Bavarian Minister of Justice, was already a secret Hitler convert, and, with the sympathetic support of the police president, Poehner, and his chief assistant, Wilhelm Frick, enabled him to avoid the efforts of Schweyer, the Bavarian Minister of the Interior, to fasten charges on him as a disturber of the peace.

Hitler was engaged in a constant round of visits and interviews – Lossow, Poehner, Roehm and Scheubner-Richter, another Balt and a crony of Rosenberg, who was closely associated with Ludendorff. Max Erwin von Scheubner-Richter had been a Russian agent in Constantinople during the war, had defected to the Germans and had found a place among the Right Wing societies in Munich as an envoy of the White Russian and Ukrainian emigrants. Part of the strength of his position was due to the fact that he had persuaded the Grand Duchess of Coburg, who was a relative of the Russian royal family, to channel funds through him to the patriotic organizations. He was another 'stab-in-the-back' propagandist, who saw in the defeat of Germany only a failure of supplies and of the home front, to be cured by gaining control of the granaries of the Ukraine and White Russia.

Hitler did not really mind what form the uprising against Berlin took as long as there was an uprising. If the situation had appeared favourable, he might even have supported a separatist Putsch and

then mounted a counter-Putsch under the old Imperial colours
which he would then direct from within along National-Socialist
lines. I used to accompany him sometimes on his endless journeys
round Munich and remember one phrase he used constantly: *"Wir
müssen die Leute hineinkompromittieren"* – "We must compromise
these people so that they have to march with us," which was typical
of the blackmailing techniques the Nazis later developed.

The key to the situation was Lossow and the *Reichswehr*. Hitler
knew that all the officers were longing to wipe out the indignities of
the immediate post-war years, when they had had their badges of
rank and medals torn off by Communist mobs. Although their hero
remained Ludendorff, they recognized in Hitler the political *deus
ex machina* of the threatened revolt and a great many of them gave
him secret support. Even the members of the infantry cadet school
were affected by the general atmosphere and had developed a complete contempt for the authorities in Berlin. One of them – it may
have been young Xylander, who came from one of the best Munich
families – was going round wearing the cockade on his cap reversed,
which was an accepted formula for indicating the famous phrase
from Goethe's *Götz von Berlichingen* '*Leck mich am A———.*' Another
popular simile for this insult was to stick the postage-stamps with
President Ebert's head upside down.

Sometimes I could only admire Hitler's effrontery. On one occasion he was addressing a small meeting in the street, outside the
Beobachter office, with a S.A. guard, when a couple of mounted
police trotted up and tried to disperse them. They really meant
business, but Hitler berated them with all the strength of his orderly-
room vocabulary and asked them what they meant by drawing
sabres against their friends. Did they not realize that they only had
sabres because people like Hitler and his Nazis were fighting the
Communists, who would have taken them away from them? He
produced such a torrent of abuse and argument that in the end the
police just gave up and went away.

Hitler's 'in fourteen days we will march' had acquired a new
urgency. His mind was wholly centred on the necessity for action.
"Hanfstaengl, the only way to organize a Putsch is at a week-end,"
he said to me. "All the people in the administration will be away

from their offices and the police will only be at half-strength. That is the time to strike." He was putting every ounce of his energy into the struggle. At one point he booked the huge Krone Circus hall for a solid week and spoke there every afternoon and evening. They were some of the best speeches he ever gave and one, specifically directed at the students, was an absolute masterpiece.

On the last day, the Sunday, the authorities had forbidden any formations to march with unfurled flags and banners. As soon as the meeting was over the S.A. tramped off to the Mars Feld with their flags furled. But either due to a misunderstanding or deliberate disregard of orders, the second battalion, under Brückner, unrolled their flags and, on turning into the Arnulfstrasse, met a strong police cordon. There was a clash, and the story as I heard it maintained that one of the flag-bearers had had his wrist severed by a police sabre. Whatever the cause there was uproar at headquarters and Hitler sent Goering and myself to see von Kahr to complain of the brutality of his security forces. Somehow the incident was smoothed over. Even Kahr was not prepared to clamp down on the Nazis, so confused had the situation become.

I was sitting in Hitler's office with him that evening and he became so restless that he decided that Goering, Ulrich Graf and I should accompany him on a reconnaissance trip round the city to see if there were any new developments. This was typical of him; you could never keep him off the streets. We ended up in the Hofbräuhaus about eight o'clock at night and Hitler had the idea of getting the people out of the big courtyard in the back to follow us in a protest march, just for the sake of raising hell. The beer-drinkers would have none of it and, after calling us all the names under the sun and telling us to get out, started bombarding us with their heavy mugs. One whistled past my nose and shattered against the wall, spraying beer all around. I had not even ducked, which shows what a greenhorn I was in such matters. We had to beat a hurried retreat.

Any reason to start a Putsch was sufficient. One week-end – it must have been in October – I found Rosenberg in a high state of excitement: "We are just getting out the proclamations." "What on earth for?" I asked him. He pulled himself together a little and pronounced, in his omniscient Baltic way, "The next few days will see the opening of a new chapter and we must be ready." I inquired around and discovered that he had concocted a crazy plan for capturing Prince Rupprecht and his staff, together with the whole Government, at the unveiling ceremony of the monument to the Unknown Soldier in front of the Ministry of War.

Hermann Esser and I managed to stop that by arguing that any attack on Rupprecht's person would inevitably bring out the *Reichswehr* in force against us. Ludendorff and Scheubner-Richter had also been behind this plan, which was a good indication of how completely out of touch they were with the true situation in Bavaria. It gave me a chance to have another dig at Rosenberg and warn Hitler of the perils of getting too closely involved with the Baltic plotters. However, it was a bad time to ride my particular hobbyhorse. "America is a long way away," Hitler said to me. "We must think first of a march on Berlin. Once we have dealt with the immediate situation then we can look around and I can find Rosenberg another job."

Hitler continued to rail at the Central Government in Berlin with impunity, and at the beginning of October von Seeckt ordered Lossow to suppress the *Völkische Beobachter*. Under pressure from Kahr, who in turn thought he might be able to use the Hitler-Ludendorff forces, nothing was done, and when Lossow failed to carry out a further peremptory order on October 20, he was dismissed from his command. In the conflict of loyalties he opted to support his neighbours. The centuries-old tradition of the formerly independent Bavarian Army reasserted itself and dislike of the General Staff in Berlin took precedence over military discipline. With von Kahr and Colonel von Seisser, the chief of the State Police, von Lossow formed a triumvirate to govern Bavaria as an independent State. Their aim was to restore the Wittelsbach monarchy, and their plan, as it later became clear, was first to use the Ludendorff-Hitler forces and then crush them. The scene was set for the next act.

CHAPTER V

FIASCO AT THE FELDHERRNHALLE

Plan for a Putsch – Cracks in the Kampfbund *– Double-cross at the Bürgerbräu – Kahrfreitag – Red wine for Ludendorff – Fusillade in the Residenzstrasse – My escape to Austria – Hitler's attempted suicide.*

MUNICH LITERALLY boiled with plot, counter-plot, demonstrations and rumour during the twenty days following von Lossow's defection with the Bavarian Army Corps. The best place to try and keep track of developments was at the *Beobachter* offices. I spent part of each day there and was sitting with Rosenberg in his room around midday on November 8 when Hitler told us he had decided to launch his Putsch.

Rosenberg was such an unappetizing fellow. He had only recently married, but his colleagues on the paper recounted innumerable stories about his unsavoury love life, which usually involved multiple intercourse with half a dozen men and women companions at a time in some grubby back-street flat. It must have been the Tartar in him. In dress he had the taste of a costermonger's donkey, and on this occasion I remember very well he was wearing a violet shirt with a scarlet tie, with a brown waistcoat and blue suit. He had some theory about it being a waste of money to wash shirts and used to throw them away when they became unwearable even by his standards.

However, there I sat with him in his little white-washed office. His desk was diagonally across the corner of the room, on it the pistol he always kept prominently displayed. We could hear Hitler stomping up and down the corridor and heels clicking as he called out "Where is Captain Goering?" It was all very military. Then he burst into our room, pallid with excitement, trench-coat tightly belted and carrying his riding whip. We both stood up. "Swear you will not mention this to a living soul," he said in a tone of suppressed urgency. "The hour has come. Tonight we act. You, Comrade Rosenberg, and you, Herr Hanfstaengl (I was still not a Party member) will be part of my immediate escort. Rendezvous outside the Bürgerbräu Keller at seven o'clock. Bring your pistols."

So that was the plan. The Bürgerbräu Keller had been booked for that evening by the ruling triumvirate for a major meeting of all the leading Bavarian personalities, to which Hitler and Ludendorff had been invited. Our informants in the ministries and the police had told us that this was to be the forerunner of the proclamation of the Wittelsbach restoration and the final break with the Socialist Government in Berlin. This was the point where Hitler and Ludendorff differed radically with their fellow-conspirators. The National-Socialists and the *Kampfbund* also wanted to do away with the Red Republic in the capital, but they wanted an integrated nationalist Germany under the black, white and red flag, and no part of Bavarian separatism under its white and blue banner. Even less were they prepared to listen to the plans of some Bavarians to join a Danubian federation with Austria.

Uneasy allies as the two groups had been, each had supported the other tactically as long as there seemed profit to be gained from the collaboration. Two days earlier the *Kampfbund* people, with Hitler, had been called to Kahr's office, where he and Lossow warned them to instigate no Putsch until the Provisional Government itself gave the signal. It was only after this meeting that Hitler learnt that the Catholic separatists had their own plans for taking the initiative. Now he proposed to unite the public ferment by a *coup de main*.

I may myself in a small way have helped to bring matters to a head. One of the journalists whom I helped to keep informed about events used to reciprocate by telling me of any remarks he had heard in Government circles. This newspaperman lived in the Regina Hotel, and in order to draw less attention to our relationship I used to announce myself as Georg Wagner, by which hangs a tale which I shall have to tell in due course. A couple of weeks or so before the Putsch, this newspaperman had called on von Kahr and had abstracted from him the information that he had no intention whatsoever of bringing Hitler into the Government in spite of their apparent alliance. The information did not come as a great surprise to Hitler when I passed it on: "That's typical of the cunning old rogue," he commented.

A similar tip had come from Count Lerchenfeld, a former Prime Minister, who still had considerable influence in affairs. I was sitting with my journalist friend in his room when Lerchenfeld was announced. There was no time for me to leave without meeting him in the corridor, so I retreated hurriedly into the bathroom. I could hear very little of what was being said, but as Lerchenfeld stood up to go he must have turned in the direction of my hiding-place and I caught the words: "No, no, we shall have no use for the National-Socialists, they are far too radical for our purposes."

This further annoyed Hitler, but was typical of the atmosphere of double-cross and triple-cross reigning in Bavaria at the time. Even some of our apparently firm allies in the *Kampfbund* were by no means to be trusted. Roehm and his *Reichskriegsflagge* could be relied upon. In fact he stormed and held the War Ministry with the officer cadets the following day. On the other hand, Ehrhardt was a much more doubtful element, although some of his *Viking* people were still on duty in the *Beobachter* offices, to outward appearances in closest harmony with the National-Socialists. I had rung up there from Uffing a few days earlier, got a crossed line and thus was witness to a conversation which made it clear that Ehrhardt's men were disposing of some of the mutual stocks of arms in a distinctly suspicious manner. I warned Hoffmann, Goering's adjutant, but as he also was a member of the *Viking* organization the matter was somehow covered up. However, my suspicions were more than justified as on the day of the Putsch Ehrhardt sided with Kahr.

Nor was Ehrhardt the only one. Captain Kautter, another of Goering's *aides*, also switched allegiances and defended Kahr's ministry when the time for decision came. Poehner, who had been superseded as police president, but still wielded great influence, was another doubtful ally. He had protected Hitler in many ways and great reliance was placed on his attitude. But when the Putsch foundered he lost his nerve and Goering and Roehm obtained no support from him, although he had made himself sufficiently suspect to stand trial later with the others.

Many of the titled officers in the affiliated patriotic organization professed dual loyalties. Crown Prince Rupprecht used to be referred to quite frequently as 'His Majesty', and a proportion of the *Kampfbund* membership was distinctly Wittelsbach monarchist in outlook. So much so that for many years Hitler appeared to let it be understood that he intended to restore monarchical forms of government, an attitude which later brought considerable Bruns-wick, Hesse and Hohenzollern support, only for all of them to complain about being betrayed in the end.

What was to prove an even more decisive factor was Hitler's disregard of the need to placate Catholic opinion. Ludendorff and a considerable proportion of the North German nationalist mal-contents who had found refuge in Bavaria were either Protestants or violently anti-Church and specifically anti-Catholic. The mistake was to assume the Putsch would succeed with their help alone. General von Epp, himself a Roman Catholic, had been so grossly offended by Rosenberg that he became indifferent to any Putsch led by Hitler and Ludendorff. Von Epp's action in ordering a Mass and Te Deum of thanksgiving to be held in Munich's largest square at the liberation in 1919, had led Rosenberg to refer to him repeatedly in sarcastic articles in the *Beobachter* as the '*Mutter-gottes-General*'. This so alienated von Epp that he would have little further to do with the Nazis. Yet he had a personal following of some 25,000 Life Guard reservists and his influence on Hitler's side might have tipped the scales.

This then was the fantastically confused situation, and here was Hitler giving Rosenberg and myself orders to buckle on our pistols and liberate Germany. That morning, in a desperate ogle in von Lossow's direction, the *Völkische Beobachter* had come out with a great picture on the front page of General Yorck von Wartenburg, who carried the Prussian Army over to the Russians against Napoleon at Tauroggen, with the caption: "Shall we find a second General Yorck in our hour of need?" Rosenberg and I had been discussing its possible effect when Hitler burst in on us. After cast-ing an approving glance at the copy on the table, Hitler said to me, as he turned to leave: "I shall rely on you to look after the interests of the foreign press." In a moment or two I followed. Hitler's announcement had at least stopped Rosenberg's infuriating habit of whistling through his teeth when I talked to him, but the time had clearly come for action rather than for further incivilities.

My first thought was to arrange for my wife, who had just become pregnant again, and my two-and-a-half-year-old son, Egon, to leave Munich. Walking quickly back to my flat in the Gentz-strasse, which I still retained as a *pied-à-terre*, I told them to pack up and go that afternoon to Uffing. I also had to pass the word round to the international journalists, such as H. R. Knickerbocker, and Larry Rue of the *Chicago Tribune*, who had come flocking to Munich in the expectation of exciting events, that they must under no circumstances fail to be at the Bürgerbräu Keller meeting that evening, although I could not, of course, tell them why. I was confused enough myself at the course events might take and although I tried to see Hitler again during the afternoon for a further discussion to clear our minds, I was unable to get in touch with him. I was told that he was in conference with Captain Eduard Dietl of the Bavarian general staff, who was one of his chief infor-mants in the *Reichswehr*, and who later commanded a division in Norway and Finland.

I learned later that the plan for the Putsch had in fact been devised by Schenbner-Richter, who had also received information that von Kahr was about to take the initiative. Be that as it may, Hitler obtained all the credit, as Scheubner-Richter was one of those killed at the Feldherrnhalle the following day.

The Bürgerbräu Keller, an eminently respectable beer-hall much frequented by a better class of people at the time, is about half a mile up the Rosenheimer Strasse from the centre of Munich, on the other side of the Isar river. I got there early, about seven o'clock, to find the area cordoned off by police, who refused to let either me or the foreign journalists who were already there through into the hall. I will never make a revolutionary, although perhaps it was an indication of the disorganized and amateurish nature of the whole affair. So there we stood, with me trying to bluff our way through and no sign whatsoever of Hitler. It must have been half an hour or more before the red Benz car he had recently acquired drew up and he climbed out with Amann, Rosenberg and Ulrich Graf. "These gentlemen are coming with me," he said peremptorily to the police inspector on duty and forward we all trotted at his heels.

I was bringing up the rear with an American woman journalist, and although the others got through, the entrance door was then slammed in our faces. I stood outside, feeling uncommonly foolish, berating the police: "This lady represents an American newspaper," I said heatedly. "Herr von Kahr is giving an important speech and there will be a first-class scandal if reports are prevented from reaching the foreign Press." What turned the tide was the fact that my companion was smoking an American cigarette, a scent so rare and luxurious in impoverished Germany that her bona fides was established. We were let past, to meet one of Hitler's bodyguards whom he had sent back to find out what had happened to us.

The entrance corridor was completely empty, apart from the vast pile of top-hats, uniform-coats and swords in the cloakroom. It was quite clear that the *élite* of the whole capital of Munich was there. I found that Hitler had quietly taken up position by one of the big supporting pillars about twenty-five yards from the platform. Nobody seemed to notice us and we just stood there looking innocent, for what must have been at least twenty minutes. Hitler, who was still wearing his trench-coat, was chatting quietly to Amann, now and again biting a finger-nail and occasionally looking sideways at the platform, where von Kahr, von Lossow and von Seisser sat.

Kahr was on his feet, droning away at some incomprehensible and boring speech. I said to myself, this waiting is dull enough, but there's no need to go thirsty. So I went over to the serving-hatch and got three litre jugs of beer. I remember they cost a billion marks apiece. I took a good swig at one myself and handed the other two over to our group, where Hitler took a thoughtful draught. It is no use just standing around, I thought, and in Munich no one will suspect anyone with his nose in a stein of beer of having ulterior motives.

The wait seemed interminable. Kahr was still mumbling away and I had a good look round the hall. Sure enough, everyone was there: the Bavarian provincial cabinet, leaders of society, newspaper editors, and officers. Not far away I caught sight of Admiral Paul von Hintze, who had been German ambassador in Mexico before the war and now lived in Salzburg, where he was reputed to provide some sort of line of communication with Otto of Hapsburg. So they are in this, too, I thought, with their plans for a Catholic Danubian confederation!

Kahr was sending us off to sleep. He had just said the words "and now I come to the consideration . . ." which, for all I know, was to be the high point of his speech, when the door behind us which we had come through flew open and in burst Goering, looking like Wallenstein on the march, with all his orders clinking, plus about twenty-five brownshirts with pistols and machine-guns. What an uproar. Everything happened at once. Hitler began to plough his way towards the platform and the rest of us surged forward behind him. Tables overturned with their jugs of beer. I saw Wutzhofer, one of the members of the Bavarian cabinet, crawl under another for cover. On the way we passed a major named Mucksel, one of the heads of the intelligence section at Army headquarters, who started to draw his pistol as soon as he saw Hitler approach, but the bodyguard had covered him with theirs and there was no shooting. Just as well, I remember thinking. If I had had to loose off the cannon I was carrying I would probably have maimed myself.

Hitler clambered on a chair and fired a round at the ceiling. It is always maintained that he did this to terrify the gathering into submission, but I swear he did it to wake people up. Kahr's speech had been such a bromide that at least a third of the people in the hall had almost fallen asleep. I had practically dozed off on my feet myself. Anyway, on home ground at last, Hitler barked an impromptu proclamation: "The national revolution has broken out. The *Reichswehr* is with us. Our flag is flying on their barracks. . . ."

I suddenly caught one glance from von Lossow at Hitler. There was such a furtive look of thinly veiled contempt on his monocled face, with its sabre-cuts, that I knew he could not be trusted to go along with us. I turned to Goering and said: "Hermann, watch your step. Lossow is going to double-cross us." "How do you know that?" Goering asked me. "One look at his face is enough," I said. I felt in my finger-tips that there was trouble brewing. Hitler and Lossow had been as thick as thieves for weeks but I knew that no binding promises of assistance had been forthcoming from the Army chief. He could never get over the fact that he was an aristocratic general and Hitler was an ex-corporal. There was still no room for self-made men in the Germany of those days and Hitler's fight against this attitude was to take him years.

Hitler invited Kahr and company to join him in one of the side-rooms to discuss their plans. There they were joined by Scheubner-Richter and Ludendorff, tremendous in full regimentals with all his decorations. After a first somewhat inconclusive session, Hitler returned to the hall alone and launched into a tremendous tirade. "Now is the time to do away with the sinners' Tower of Babel in Berlin," and so on. Announcing that he had entered into coalition with the triumvirate and careful to hide the fact that they had been notably frigid about it, he soon had the audience bawling its enthusiasm. This may have been partly due to the fact that in his excitement he talked about "His Majesty the Crown Prince of Bavaria". Or it may have been deliberate in order to get the people on his side, under the impression that he was supporting the Wittelsbach restoration. In any case it worked. He went back to inform his reluctant allies that the whole sense of the meeting was on his side and that action against Berlin could commence.

For Hitler's words to achieve such immediate effect, they needed to reach receptive ears. To a great many staid and established members of the audience he represented little more than an adventurer. Nevertheless, they had been tempted by the voluptuous picture of power he had painted for them. Since Bismarck had founded the Second German Reich, Bavaria had been little more than a provincial vassal and here opportunity was being offered for Munich to assume the leadership of Germany and take it away from the despised Prussians in Berlin. There were a good many women in the audience, distinguished local matrons with heavy, provincial furs, and they had applauded the loudest. It was another example of the way women will respond to sheer effrontery.

In the main hall the S.A. was in complete command. All the police had disappeared and this, in fact, was the main service of Poehner, who still had enough authority with Frick at police headquarters to tell him to instruct his men not to interfere with the proceedings. Goering jumped on to the platform and, with his matchless lack of tact, informed the audience that the leaders had now gone into conference and that everybody else was to remain where they were. "In any case, there is beer to drink," he said in the unmistakable tone of contempt of the northern German for the Bavarian, as if to suggest that as long as they had a stein in their hands there was little else they needed.

Somewhere about this time I, in my turn, climbed on a chair with the more peaceable and almost absurdly normal announcement that representatives of the foreign press should join me. Then I held an impromptu press conference, explaining that a new Government had been formed, that all persons and property would be respected, that order and discipline would be restored in the country, and so on – all the things I truly believed in at the time. Seeing my six-foot-four on the chair had also attracted a number of German friends. There was von Borscht, the former lord mayor of Munich, Dr. Gerlich, the editor of the *Münchener Neueste Nachrichten*, and others who came clamoring round. "Ah, my dear Hanfstaengl, what a pleasure to see you here," said Borscht, who was an old friend of my father's. "Can't you help me to get out, we are being kept prisoner."

I took him over to the main door, where an S.A. man, Schreck, who in later years became Hitler's driver, was on duty. "No one is to go out. I have my orders. Only people in uniform can give commands here, civilians must do what they are told." This uniform-complex, I thought! And with the years it got infinitely worse. So Borscht and I retreated and I got him a stein of beer from the serving-hatch, where, after a word with the girls who were doing the serving, I managed to whisper in Borscht's ear: "Get out through the kitchen." So off he went. In due course I got Knickerbocker and Larry Rue out the same way, and also Gerlich, who was in a state of high exaltation about the evening's proceedings. "What a magnificent thing, Germany will be reunited again," he was burbling. As soon as he got back to his newspaper he dictated a tremendous article praising the national revolution, which came out the next day, before the march on the Feldherrnhalle, and provided most useful evidence at Hitler's trial because it gave a full description of Kahr and Lossow participating in the Putsch.

After nearly half an hour the chief conspirators returned to the hall. Hitler had taken off his trench-coat and was revealed in his so-called good clothes, a black tailcoat and waistcoat, but cut in the Bavarian provincial fashion. He could not have looked less like a revolutionary; he was more like a collector of taxes in his Sunday best. This was the extraordinary thing about him, he still looked utterly mediocre in repose. A certain quality in his eyes and a certain reserve in his manner were all that made you look twice. He was still distinctly subservient in his attitude, except, of course, when he began to speak, as he had just shown. Then he rose into something super-human. It was the only element in which he felt himself totally at home. It was like the difference between a Stradivarius lying in its case, just a few bits of wood and lengths of catgut, and the same violin being played by a master. Just now he was quiet, looking like the slightly nervous sort of provincial bridegroom you could see in scores of pictures behind the dusty windows of Bavarian village photographers.

They all lined up on the platform: Kahr, Lossow and Seisser, Ludendorff, Frick, and Poehner, all looking very grave and history-conscious, and Hitler in that baggy, flabby suit, with a big swastika button in his lapel and the iron cross on his left breast. He was determined to lose no time. He made a short announcement that a new National Government had been formed. A solemn oath was taken by all the partners, following by the most impressive singing of *Deutschland über alles* I have ever heard. I caught sight of Gottfried Feder worming his way into the group from the back and trying to look important. He had some idea that he was going to become Minister of Economics in the new Government, but unfortunately there was no photographer present to record his momentary mingling with the great.

It had, in fact, all been highly dramatic and things had not yet started to go wrong. With his innate sense of mass psychology, Hitler had hit on exactly the right formula to sway the different sections of the gathering. Most of them educated men, they had sensed in the conspiratorial oath taken from the platform something of the tone of the Rütli oath in Schiller's *Wilhelm Tell* and their naïve political romanticism had been fired. The Gambetta quality in Hitler had magnetized them.

Some of the side-shows, of course, were less romantic. Hess had been entrusted with the task of segregating the other members of the Bavarian cabinet and I had watched him shooing them unceremoniously up a narrow flight of stairs into another room. Some of the brownshirt fanatics were all for liquidating them out of hand, but I managed to bustle my way in and keep the hotheads out. My trouble was I was too civilized for this sort of thing. Brought up on the old idea that you do not kick your enemy when he is down, I tried to make myself pleasant by offering the ministers tankards of beer. Schweyer, the Minister of the Interior, who had been one of the few to have no truck whatsoever with Hitler, refused haughtily and just sat on, thirsty, which is about the worst punishment a Bavarian can endure. But Wutzhofer grabbed his stein, as did most of the others. However, that was another six billion marks out of my pocket and was literally all I had, so for the rest of the evening I had to go dry myself.

Then there was something of a lull. I found my way back to Goering, who said, "Putzi, go and ring up Karin and tell her that I shall probably not be home tonight, and when you get out, put this letter in the post for her." Somehow one sensed that all was not going well with the Putsch plans in the city. We had the news that Roehm had succeeded in taking over the Army headquarters with the officer cadets he had suborned, but elsewhere matters were by no means going so smoothly. Some of the other barracks were not under control and the attitude of the police was doubtful. When Hermann Esser turned up – he had been in bed with 'flu' and still had a temperature – I suggested to Hitler that we ought to make a reconnaissance. It had occurred to me that we had not made sufficiently sure that the police were not calling up reinforcements from outside Munich, so we drove down to their headquarters with the intention of taking over the communications centre. However, we were fobbed off and had to return to the Bürgerbräu. In fact, we must have been away for some time, as when we returned it was to find that Hitler, in an ill-advised moment, had also left for the centre of the city to encourage flagging spirits.

As Esser and I got back we were disagreeably surprised to find that the whole meeting was breaking up. Most of the people in the main hall had already left, as had Kahr, Lossow and Seisser, after giving Ludendorff, who had also decided to leave, their word of honour not to alter the course of events. This seemed a very sinister development to Esser and me, and when, after some time, Hitler returned, only his brownshirts were left. He had put on his trench-coat again over that frightful tailcoat outfit and paced up and down like a desperado. I taxed him once more about von Lossow, but although he seemed worried he had by no means lost hope. He seemed to have accepted the argument of Scheubner-Richter, who was acting as Ludendorff's deputy, that 'you could not keep an old gentleman like Kahr sitting in a poky room in a beer-hall all night'.

I reminded Hitler of a recommendation I had made before the Putsch, that we should requisition an hotel into which the entire Government could be put under guard. The reason why I had tried so desperately to see Hitler again in the afternoon was to get his authority to take over the Leinfelder, which was a very respectable establishment catering for diplomats and aristocratic families. I was, heaven knows, a mere amateur in the business of revolutions – my chief claim to fame was as a player of the piano – but I knew enough from my history books to realize that if you are going to supplant a government by force you have at least to control the movements of your predecessors. In those days Hitler must have been even more of an amateur than I was because he neglected even this simple precaution.

Instead he retreated into a mood of exaltation: "Tomorrow either we are successful and masters of a united Germany or we shall be hanging from the lamp-posts," he said in that dramatic voice, and sent one confidant after another down to the *Reichswehr* head-quarters to find out how things were going on, but they learnt nothing to their advantage. I stood next to Goering as he tried to ring up the Bavarian Government offices, where von Kahr was sup-posed to have gone. Who should answer the telephone but Kautter, the Ehrhardt Organization Consul man, who pretended he did not know where Kahr was. It was my first indication that some double-crossing was in progress and that the situation was going awry. Captain Streck, Ludendorff's adjutant, was sent down to find out what was happening, but he had an inconclusive parley with Captain Schweinle, a police officer, through a window – he was wise enough not to accept an invitation to go in – and came back with the cryptic report: "The situation stinks."

A Major Siry was dispatched to find out what was happening at the Army barracks and came back with even worse tidings. He had only by great good fortune escaped being arrested. The worst news came from Lieutenant Neunzert, who had been sent with a message to Crown Prince Rupprecht begging him to throw his prestige behind the Putsch and offering him the post of Regent *ad interim*. He had a cold reception and came back empty-handed. In fact, Kahr, Lossow and Seisser had retired to the 19th Infantry Regiment barracks, but what we had no means of telling at the time was that an urgent emissary from Rupprecht had informed them that he would play no part in any Putsch connected with Ludendorff and that they must take all necessary measures. Seeking to save their skins by energetic action, Lossow and Seisser were preparing to use force to counter any Hitler march, and Kahr was about to leave for Regensburg to perpetuate his government of Bavaria in safety.

With the situation looking increasingly doubtful, Hitler decided to spend the night in splendid isolation in the Bürgerbräu, more or less in a state of siege. He thought I would be more useful testing the atmosphere in the city, so I left them and, prosaically enough, went to bed.

*   *   *

The following day has come to be known as *Kahrfreitag*, a play on the German word for Good Friday, *Karfreitag*. When I got back to Bürgerbräu about eight in the morning, I found that Hitler had apparently been up all night. Ludendorff had returned with his own followers, but all in civilian clothes. They were no longer in the small room on the ground floor where Ludendorff had so mis-guidedly accepted his fellow-generals' word of honour, but had moved to a larger private room upstairs. The old quartermaster-general was sitting there stony-faced and frightening in his unper-turbed calm, sipping away at red wine, the only sustenance the conspirators had enjoyed. The air was thick with cigar and cigarette smoke. In the ante-room there was a little orchestra platform and on it, in a pile about five feet high, thousands of million- and billion-mark notes, in neat banker's bundles, which the brownshirts had 'requisitioned' somewhere during the night. I could have done with a few of them myself, as my hospitality the night before had left me without a penny in my pocket, but evidently they were to be expended in a legal and formal fashion whatever their origin.

This even applied to the civilian brass band, which Brückner, Hitler's adjutant, had rustled up from somewhere. By this time there were about 800 uniformed men in and around the hall, all somewhat dispirited. It was an unlikely day for a Putsch, cold with flurries of snow, and most of the S.A. and *Kampfbund* men were in thin cotton shirts and had had nothing to eat since the night before. Anyway, this morose and resentful band was produced and demanded first breakfast and then prepayment, neither of which they received, so Brückner bawled them out, sent them up on to the platform and ordered them to play. We could hear them tootling away without any life in the music, even making a hash of Hitler's favourite *Badenweiler* march.

They were still undecided what to do next, although Ludendorff was pressing firmly for a march on the centre of the city. Hitler said he was relying on me to keep him informed about the general feeling in Munich and I spent most of the morning travelling by car between the Bürgerbräu and the *Beobachter*. I had to find some version to satisfy the suspicious foreign correspondents, who were more or less encamped at the newspaper, and the best I could do was to suggest that a few personal differences had arisen between the leaders of the conspiracy and that all would soon be settled. Rosenberg was under no illusions. "It is no good, the whole thing has failed," he said despairingly. By eleven o'clock I was back in the Bürgerbräu again, after great difficulty with ominously increasing police cordons. I found uncertainty and glum faces. No one was talking very much. Goering was all for retreating in the direction of Rosenheim and there collecting reinforcements for a fresh start. However, Ludendorff put a stop to that: "The movement cannot end in the ditch of some obscure country lane," he said tersely, and, sipping his red wine, froze them into submission.

They soon sent me back into the city to report further developments. I got through to the *Beobachter*, where it became clear that

the game was up. The police were openly ripping down the proclamations of the setting up of the national republic, signed by Hitler,
Kahr, Lossow and Seisser, and *Reichswehr* formations were closing
in on strategic points in the city. There was no further sign of
Streicher, the Nazi leader in Nuremburg, whom I had seen harangu-
ing a crowd and distributing leaflets in front of the Feldherrnhalle,
and other speakers had disappeared from the Marienplatz, although
there was still a big crowd there. The situation seemed hopeless and
I decided to hurry home and prepare for a get-away.

I had not been there long when the telephone rang; it was my
sister Erna, who lived in Bogenhausen across the river. "Putzi," she
said. "Ferdinand Sauerbruch [the famous surgeon] has just been
on the line. They are all marching into town and are over the bridge
and in the Tal already." They had made up their minds to relieve
Roehm, now besieged in the Army headquarters in the Ludwig-
strasse. Most of the approaches were sealed off by the *Reichswehr*,
with the exception of the Residenzstrasse, the narrow street which
leads into the Odeonsplatz by the Feldherrnhalle, which was held by
Seisser's gendarmery, 'the green police', as they were called, commanded by Freiherr von Godin, who gave the order to fire on the
marching column.

I tore out of my flat and half ran in the direction of the Briennerstrasse. I was past the Pinakothek museum – nearly there – when
a great mass of people came flooding up from the direction of the
Odeonsplatz. I saw one face I knew, a sort of first-aid man in one
of the S.A. brigades, being helped along in a state of collapse. "What
on earth has happened?" I asked him. "My God, Herr Hanfstaengl,
it's too terrible," he said. "It is the end of Germany! The *Reichswehr*
opened fire with machine-guns down at the Feldherrnhalle. It was
pure suicide. They're all killed. Ludendorff's dead, Hitler's dead,
Goering's dead. . . ." Heaven preserve us, I thought, and helped the
man up to his flat and then hurried back home to prepare for flight.

The three leaders were, of course, still alive, although Goering had
two bullets in the groin. True to their wartime training, all the old
soldiers had thrown themselves to the ground at the sound of
machine-gun fire. Ludendorff, however, had marched through
unscathed and Hitler had been borne to the ground by the dead

Scheubner-Richter, whose arm was linked with his, dislocating Hitler's shoulder. Fifteen others had been killed and scores wounded. The police had mostly fired into the ground and the ricocheting bullets and splinters from the granite setts had caused many nasty wounds. The leaders and most of the wounded were dragged away by the S.A. men without further interference from the police.

As I was hurrying up the Arcisstrasse on the way to my flat I saw an open car coming down it from the north. It screeched to a halt and in it sat Esser, Amann, Dietrich Eckart and Heinrich Hoffmann. In the hubbub of mutual inquiry I told them the news as I knew it and we all made for Hoffman's flat, which was nearby, to concert our plans. "There is only one thing to do. We must get out of Munich immediately," I told them. "Over the border to Salzburg or Innsbruck and see what we can reorganize from there." We all bid each other a hurried farewell and dispersed.

It suddenly occurred to me that Admiral von Hintze, whom I knew well, might help me to get away. I was expecting to be picked up by the police at any moment. I was an easily recognizable figure and by now well known for my close relationship with Hitler. However, I decided to pay a quick call at the Hotel Leinfelder, where the admiral was living. "Do you have a passport?" Hintze asked me. I had to confess I had not – it will give an indication of how poorly organized we were. "Good heavens, man, I have three," he told me. However, he gave me a couple of names and that evening I was already in Rosenheim on the Austrian border. There a doctor's secretary helped me to cross the frontier illegally and the following night I was in Kufstein, where there was a little group of fourteen railwaymen who were Nazis. The family of one of them, with a Czech name, kept a small flower-shop and I spent the night sleeping on the tiled floor underneath a bank of chrysanthemums. I suppose you might call it my first political interment.

The last place it would have occurred to me to go was my own home in Uffing, where I would surely be sought and arrested. To my astonishment, I was to learn that Hitler had chosen it as his hiding-place. Konrad Heiden has written a completely garbled version of this episode, in which he suggests that my sister was in residence there and that Hitler spent the next forty-eight hours in her bed. Nothing could be further from the truth. My sister Erna remained in Munich, and although for family reasons the Uffing house was registered in her name, the only occupants were my wife, who was in the first month of pregnancy of our daughter, Egon and a maidservant. Hitler certainly entertained one of his unproductive passions for Helene, but she treated his *Schwärmerei* rather as a doctor treats a patient.

Late on the evening of the Putsch a knock came at the door and outside stood Hitler, Dr. Walter Schultze, a physician in one of the S.A. battalions, and two or three others. Hitler's dislocated shoulder was drooping and he was in considerable pain. In fact it was not finally set until he arrived at Landsberg prison three or four days later, and it would take a better writer than Heiden to explain how a man with a dislocated shoulder could spend the next two days behaving like Tannhäuser in the Venusberg.

Hitler asked if he could stay the night. My wife, in total ignorance of all that had occurred, let him in and the others went away. She gave him a little attic-bedroom I had fitted up with my books, while she slept downstairs with Egon and the maid. Hitler was completely despondent and almost incoherent, but she managed to piece together some sort of account of what had happened. One of his chief concerns was the conviction that his bodyguard, Graf, who had flung himself in front of Ludendorff and Hitler just as the police opened fire, was dead. In fact, the man, although severely wounded, recovered. Later, Hitler, for reasons which I could never understand nor forgive, simply gave Graf notice, employing in his place a boorish character named Julius Schaub, and paid no further attention to him.

The next morning my wife told him, "Herr Hitler, for your own sake you ought to find somewhere else to hide. The police are sure to come here, even if only to look for my husband, and it is too much of a risk." This he fully understood. The plan was for him to wait for the Bechsteins' car to come and pick him up and take him to safety. So, for the time being, he stayed, spending most of the day in the attic-room, where the bed was covered by the two English travelling-rugs I had acquired in my student days, which he later took with him to Landsberg prison.

On the Saturday afternoon came another visitor. It was 'friend' Greinz, Goering's gardener, about whom I had entertained such justified suspicions. He asked to speak to Hitler, but when my wife told him he was not there went away and spent the night at an inn in Uffing. I have not the slightest doubt that he put the police on Hitler's track, as on the Sunday evening a couple of lorries appeared in the front of the house, full of green-uniformed gendarmery. My wife hurried up to the attic and found Hitler in a state of frenzy. He had pulled out his revolver with his good hand and shouted, "This is the end. I will never let these swine take me. I will shoot myself first." It so happened that I had taught my wife one of the few ju-jitsu tricks I know, for wrenching a pistol out of someone's grasp. Hitler's movements were awkward with his dislocated shoulder and she managed to get the thing away from him and fling it into a two-hundredweight barrel of flour we kept up in the attic to combat the recurrent shortages.

Hitler calmed down somewhat and in the few moments left sat down and scribbled out a political testament on a piece of paper. Rosenberg was appointed leader of the party, with Amann as his deputy, and Hermann Esser and Julius Streicher as the other members of the quadrumvirate. Underneath, Hitler wrote, "Hanfstaengl will be responsible for gathering funds for the party," although where he thought I was going to get any more from is a mystery to me. Moreover, I did not like the company in which I had been placed. Of Goering there was no mention, the beginning of a long period of eclipse during which Hitler, still smarting from the double-cross of von Lossow, condemned almost all members of the officer class as totally unreliable.

By this time a lieutenant and a couple of gendarmes were at the door. They had just come from my mother's farm, which was near by, where they had been sticking bayonets in haystacks looking for Hitler, but now felt sure of their quarry. Hitler came downstairs and made no physical resistance, but gave them a terrible tongue-lashing at the top of his voice, accusing them of breaking their oath, conniving at the splitting of Germany, and so on, in the same vein. All this was above the heads of the police, whose loyalties had been veering like windvanes over the previous three or four days at the behest of their senior officers. So they presented their excuses and politely carried him off.

There is little doubt that Hitler could have escaped to Austria if he had wanted to, and, although we never talked about it in detail, it is a fair assumption that he had specific reasons for not doing so. Years later, at the time of the Anschluss, the Gestapo made straight for the Vienna police headquarters and impounded a number of dossiers. One of them, I am convinced, related to Hitler and dated back to his early youth in the city, although what the charges were we shall probably never know. In fact, the Bechstein car did finally arrive at the Uffing house – half an hour after he had been arrested.

CHAPTER VI

TWILIGHT AT LANDSBERG

*Goering in exile – A first sight of Geli Raubal – Hitler's hunger
strike – The acrobat of the cells – Duel for the leadership –
Welcome with* Liebestod *– The narrowing of a mind – Operatic
eroticism – The man on the tight-rope.*

THOSE OF us who had escaped to Austria – Goering, Esser, Ross-
bach and myself – soon regained touch with each other and I was
able to exchange news with my wife. We received word from Hitler's
lawyer, Lorenz Roder, that we were to remain away, if possible, as
any addition to the list of those arrested would only complicate his
defence problems. Goering I found in hospital in Innsbruck. He
really had been badly wounded, although he was over the worst
when I saw him. He told me how he had managed to crawl up
behind one of the monumental lions in front of the Residenz Palace
after he had been hit. Some of the brownshirts had then carried him
to the first doctor in the Residenzstrasse, who happened to be a Jew
and for many years afterwards Goering spoke warmly of his kindness
and skill. Goering was never one of the crazy anti-Semites of the
Party, and, as one of the few unmistakably Aryan members of
Hitler's entourage, was the least fervent exponent of their racial
theories.

From Munich he had been smuggled over the border, and in
Innsbruck had to be operated on. He was suffering severe pain and
had to be given two morphia injections a day. It was always maintained that he later became an addict. I have no personal and
positive proof of this, but this treatment in the Innsbruck hospital
very likely provided the inception of the habit.

I went back with Karin to her hotel and found to my surprise that
she was living in opulent fashion. The rest of us exiles were going
around like tramps, but this was never the Goerings' way, and their
ostentation caused a lot of bad blood in the Party. He simply had no

sense of the value of money, and when he finally left Austria via Venice for Sweden, I helped to finance the trip. I received little thanks and never saw my money back. Yet somehow this did not cause offence. He was a very attractive, rollicking fellow, the type that can get away with this sort of thing. In many ways it was a pity that he spent so long away. He was an intelligent and travelled man, with a much broader fund of common sense than the other Nazis. Hitler was now shut up in gaol with the worst of them, Hess, Weber, Frick and others, really narrow-minded doctrinaire provincials who, in the confined space of a prison, were able to imprint their half-baked *Weltanschauung* firmly in his mind. The only other man of value, poor old Dietrich Eckart, had a heart attack during one of the Landsberg prison governor's mock escape exercises and was released, only to die a few days later.

At one time we exiles concocted a plan for taking a few people over the frontier with a couple of machine-guns to raid Landsberg and set the prisoners free. It was a good thing we did not, as the authorities would have been fully prepared for us. Hitler himself dreaded such an attempt, as he was afraid he and his companions would be shot by the guards in the *mêlée*, and smuggled a message out ordering us to desist from any such enterprise. The prison governor used to tell off a couple of his guards to attempt a mock escape to test his security precautions, with all the necessary sound effects. It was a burst of machine-gun fire in the small hours from an alerted sentry which startled Eckart, literally, to death.

I took advantage of my involuntary stay in Austria to look up Hitler's family in Vienna. I was interested to find out all I could about his background and although I had no reason to suppose that his family had the slightest influence on him, thought it might be a good idea to plant a few facts about the more sinister members of his entourage, particularly Rosenberg. I could probably have saved myself the trouble, as when I finally tracked down his half-sister, Frau Raubal, I found her living in abject poverty on the third or fourth floor of a crumbling tenement block. She would not open the door more than a slit, as she was obviously ashamed of their miserable surroundings, but even through this crack I could see that the place was bare and dirty and that on the floor of the hall there was nothing but a decrepit straw mattress. But she accepted an invitation to come out to a café and brought her not unattractive blonde daughter Geli, who was probably about sixteen at the time.

It was rather as if I had taken my charwoman out for a meal. The mother was diffident and confused, although the daughter was quite bold and pretty. They were dressed in cheap, nondescript clothes, but I thought I might as well get them on my side and asked Geli if she would like to come to a music-hall with me. It was some second-rate operetta and there was a fat tenor who sang a dreadful doggerel ballad about "who will cry when we must part, and another has found his way to your heart" or some such thing. This was just the sort of entertainment which appealed to Geli's mediocre mind. Here we have gone through this Feldherrnhalle thing, I thought, and here is Hitler's niece clapping her hands off at this drivel.

My worst experience in Austria was meeting my old friend Luigi Kasimir, the etcher. Not that I was not delighted to see him, as he was able to bring me news of home and take back mine. However, I was using again the name of Georg Wagner as a cover in Austria, and when he started addressing me loudly in a public restaurant as 'Putzi' I whispered to him: "Luigi, for heaven's sake drop this Putzi and call me Georg. I am going under the name of Georg Wagner while I am here." He looked at me appalled: "Good Lord, man," he said, "that is the fellow who has been making these forged twenty-pound notes. The police are looking for him all over the place. There is an immediate arrest order out for him in half a dozen European countries." That is what comes of being a Wagner enthusiast.

I went back in disguise to spend Christmas with my family. This involved traversing a single-track railway tunnel called the Hanging Stone near Berchtesgaden, a somewhat hazardous enterprise, as you had to run between trains alternating in both directions. It was more of a risk than I knew, as ten years later I managed to look at my own police record and saw that an order had been issued to arrest me on sight the moment I crossed the frontier. I had grown a set of Franz-Josef mutton-chop whiskers, wore dark glasses and walked with a limp. Strangely enough no one recognized me, even when I walked down to the *Beobachter* offices and talked to a couple of the drivers. The newspaper had, of course, been banned. By the time Hitler came up for trial, the arrest order had been rescinded and I was free to move about again.

While on remand at Landsberg, Hitler, taking his example from the Sinn Feiners, had attempted a hunger strike. He refused to talk to the guards or any of his old comrades, so Roder, his counsel, got in touch with my wife. She sent a message through to say that she had not prevented him from committing suicide in order to let him starve himself to death and that this was the very thing his worst enemies hoped for. Her advice turned the scale. Hitler had a great admiration for her and his whole appearance at Uffing after the Putsch must have been part of some subconscious urge to turn for succour to this woman, who corresponded so closely to his repressed yearnings. Also, amidst the annihilation of all that he had organized, the Uffing house must have acquired the aura of an extra-territorial asylum.

I visited Hitler a couple of times in gaol, first when he was brought back to the cells under the court in the Blutenburgstrasse for the trial, and then back to Landsberg after his sentence. I even took little Egon along with me to the Blutenburgstrasse and Hitler was delighted. "Well, it is nice to see you, Hanfstaengl," he said, "and there is little Egon," taking the child on his knee and letting him choose some of the sweets and cakes which had been sent in by sympathizers. He had this extraordinary quality of immediate appeal to children and the boy adored him.

"I am so sorry about that business at Uffing," he said. "I had no idea your wife was pregnant and it was all a very stupid idea." He looked well and was full of confidence about the outcome of the trial. "What on earth can they do to me?" he said, "all I have to do is to tell some of the things I know about von Lossow and the whole thing will collapse." This was a little over-confident, but in spite of the five-year sentence he received, he turned the trial into a major triumph, making Kahr, Lossow and company look so foolish that he largely restored his prestige in Munich. The trump card he held was his inside knowledge of Lossow and Kahr's own plans, in which a number of authorities, both in Berlin and abroad, would have been more than interested. This was the threat he was able to hold over the head of his dubious accusers, and his final sentence was more a matter of convenience than anything else, as it was understood from the first that he would not have to serve the whole of it.

The ascendancy he gained over the officials and guards at Landsberg was quite extraordinary. The gaolers even used to say *Heil Hitler* when they came into his cell. This was partly due to the extraordinary magnetism of his personality, and to his political martyrdom, which found a wide acclaim across many varied sections of the community. He received favoured treatment, which included freedom to accpt gifts of food from outside, and this again gave him a further hold over his warders. It was very easy to say 'take this box of chocolates home to your wife' when he had almost unlimited quantities available. He and Hess had not so much cells as a small suite of rooms forming an apartment. The place looked like a delicatessen store. You could have opened up a flower and fruit and a wine shop with all the stuff stacked there. People were sending presents from all over Germany and Hitler had grown visibly fatter on the proceeds. Frau Bruckmann had been one of the most generous donors, but food supplies and money had also come in from Siegfried and Winifred Wagner, who in 1924 had restarted the Bayreuth Festival and were making collections among their friends for the political prisoners in Landsberg. Winifred Wagner is another of the women whose name has been mentioned in connexion with Hitler, but she again was an older woman, the motherly type, who found some outlet in making a social protégé of him.

"You really must take part in some of the gymnastic exercises and prison sports," I told him. – "No," he said, and the reply was very typical of his mentality, "I keep away from them. It would be bad for discipline if I took part in physical training. A leader cannot afford to be beaten at games." There on the table were Westphalia hams, cakes, brandy and everything one can imagine. It looked like a fantastically well equipped expedition to the South Pole. "If you don't watch out you'll get as fat as old Walterspiel [the massive owner of the Four Seasons Hotel]," I told him. "No," he insisted. "I shall always be able to get the extra pounds off by speaking."

I had taken along a couple of Hanfstaengl books of old-master reproductions of the Pinakothek and Dresden collections, which were accepted with grudging thanks. A recent copy of the German satirical weekly *Simplicissimus* did more to cheer him up. It had a mocking cartoon in colour on the front page, showing Hitler entering Berlin on a white horse, surrounded by admirers, for all the world like Sir Galahad. "There you are," he said, delighted, "they can laugh but I shall get there yet," although his mood was not particularly optimistic at the time. "What are people in Munich saying?" he kept asking me eagerly. I told him that the mood was still very much in favour of a parliamentary monarchy, something after the style of Horthy's régime in Hungary, and that if Rupprecht would give his support it could be achieved with comparatively little effort.

This was by no means to the taste of Hess, who only grudgingly left Hitler's side while I was talking to him. This was the period of his greatest and lasting influence, helping Hitler to collect his ideas for *Mein Kampf*. Hess was another whistler, like Rosenberg, to which he added the exasperating habit of fooling around with the chair he was sitting on. He would sit on it the wrong way round, pass it through his legs, sit on the back, twirl it on one leg, like an amateur acrobat trying to show off. He could not bear to see Hitler exposed to any views other than his own and was always trying to distract attention. All Hess could do was talk in catch-phrases. "We must learn to be much more brutal in our methods. That is the only way to deal with our enemies," he would chant. "A little more of that and the Bürgerbräu affair would have ended differently." He loved the word 'brutal', which in German is pronounced with a rolling 'r' and equal stress on both syllables, and Hitler also seemed to take pleasure in the sound of it. You could almost feel him quicken as he roared the word out at Hess's prompting. There was a very close bond between the two during this period, and for the first time I heard them speak to each other on 'thou' terms, although later in public they did not. Drexler and Eckart were the only other people I heard Hitler do it with, and one or two of the old comrades from his war days. Roehm used to try it on, but he never got thou'd back, which did not seem to discourage him.

For all that, I was extremely worried about the narrowing of his prejudices in Hess's company in gaol, and I made one somewhat forlorn effort in an interview with Rupprecht's adjutant, von Redwitz, to have Hitler amnestied before it was too late. I tried to persuade the monarchists that if they placed Hitler under a debt to them, they would be able to exercise a restraining influence on him. On their side, his gifts as a demagogue might well bring the triumph of their cause. I tried to get them to release him with others on the occasion of the approaching tenth anniversary of the outbreak of the Great War on the first of August. As a volunteer he could have qualified. However, I could make no impression. Von Redwitz himself, with whom I had gone to school, was sympathetic enough, but the other members of Rupprecht's entourage were not prepared to take the risk. As it was, Hitler had to stay in gaol until just before Christmas, with only tragic blockheads for company.

It was hinted to me that Hitler was engaged in writing the political biography which, the following year, emerged as the first volume of *Mein Kampf*. At first Hitler used Emil Maurice as his secretary, but Hess soon ousted him, pecking out the pages on a decrepit Remington typewriter. The difficulty was to get it published. The *Völkische Beobachter* had been closed down by the authorities after the Putsch and although the publishing company and offices were still intact under Amann, there was no money coming in. Bills were unpaid and the creditors were about to move in and seize all the office furniture and property and put them up to auction. Amann rang me up one day and begged me to come to see him. I think we met in front of the Munich synagogue and he led me round the corner into the garden at the back, where we walked up and down. The organization was on its last legs, he said, if help was not immediately forthcoming, it would be broken up and dispersed.

Half the manuscript of *Mein Kampf* had been smuggled out from Landsberg gaol and they were in the process of setting it up in type, but if the duns moved in the whole thing would be lost. "You are the only man who can help us, Herr Hanfstaengl. You must do it if you believe in Hitler at all. Otherwise it is the end." I had a great many obligations at the time myself. I had received another instalment from the States, but part of it had gone on helping the families of those killed and injured at the Feldherrnhalle, and I had also made up my mind to move back into Munich and find a house so that I could start living a more normal and profitable life. Amann was so insistent that in the end I gave way. There were about half a dozen notes of hand of three or four hundred marks each but I paid some of them and backed others and this sufficed to keep the offices going. I was not alone in this. I think Gansser helped again, but the fact that Hitler found a functioning staff when he was released from gaol was entirely due to our efforts.

The National-Socialist Party had of course been dissolved by decree after the Putsch, although certain sections of it had re-formed and did very well in the elections of spring 1924 under the name of the People's Block. This was largely due to the moral triumph Hitler had gained during his trial, which made him for the first time a national figure. Riding in on the coat-tails of his prestige, the Block actually became the second largest party in the Bavarian parliament and obtained thirty-two seats in the *Reichstag*. Hitler tried to maintain a measure of control from the prison over the list of candidates to be presented and I remember him working on it during one of my visits. In fact it was at my suggestion that he included our eccentric bomb-manufacturing friend Emil Gansser in the roster.

However, his leadership was by no means unanimously acknowledged, while on the other hand the ill-assorted groups which had banded themselves together for electoral purposes were soon at loggerheads and the flimsy coalition fell apart. At the *Beobachter* offices there was a running fire of partially justified criticism against Hitler himself, led particularly by Anton Drexler, with the active backing of Gottfried Feder. Drexler wanted to remodel the party along his own less revolutionary lines and Feder was probably playing his own game. They called Hitler a dictator and a *prima donna* and proclaimed that he must be brought under greater control if the Party was ever to be built up again. He was generally blamed for the failure of the Putsch, which in retrospect they regarded as an over-hasty and ill-organized attempt to seize power.

More dangerous still was the determination of Ludendorff to centre the control of the nationalist groups in his own hands and take advantage of Hitler's absence to neutralize him permanently. To achieve this and bring the banned but still functioning Nazi Party under his wing he called in Gregor Strasser to act as political leader and organizer. I had not had a lot to do with Strasser, who had a chemist's shop down in Landshut, where he had organized a small

S.A. battalion which was in fact very much better disciplined and more effective than the group in Munich. Strasser was a gifted organizer and was to play an important, but frequently independent, rôle in the years that followed. Between them Strasser and Ludendorff obtained the adherence of Rosenberg, Hitler's nominated successor, but this only hastened the split in the party, as the anti-Rosenberg faction was growing in strength, led by his three nominal co-regents.

I was in almost constant communication with Hitler through Roder and helped to keep him informed about the intrigues within the Party. It had become clear to me that street marches and demonstrations would get us nowhere and, in advocating a campaign through parliamentary channels, I had found myself, as usual, in opposition to Rosenberg. I had little confidence in any of the lesser lights and kept pointing out that if the movement was to get anywhere in a resuscitated form, it would only be under the leadership of Hitler. One malicious act of Rosenberg's I could not prevent was when he had Goering struck from the roster of the Party, which seemed to me a monstrous piece of pettiness from a man who had come scot free out of the whole affair.

It became clear to Hitler that he could not control these manœuvrings from his comfortable gaol and in July he smuggled out a letter formally dissociating himself from this internecine brawl and in effect resigning the leadership of the Party. His sound political intuition had told him that the best thing to do was to let the various factions fight and avoid drawing too much attention to himself for the time being. A moderate government of the Bavarian People's Party under Dr. Heinrich Held had assumed political power and von Lossow had been superseded by General von Kressenstein. In fact it was being seriously considered whether Hitler should not be expelled to his native Austria on his release. We know now that he was not repatriated only because the Austrian Government would not have him. By the time he got out, the Party wheel had come full circle and he was acclaimed as the only man capable of putting the pieces together again. From that time on his position was never seriously challenged.

The day he left Landsberg, he came to my new Munich home in

the Pienzenauer Strasse for a quiet celebration dinner. The invitation had been forwarded through Roder. I had in the meantime received the last payment on the liquidated Hanfstaengl interests in America and had been able to buy this very attractive house in the Herzog Park quarter. It had a huge studio and much charm, and after all these years I am now living in it again, although we have rebuilt it and the studio has disappeared.

He arrived about half past six, in the little blue serge suit of which he was so proud, straining at the buttons with the weight he had put on in Landsberg. Egon was with me to greet him at the door. "I am so glad to see you again, Uncle Dolf," he said and Hitler took his hand as we walked down the corridor. I had a big concert grand in the studio and before I could gather my wits or offer any hospitality, Hitler, who seemed tense and wound up, said, almost pleadingly: "Hanfstaengl, play me the *Liebestod*." It was one of my party pieces. So down I sat and hammered out this tremendous thing from *Tristan and Isolde*, with Lisztian embellishments, and it seemed to work the trick. He relaxed. My wife came in and he was charming to her, apologizing again for the scene at Uffing a year earlier and crooning over our new little daughter Hertha. In his curious frustrated way he was somehow jealous of me for having such a good-looking wife.

First we made small talk. "Well now," he said in that diffident tone which was one part of his character, "after that little flat of yours in the Gentzstrasse who would have thought we would meet again in a fine house in the best part of town. You are the most feudal acquaintance I have." He was most impressed and kept repeating the phrase about the *feine Gegend,* which indeed it was. It was the most fashionable part of Munich. Suddenly he looked over his shoulder and stopped in mid-sentence. "I am sorry," he apologized ruefully, "that is the effect of prison. You always expect someone to be listening," and he launched into a graphic description of the psychological effect of the peep-hole in the prison door.

We had prepared a real welcome dinner, turkey, followed by the rich Austrian pastries that he loved. I noticed that he was hardly drinking at all, so there was no need to keep the sugar castor out of his reach. In fact it was about this time that he started to develop the vegetarian eating habits which later became so marked. It may have started with the necessity of dieting off his extra poundage, but as usual he made a personal issue of it. "If I feel that meat and alcohol are damaging to my system I hope at least I have enough will power to do without them however much I enjoy them," he used to say. But there was nothing wrong with his appetite that evening.

After dinner he started warming up, striding up and down the room like a soldier, hands clasped behind his back. He was never much of a man for sitting down. Somehow he got back on to the subject of the war again and we discovered that his powers of mimicry did not only cover the human voice. He was describing some recollection of the Western Front and started imitating an artillery barrage. He could reproduce the noise of every imaginable gun, German, French or English, the howitzers, the 75's, the machine-guns, separately and all at once. With that tremendous voice of his we really went through about five minutes of the Battle of the Somme and what the neighbours must have thought I cannot imagine. Fortunately the windows were closed and there was quite a large garden surrounding the house. As an encouragement to his morale I had just given him as a homecoming present an autographed document signed by Frederick the Great, which had come down through my family. "Don't forget how even *der alte Fritz* sat on a drum chewing his nails after the Battle of Hochkirch, wondering what on earth he was going to do next," I tried to encourage him. His eyes brightened. You could almost feel the head of steam building up.

Suddenly he launched into a great political tirade. To my horror he spouted a still further distilled essence of all the nonsense that Hess and Rosenberg had been concocting. All those ridiculous prejudices of little infantry minds, incapable of appreciating the balance of world forces and concentrating instead on the internecine conflicts of purely Continental war and politics. "We shall reach the decision in France," Hitler screamed. "We will reduce Paris to rubble. We must break the chains of Versailles." Oh! my God, I thought, Paris in ruins, the Louvre, all those art treasures gone. Each time Hitler got into this mood I felt almost physically sick.

He seemed to have come out of Landsberg with all his worst prejudices reinforced. I am sure that this is the point at which his latent radical tendencies started to crystallize, although there were still years to go before he became the unteachable, unreasonable and unapproachable fanatic whom the world knows from his days of power. The year he spent in Landsberg, instead of giving him time to sit back and take a broader view of political problems, had only given those imprisoned with him an opportunity to narrow his mind within their own confined limits. His anti-Semitism had acquired even more specific racial undertones. Between them, they had filled his mind with fury about the French use of Senegalese troops in the Ruhr during the occupation, and I am not at all sure that this was not the starting-point of the racial purity laws which the Nazis finally evolved. They would pick these ideas up and embroider on them and, to bolster their arguments, even quote such respected sources as Bernard Shaw, who was not averse to advocating the necessity of breeding human beings according to the standards we have developed in the domestic animal world. Of course G.B.S. had the advantage of a full beard, so that no one could see he was smiling all the time and that it was not necessary to take him seriously. But Hitler only had his little moustache and he was taken seriously and he took himself seriously and the whole thing became an obsession with him.

That was bad enough but what really worried me was the way in which Hess had succeeded in pumping his head full of the Haushofer thesis of getting the Russians to be knocked out a second time by the Japanese, who were Germany's only possible ally in the world and so on. America had simply been banished from his mind and I was right back to where I started. In a way the racial obsession played a part in this. He was not really anti-American. He had failed to absorb any of the information I had kept trying to give him and merely regarded America as part of the Jewish problem. Wall Street was controlled by the Jews, America was run by the Jews, and therefore he could not take them into account. They were out of his reach and not an immediate problem. As *Mein Kampf* was to show, he was right back in the politico-military conceptions of Frederick the Great and Clausewitz. He thought only in European terms and was juggling with the idea of making England or, failing that, Italy, into an ally for his day of reckoning with France. It was just as if the man who really turned the tide of war, Pershing, and his millions of fresh troops transported across the Atlantic had simply not existed. Nor did it occur to him that in another war the same miracle of amphibious organization could be repeated, even faster and even more to Germany's disadvantage.

When he calmed down I started to reason with him. I was one of the few people to whom he would listen, perfectly reasonably and soberly, when we were alone, although he never gave an indication whether he agreed with one or not, or what he proposed to do about it. The moment another person was present Hitler would revert to his declamatory platform style, and it became impossible to try and make him see something in a new light. "It is no good," I told him, "you have got to get rid of this fellow Rosenberg," and I showed him one of the old articles in the *Völkische Beobachter,* in which there were no less than fourteen grammatical errors. Rosenberg was intrinsically illiterate, carried along by his ridiculous Nordic race resentments. "In another fifty years this mythos of his may be recognized as one of the great masterpieces of philosophy," said Hitler. "It is tripe," I insisted, "and tripe remains tripe." I really did talk to him like this, any number of witnesses will confirm it. "If you fold a piece of paper over an ink blot no one is going to mistake it in fifty years for a Rembrandt. Rosenberg is a dangerous and stupid man and the sooner you get rid of him the better." As events turned out I might just as well have been talking to a brick wall.

Another quirk Hitler had developed was a passionate dislike of the officer class. First Lossow, then Ludendorff and somehow Goering got included in the condemnation. He would never trust any of them again, he said, and embroidered great plans for so building up the brownshirts that they would swamp and neutralize the *Reichswehr.* It may seem far-fetched, but I have a private theory that the lunatic contempt and suspicion which Hitler later showed for his generals and field-marshals had its roots in this 1923 Putsch. He never lost his wildly romantic ideas about the rôle of the Army, but the officers he never trusted again. "As far as I am concerned I will never believe an officer's word of honour in my life," I remember him saying that evening. "One of these days these gentlemen will know how I feel about them."

The other strong impression he left me with that evening was the emotional quality of the friendship that had developed with Hess. *"Ach, mein Rudi, mein Hesserl,"* he wailed as he stomped up and down. "Isn't it appalling to think he's still there. [Hess was not released from Landsberg until later.] I will not be a happy man until I see the last of them is out." It is probably not true to say there was a physical homosexual relationship between the two, but in a passive way the attraction was there. I certainly did not trust the manhood of either. You can drink very weak tea, or very thin absinthe and you can suffer from very diluted sex-inversion. These are border emotions and in the science of sexual derangement we still have a long way to go before tracking them down.

I felt Hitler was a case of a man who was neither fish, flesh nor fowl, neither fully homosexual nor fully heterosexual. Somehow the very rootlessness of his background, his very capacity for balancing out a situation and his intuitive gift of always remaining above the petty personal jealousies of his supporters were all a reflection of his sexual isolation. You could never pin him down, say that he was this thing or that thing, it was all floating, without roots, intangible and mediumistic. He had these people of unsavoury habits round him, from Roehm and Heines on the one side to Rosenberg on the other, and seemed to have no sense of moral displeasure at their behaviour. Ernst, another homosexual S.A. leader, hinted in the 'thirties that it would only need a few words from him to silence Hitler when, for political reasons, he started to complain about Roehm's behaviour. Perhaps that is why he was shot as well.

From watching Hitler and talking to those near him, I had formed the firm conviction that he was impotent, the repressed, masturbating type. To adopt scientific jargon for a moment, he had an Oedipus complex, which often ends up that way. He had hated his father, a stupid, petty, brutal, small-time, provincial customs inspector, and adored his mother. Hitler's repressed homosexuality probably dated from the time when he caught syphilis in Vienna about 1908. From the time I knew him, I do not suppose he had orthodox sexual relations with any woman. He was probably incapable of a normal reaction to their physical proximity. In due course he did become identified with various women and the case of his niece Geli Raubal will have to be studied in some detail, as to my mind it was a psychological turning-point of the most sinister nature. But his eroticism was purely operatic, never operative. An impotent man with tremendous nervous energy, Hitler had to release this tension somehow. He was in turn sadist and masochist, and in the sexual half-light of his life, he never found the physical release which similar unfortunates can sometimes achieve, often due to some trick of circumstance or the attentions of one particular person. In his relations with women Hitler had to dramatize himself, as he had to dramatize himself in his relations with the world as a whole. The barren hero, I suppose you might call him.

Some part of this uncertain and strange sexual constitution had reacted to the presence of Hess, a fine, but rather repressed looking young fellow at the time, during their confinement in Landsberg. The moral side of it did not bother me particularly, but this curious borderline inner bondage had its effects on Hitler's mind, which became further impregnated with the *borné*, limited doctrines of the Hess-Haushofer coterie, with their pro-Japanese and anti-American aberrations, and I and my friends could never winkle them out again.

It is useless to speculate on the reordering of historical events, but in a way it was a pity that this Putsch did not enjoy some modest success. It would not have led very far and would have had few consequences, except ensuring the territorial integrity of Germany, which, with Rhineland and Bavarian separatism rampant, seemed so dangerously threatened at the time. Hitler would have been only one of the leaders and instead of having to accommodate the passions of a couple of million brownshirts in the midst of the worst economic depression any European country has ever suffered, such as he had to in 1933, with his own prejudices finally reinforced, the ten thousand brownshirts of 1923 would have found some peaceful place in a more ordered community.

As the evening wore on Wilhelm Funk, our painter friend (he had been a friend of Zorn and Sargent) rang up and said: "Of course, he's there, isn't he?' The whole of Munich was agog to know where Hitler had holed up, so in the end I invited him over. He was a curious combination of the Englishman-about-town and the fulsome

American. He started giving Hitler a great pep-talk about how he must start anew and how great his chances were, and so on. After this tirade Hitler was in his modest mood again: *"Ach, Herr Professor,"* he said (he still had the petty bourgeois complex of addressing any man of some attainment with a title of some sort), "that is all very good advice, but you must never forget how terribly difficult it is for someone without a name or position or academic qualifications, to work himself up to the position where his name is identified with a political programme. You underrate all the bitter hard work involved." And then turning to me he added: "Perhaps, after all, Hanfstaengl, this Putsch was a good thing, at least no one can say I am unknown now, and that gives us a basis to start on again."

For the benefit of the new guest, he started giving a long explanation of his reasons for organizing the Putsch, the imminent danger of the separatist movements, the disorganization and disunity, the need to restore German pride and prestige, and then, coming to the point, almost musing to himself: "What else could we have done? The *Beobachter* was almost in the hands of the receivers and we had no money. There was simply no money left in the Party. What else could we be expected to do? We had to do something." He looked up at my wife: "It has all been a terrible disappointment, dear Frau Hanfstaengl, but the next time I promise you I will not fall off the tight-rope."

CHAPTER VII

HITLER AND HENRY VIII

A revision of Mein Kampf *– No waltzes for the Führer –
Ludendorff for President – The return of Rosenberg – A world
tour rejected – The scaffold block at the Tower – Hitler on
his knees – Forced repayment of a debt.*

FOR A FEW weeks, Hitler seemed to be trying to get his political
bearings. He visited us again before the turn of the year and I impressed upon him the absolute necessity of reaching some sort of
modus vivendi with Heinrich Held, the head of the new Bavarian
Government. "Unless you can persuade him that the Party has
moderated its views, they will simply ban it for good," I told him.
"You have got to remember that Bavaria is predominantly Catholic.
You will never get anywhere by constantly offending them or letting
Rosenberg loose again with his diatribes in print. You have reached
the parting of the ways with Ludendorff, and if you can reassure
Held on this point it will make a very good impression." A few days
later, to my surprise, Hitler called again and said that he had in fact
seen Held, had had a friendly half-hour's conversation with him and
hoped for the best. He must have been unusually persuasive as
within a couple of months the Party was legally permitted to
reconstitute itself.

I had a little study in the Pienzenauer house where I used to work.
There was no central heating, and the big studio cost such a fortune
to warm that I spent most of my time in this cubby-hole. It was full
of books and I had hung up a few pictures and photographs on the
wall. One of them was a portrait of Mussolini, which I had put there
more as a warning than anything else, with his eyes rolling and looking like a ham actor playing Othello. It also made nonsense of his
claim to be a Lombard of ancient ancestry. You could see he was
two-thirds Moorish. There was also a Hanfstaengl print of a Van
Gogh sunflower, which I had persuaded my brother, much against

his will, to include in our catalogue. Perhaps I had been a little ahead of public taste, although in later years it proved one of our most popular reproductions and sold in enormous numbers. Hitler did not like it. "The colours are too loud for me," he remarked, but he liked the Mussolini portrait and another photograph of Toscanini conducting.

Roehm was up there with us one afternoon in February. I had asked him along to get Hitler away from his café cronies. "There is a real emperor's head," said Hitler, pointing at the Mussolini picture. "He looks like Tiberius, one of the busts in the Vatican museum." Roehm was much less impressed. *"Mein lieber Addolf,"* he said in his thick Bavarian accent, "the man looks like an Abyssinian. You will never make a Fascist out of me. I remain what I have always been, a Bavarian monarchist." I looked at him, but he did not seem to be joking and I never forgot his remark. The day was to come when I wondered whether Hitler had remembered it too.

For a short period it really seemed as if Hitler was prepared to listen to the voice of reason, and in the first few weeks of 1925 I seriously considered giving most of my time again to the guidance of this unpredictable genius. Politically his stock was at a low ebb. The Party had yet to be reactivated legally, there was a ban on his making public speeches, the Central Government had been stabilized, Dr. Schacht's new mark had cured inflation and robbed the Nazis of one of their most effective arguments and Hitler yet had to reimpose himself on his nationalist allies. One day he came to me and said: "We must have 100,000 marks, with that money everything could be built up again." His chief hope lay in the success of his book, the manuscript of which was now complete. Here I felt was a means of making him beholden to the camp of respectability. I told my brother Edgar the book was available and that it was well worth the while of our firm to acquire the rights. We had published a few political biographies and I suggested that this would be a very profitable title to have on our list. But Edgar, who was a very conservative business man, turned the idea down, which was highly indicative of the way a great many people felt about Hitler after the failure of the Bürgerbräu Putsch.

By this time Amann's people had started producing the galleys and one morning Hitler appeared with a bunch of them in his hand. "Would you help me correct them?" he asked, to which I agreed only too readily, until I started to read them. It was really frightful stuff. I suppose I did not see more than the first seventy pages or so, but already his impossible political premises were evident and, quite apart from that, the style filled me with horror. Heaven knows the German language offers endless opportunities for diffuseness of thought and an infinite number of dependent clauses. Here it was combined with a schoolroom phraseology and blatant lapses of style.

I set to work first of all crossing out his worst adjectives, *furchtbar* and *ungeheuer*, and the excessive use of superlatives. Some of the faults were highly indicative. In village schools you were taught it was polite to write *mein Vater besass ein Haus* and not the more colloquial *mein Vater hatte ein Haus* for 'my father had a house'! There on page 22 it came up: *mit mir besass das Schicksal in dieser Hinsicht Erbarmen* – 'fate was kind to me in this respect'. Somewhere else he spoke of his talent as a painter. "You cannot say this," I told him. "Other people may say you have talent, but you cannot say it yourself." There were little dishonesties, like describing his father as a *Staatsbeamter,* who is a senior official, which his father never was. His limited outlook was reflected in his use of the word *Weltgeschichte* – world history – in connexion with quite minor European quarrels.

He soon lost patience with me and said "yes, yes, I will see to it," but of course he never did, and the book still reads like one of Fafner's monologues out of Wagner's *Siegfried*. But if you cut your way through the verbiage it reveals the essential Hitler, with all his blind spots, combined with the fantastic energy and single-mindedness with which he adhered to this rigmarole. When I found one set of sheets was missing, I asked what had happened to the others and was told that they were being corrected by Stolzing-Czerny, a Bohemian German who was on the staff of the *Beobachter*. I told Hitler that unless I had the whole text I could not hope to correct it properly, but I never did see the rest and had to read it in book form when it came out.

It was, I suppose, a forlorn hope, but my wife and I even thought of instilling in him some of the social graces as a means of resisting the threat of increasing radicalism in his views. We wanted to soften the manner he still had of a non-com in civilian clothes and suggested that he should go to a dancing school, where we knew they usually taught social deportment as well. The Charleston was the rage at the time, but we intended to avoid that at all costs and hoped that a well learnt waltz might be more conducive to inner harmony. It was odd for a man with such a musical sense that he seemed completely allergic to this expression of it. Even my wife's charm could make no difference. "No," he declared, "dancing is an unworthy occupation for a statesman." – "But, Herr Hitler," I interjected, "Napoleon enjoyed dancing very much, and Washington and Frederick the Great could always be relied upon to attend a ball." – "No, I won't do it. It is a stupid waste of time and these Viennese waltzes are too effeminate for a man to dance. This craze is by no means the least factor in the decline of their Empire. That is what I hate about Vienna."

Although we continued to see quite a lot of Hitler, I could feel that the rabid extremists of the Party had got their claws into him again and the arguments of the more reasonable of us were constantly being countered. Even the march of events conspired against us. The authorities legalized the existence of the Party again on February 24. On the 27th Hitler spoke again for the first time in the Bürgerbräu Keller. Although he seemed reasonably circumspect to me, there was a sufficient hint of the old threats for Held to become alarmed at the liberty he had allowed him, and he was prohibited from speaking again, a ban which was to last for over two years in Bavaria and until September 1928 in the rest of Germany. I had been sitting next to Hess, who by now was also out of gaol. We were quite near the platform and I tried to raise this gloomy young man's spirits by betting that I could foretell the exact words with which Hitler would start his speech. "What do you mean?" asked Hess. "I will lay any money he says 'wenn wir uns die Frage vorlegen' ['when we ask ourselves . . .' his old formula for a résumé of events]." And sure enough he did.

The next day President Ebert died and Germany was suddenly in the throes of an election. Immediately the Party was faced by the problem of what to do. I thought it was much too soon to take a stand for any of the candidates. The Party was still split and disorganized and it seemed to me to make much greater sense to remain neutral and exact a price for political collaboration at a later stage. There was a conference on the subject at the house on the Tegern Lake of old Müller, who was the *Beobachter* printer, and I can remember my arguments were supported not only by Hermann Esser but by Himmler. However, Hitler was intent on a trial of strength and he was more or less forced by his nationalist allies to support the candidature of Ludendorff.

There had been no love lost between the two men since the Putsch trial, when the general had taken up a completely independent attitude and repudiated much of his association with the Nazis. Hitler regarded this as a gross breach of faith and never really trusted him again, although he made the best of a bad job and repeated his allies' arguments about Ludendorff being the one man with the right sort of name and providing the only rallying point for patriotic citizens. This shows how little they had learnt.

The result was complete fiasco. Ludendorff did not even obtain one per cent of the votes. However, no candidate obtained an absolute majority and it was necessary to hold a second round of voting on April 26, when Hindenburg stood successfully as the candidate of the Right. The radical nationalists gave their vote to him, but only half-heartedly, as they considered him too old and not politically-minded enough for their purposes. Hitler, with one of the quick switches of which only he was capable, professed to be pleased at the defeat of Ludendorff and went round saying: "Well at least we are rid of him at last." The result had also been a blow for Gregor Strasser's prestige, which pleased him even better.

The whole imbroglio had disillusioned me badly and I began to wonder whether it would ever be possible to tame this extraordinary creature. But then that was the problem which was to haunt me for another ten years, as I never lost my conviction that he must somehow fight his way to the top. In that I was right. My mistake was to assume that the likelihood of redemption ever existed. I still have the copy of a letter which I wrote on Hitler's birthday, April 20, to a friend of mine, Karl Oskar Bertling, who had been a German exchange student in Harvard, and was director of the American Institute in Berlin. "Recent developments in the Party (I was referring to the Ludendorff candidature) almost convinced me that these people are beyond help," I wrote. "All they think about is force and military display and parades and the old Friedrich Naumann principles of a workers' party have gone by the board. All I can see is total eclipse. Once you start introducing the tone of the orderly-room into politics it is the end. ..."

Worse was to come. Early in the year I had enjoyed the temporary satisfaction of hearing Hitler give Rosenberg the most tremendous tongue-lashing, accusing him of disloyalty, incompetence and all the crimes in the calendar. On April 1, between the two elections, the *Völkische Beobachter* had reappeared as a daily again. And who was reinstalled as editor, in spite of all my pleadings and arguments? – Rosenberg, the insufferable, *borné*, mock-mythologist, the anti-Semitic half-Jew, who, I maintain to this day, did more harm to the movement than any man except Goebbels. God help us, I thought, this is where I came in.

Hess, in his turn, was contributing his own part to Hitler's gradual divorce from reality with the inception of the *Führer* cult. Up to the time of the Putsch no one had thought of calling him anything but 'Herr Hitler'. After they both got out of Landsberg, Hess started referring to him as *der Chef* and then produced this word *Führer* in imitation of the *Duce* of Mussolini. The 'Heil Hitler' greeting also started to gain currency at this time. There was nothing particularly sinister in its inception. It was an old custom of the Austrians, who have said Heil so-and-so or *Heil mein Lieber* for generations. Even a group of cyclists passing each other would shout *All Heil* to each other even if they did not know each others' names. In fact we were saying 'Heil Goering', 'Heil Hess', before the Putsch without any sinister motive. It was just a way of saying 'good day'. Then the Party people started to use 'Heil Hitler' as a sort of pass word and from that time on it became almost *lèse majesté* to say 'Heil Schmidt' or 'Heil Hanfstaengl'. I would never go along with this nonsense, and right up to the end used to address Hitler either as Herr Hitler or Herr Reichskanzler, as the case might be, which provided the others with one of the many black marks they chalked up against me. It is not true to say that Hitler openly sponsored this development. He never ordered anyone officially to address him as *Mein Führer*. On the other hand, he never objected and took a secret pleasure in it, and so the custom grew.

Nevertheless these were the gestures of a truncated clique spitting into the wind. Only a drastically reduced rump of the old faithfuls was left. Goering was still in exile in Sweden. Roehm, whose energetic reorganization of the *Kampfbund* and S.A. while Hitler was in gaol had been regarded as probably delaying his release, had fallen out of favour. The fault he was to repeat later of wanting too much independence led to a break, and at the end of April he resigned all his offices. Strasser was estranged and had transferred his activities to Berlin, the Rhineland and Saxony, the Communist strongholds, in an almost autonomous capacity. Ludendorff was discarded. Hitler had deliberately permitted the coalition of the radical Right to collapse in order to rebuild the Nazi Party under his complete control. A distinct hiatus period ensued.

I was sharply disappointed in the turn events had taken and made a private resolution to devote myself to my personal interests. There seemed little point in continuing to associate with this discredited group of political adventurers and I felt that only some fundamental broadening in Hitler's views would maintain my faith in his future. His personal habits did not change. In the late summer of 1925 he acquired, I think with the Bechsteins' help, the villa at Berchtesgaden, Haus Wachenfeld, which, with later additions made at the expense of the State, remained his private residence. It was there that he installed Frau Raubal as housekeeper with her daughter Geli. But until that time, and whenever he was in Munich, he was usually to be found with his inner circle at the Café Heck, in the Galleriestrasse, which became his *Stammtisch* after leaving Landsberg. In fine weather they usually met out in the Hofgarten.

I continued to join him there not infrequently, in a final attempt to wean him away from his vulgarian entourage. There were, it is true, one or two exceptions. Karl Anton Reichel, an art expert, was a man of some education, and another adherent was Father Berhard Stempfle, who had been in his time the editor of a small anti-Semitic paper called the *Miesbacher Anzeiger* and had helped with the corrections on *Mein Kampf*. Apart from these two, most of the people at the *Stammtisch* were the sort of men who lose their way after any war and make a precarious living selling life assurance or something of the sort.

Whether one got to talk to him at any length depended on his mood or the strength of his company. The pin-headed provincials who had remained faithful to him objected to my presence, as they did to that of anyone they thought might bring any influences to bear apart from their own. I had been trying to interest him for some time in the idea of learning English. I thought that if he was able to read the British and American papers himself he would at least realize that another world existed and functioned outside Germany. "Give me two afternoons a week, Herr Hitler," I told him, "and in three or four months you will know all you need to start with." He was half suspicious and half fascinated by the idea, but would never make up his mind. Like most basically ignorant people, he had this complex about not needing to learn anything.

I tried to get him to realize that there was more than one view of a problem and to illustrate this described the working habits of such classical painters as Albrecht Dürer and Vermeer. They used to have a mirror standing behind them so that from time to time they could turn around and see the whole picture in reflection, checking on one plane the details of what they were trying to paint. "You must look at a problem from several angles," I told him. "You cannot have a *Weltanschauung* unless you have viewed the world. Why don't you take advantage of this lull to travel abroad? You would get a completely new view of Germany's problems." "*Um Gotteswillen*, Hanfstaengl, where would I find the time?" "You forget, Herr Hitler, that the world is growing smaller every day. Three or four months, or half a year at the most, and you could see America, Japan, India, and even if you spent the last few weeks in France and England you would have a picture of what a small part of the globe Europe – to say nothing of Germany itself – occupies. To see Germany from outside will be a revelation for you."

"You make it sound too easy," he replied. "What would happen to the movement if I did that? The whole thing has fallen apart since I was in gaol and everything has to be built up all over again."

"That may be so," I said, "but you are not going to do that over-night. Besides, don't forget that you might easily have spent another couple of years in Landsberg and you ought to look on this period as a gift from Providence. Nothing much can happen in the mean-time. Germany will not run away from you and you will come back full of new plans for the future."

"What curious ideas you have," he answered, slightly nettled. "Where do you think I spent the war? After all, it was fought out-side Germany's borders, I don't need to tell you that, and I spent months, years, as a soldier in Belgium and France." I almost gasped. "But Herr Hitler, you cannot possibly judge a country by the impressions of a soldier. You have a gun in your hand and the inhabitants either crawl to you or treat you with contempt. You never see their true face and cannot possibly form any judgement. You must meet them as equals in times of peace to get to know their real qualities."

"I know them, I tell you," he went on. "I used to see those French women coming out of their houses late every morning in dirty aprons and carpet slippers to go and buy the day's bread and vegetables, slopping around unwashed. They won't have changed. What do you think I can learn from them? And why should I try to learn any-one else's language. I am too old and have no interest and no time. Besides, German is my language, and quite sufficient for me. After all, your British friends also refuse to talk any other language."

Nevertheless the germ of the idea had lodged, and he had obviously been thinking about it, if only because of the new objec-tions he kept finding. I tried to bring up the subject whenever I could. No, he could not possibly travel under his own name. But, I told him, I had friends in the big German shipping companies and it would be perfectly possible to arrange for him to travel incognito. I even offered to go with him and was accused of talking like a travel agent when I told him of the fascinating contrasts in the United States, the vast distances of the Pacific Ocean and the enticements of the Far East, which my father had so well remembered.

When I talked about Japan I thought I had succeeded, as he started to wax lyrical about this warrior nation with its sacred tradi-tions, Germany's true ally and so on, the Haushofer stuff. I should have bitten my tongue, but I could not stop myself producing the counter-arguments of how Germany and Japan were deadly rivals in the field of world trade, with the Japanese undercutting us wherever we met and imitating German trade-marks to cheat our competition, quite apart from the political dangers of antagonizing America.

"That is typical of your bourgeois mentality," Hitler broke in sharply. "You, with your family connexions and friends. You think of everything in terms of trade. You forget that this is only the material side of things and can be changed overnight on the basis of agreements. The most important consideration is that we should think alike in terms of policies and *Weltanschauung*. We Germans have learnt to think in military terms and it is the reflection of our own ideas in Japan that we find so attractive. Besides what part could America play? You would only have to blow up the Panama Canal and they would not be able to exert pressure either way with their navy."

"Well, what about sailing through the Panama Canal while it is still there?" I interjected hoping to retrieve my *faux pas*. Even Hitler smiled resignedly, but we got no farther. During my next two or three visits to the café I could not get a word in edgeways. Local politics had taken hold again and there was always a constant coming and going of political acquaintances discussing affairs in the Bavarian *Landtag*, the situation in north Germany, articles in the *Beobachter*, the problem of enlarging its illustrated weekly edition and the endless personal quarrels on which Hitler thrived. When I got him alone again he had shifted his ground. "Mind you, I would quite like to do it," he admitted. "But I simply cannot get away for that length of time. I wouldn't mind spending a week or two in England though." Well, I thought, this is better than nothing. It is only part of the world problem, but at least he would see something else. So I tried to fire his enthusiasm by talking about Windsor Castle and the National Gallery and the Houses of Parliament. . . . Hitler was quite carried away and started sketching on the back of a menu-card from memory a drawing of the Palace of Westminster. This was the sort of parlour trick he could pull at a moment's notice and the drawing was perfectly accurate. It was no more than an architect's elevation but all the details and proportions were correct, and he had obviously carried them round in his mind from reading the old copies of Spamer's or Meyer's encyclopaedias I had often noticed in his flat.

"Of course the Tower is always worth seeing and Hampton Court which is still just as Henry VIII left it. . . ." At this he got genuinely excited: "Henry VIII, now there was really a man. If anyone understood the art of politics he did, both abroad and at home. How many wives was it he had?" – "Five or six I think," I answered, racking my brains for their names and then trying to explain that this unusual turnover had been due basically to Henry's need for ensuring an heir and the stability of his line. "Six wives," mused Hitler. "That is not bad, even when you leave the scaffold out of account. We must go to the Tower and see where they were executed. I really must get away. That would really be something worth seeing." And that was all that was left of my world tour plans. He wanted to see the scaffold at the Tower of London. He was quite obviously gripped by the successful ruthlessness of this British monarch, who fought the Pope and imposed his will and enhanced the strength of the Tudor line. Is it too fanciful to see in this exchange an indication of the terrible complexes which were to lead to Dachau and Auschwitz and Majdanek?

I had completely lost heart by now. There was no one left in the Party to whom I could turn for any support. Eckart was dead, Toni Drexler was still around, but completely deprived of influence. I remember seeing his wife Anna one day who told me: "You know, we met Adolf on the street and asked him why he never came to see us. Do you know what his answer was? – 'As soon as I have my new car I will come and call on you' – And Toni told him: 'You know you can come and see us in your old car,' but he has never been."

Goering might have helped me, but a warrant was still out against him and he dared not leave Sweden, although we used to correspond. I was unhappy to hear Hitler planning the future without taking Goering into account at all. It was partly his anti-officer complex and partly the fact that his remaining intimates had no time for Goering at all, claiming that he was no National-Socialist, and in the sense which they gave to the words they were right. Gottfried Feder, who was a fairly harmless crank, had also fallen away. In fact he saw the light if anything more clearly than I did. "How can you take over power with no reserves but that bunch of illiterates?" he said to me once. "Hitler will have to have a better second team to back him up in the long run."

Hitler had found no outlet to his personal repressions, although that did not prevent him from indulging in the preliminaries. On one occasion at the Pienzenauerstrasse house, when I had gone out to call a taxi, he went down on his knees in front of my wife, proclaimed his love for her, said what a shame it was he had not met her while she was still free and declared himself her slave. Helene managed to get him on his feet again and, when he had gone, asked me what she should do about it. I knew he had acted out this scene with several other women, so I told her to ignore it and just treat the whole affair as an aberration of loneliness.

He made another attempt with one of the daughters of his early benefactor Ohnesorge. Hitler was staying in his home in Berlin when Ohnesorge was called away, leaving his daughters in the house. Hitler made passionate advances to one of them, and at one point again went down on his knees. He said he could not marry her, but asked her to come and live with him in Munich. Ohnesorge was, of course, furious when he returned and in fact broke off relations with Hitler from about this time. They only came together again in 1931, by which time his offspring were safely married.

At one party out on the Tegern Lake, Hermann Esser took Hitler out with some ladies in a rowing-boat. It would be too much to say that Hitler was shivering with fright, but he was completely out of his element and kept suggesting reasons why the young ladies should be returned to dry land again. He seemed absolutely convinced that the boat was going to capsize and Esser told me afterwards that Hitler had an unreasoning fear of the water. He could not swim and would not learn. In fact I can never recall having seen him in a bathing costume, nor had anyone else. A story, probably authentic, was frequently told that Hitler's old army comrades, who had seen him in the wash-house, had noted that his genital organs were almost freakishly underdeveloped, and he doubtless had some sense of shame about displaying himself. It seemed to me that this must all be part of the underlying complex in his physical relations, which was compensated for by the terrifying urge for domination expressed in the field of politics. This fear of the water must also have played its part in his total incomprehension of naval matters and anything to do with the sea. Looking back it all makes sense.

Hermann Esser had his faults and lived a pretty Bohemian sort of life, but at least he shared my dislike of Rosenberg, whom he would have consigned cheerfully to a dung heap. But with Rosenberg installed again in the *Beobachter,* which was still the only printed outlet for the Nazi programme, there was nothing Esser or I could do. My own personal problems had grown in the meantime. Our little daughter was sick, the start of a distressing illness, during which she wasted away for nearly four years and I was faced by the first mountain of doctors' bills. I had made up my mind to study for a doctor's degree in history and start paying more attention to my obligations to the family firm, and I was really very short of money. The same could not be said of Hitler and his immediate clique. Wherever it came from, they were still tearing round Munich in big cars and their Hofgarten café sessions were certainly not run on credit. I thought well, I helped them out of a hole once over the *Beobachter*, which after all was only ever a loan. I will see if I can get at least some of it back.

I went down to Amann and explained the position, but he was first stupid and then obstinate and then rude. To give an example: I had Egon with me and he looked at the boy and said: "Well he does look nice and tidy, has he just had his hair cut?" So I said yes, he had just been to the barber, whereupon Amann commented: "I have to cut my boy's hair myself you know, to save money. You could do the same if you tried, it is quite easy to learn." That was his tone, and when I said that was neither here nor there and that I needed the money he just turned obstinate again, the Party had no funds and so on and so forth. I was not even asking for the dollars back, although they had represented a fortune at the time. I was perfectly prepared to accept the equivalent in new marks.

The thing went on for months. My wife even brought up the subject once with Hitler himself in Berchtesgaden, where we happened to be early in 1926. He was complaining about our not coming to the meetings and our general aloofness. So my wife asked him what to expect when he still allowed a man like Rosenberg so much influence and then taxed him about Amann's behaviour over the loan. He tried to talk his way out of it by saying that Amann had told him nothing of my situation. He contended that the Party was at its wits' end for finance and used more arguments of the same sort.

In the end I lost patience and went along to see Christian Weber, the tough, brawling horse-dealer who had still managed to keep his position in the Hitler circle, although in his rough way he had started to see through his chief. "What does Hitler mean by calling his book My Struggle," I asked him once. "I should have thought the least he could have done would have been to call it Our Struggle." Weber gave his great beer-belly laugh: "He ought to call it *Mein Krampf*," he said. He was still loyal but did not mind roaring his criticisms. He was an old bandit with an underlying yearning for respectability. We had always got on very well together and he thought I was being scurvily treated so, good horse-dealer that he was, he agreed to take over my claims at a 20 per cent discount and paid me the balance in cash. He had made a good bargain and of course got the whole amount back in no time. He knew exactly how to deal with Amann, who was, needless to state, absolutely furious. Hitler was no better pleased, although he pretended to be above such petty considerations and for some time relations between us were more or less broken off.

CHAPTER VIII

THE BOHEMIAN AT THE BROWN HOUSE

*Art versus politics – The return of Goering – A red ground for
the Swastika – The radicalism of Goebbels – Appearance of a
Hohenzollern – An electoral triumph – Picking the first team
– Interlude with the Press – A letter from the Kaiser – Committed to the Nazis.*

FOR THE next couple of years or so, my contact with Hitler was more
or less spasmodic. I immersed myself in my history books again and
in February 1928 obtained a rather belated Dr. Phil. from Munich
University with a thesis on the problem of Bavaria and the Austrian
Netherlands in the eighteenth century. It was still very much a sign
of respectability in Germany to be able to call yourself 'Herr
Doktor', and I thought the least I could do was to conform. My wife
and I had also spent some time abroad the previous year, chiefly as
a respite to her from the continued and harrowing illness of our little
daughter. We stayed in Paris and London and I had a good look at
all the art galleries, making notes for possible new reproductions for
the family firm. It all seemed so much more civilized and satisfying
than the rowdy complications of life with Hitler.

These of course were the years of his political eclipse. He was not
allowed to speak anywhere and although he was slowly reorganizing
the Party it was a very gradual process and he was making little real
impact. Economic conditions were improving out of all recognition
with the flood of American capital which was streaming into the
country and the apparent stabilizing of the Central Government. As
a result his programme and slogans lost much of their impact. He
was spending most of his time out in Berchtesgaden, but we were in
touch in a desultory fashion through Hermann Esser, who still kept
in with him and seemed to have been deputed by Hitler to render
occasional reports of our attitude. Quite apart from the fact that I
was now fully occupied in other directions, I let him know that as

long as the Rosenberg and Hess factions maintained their influence, I was not particularly interested in associating with him further.

Nevertheless, we continued to see him from time to time, although I cannot say it was an unmitigated pleasure. There was a new air of truculence and impatience about him in his private manner, which I had not remembered. His *obiter dicta* were somehow acquiring a slightly nightmarish tinge. He gave my wife and me a lift across Munich one day in his car and I remember him saying, although what brought up the subject I cannot recall: "There are two ways of judging a man's character; by the woman he marries and by the way he dies." That sounds a little morbid I thought, but the next one was worse: "Politics is like a harlot; if you love her unsuccessfully she bites your head off." It seemed a lurid turn of phrase and I wondered in what directions his thoughts were running. However, in his general attitude to politics he seemed reasonably conciliatory. We were having lunch together at a little wine pub in the Sonnenstrasse with some others, and the conversation turned to the Party's twenty-five point programme, which was an awful hodge-podge, but had long since been declared immutable. Somebody was suggesting that it should be modified and pruned of some of its contradictions, but Hitler did not agree: "What do the contradictions matter?" he said. "The New Testament is full of contradictions but that did not prevent the spread of Christianity."

In public he was professing himself a convert to the tenets of political legality and parliamentary processes, which somewhat reassured me as it was a point I had advocated very strongly after the collapse of the Putsch. The Party diehards were dead against it and failed even to draw any conclusions from the rise of Mussolini, whose march on Rome had after all only been made possible by an electoral success. Hitler appeared to have overcome their objections and earned a nickname in press circles in the process. It was coined by a Swiss journalist who had interviewed him. I forget his name, but he was a tall, pleasant fellow with a very white face, who described Hitler to me as a baffling combination of the ultra-Conservative and the ultra-radical, "in that respect he is very like Philippe Egalité, or should we perhaps call him Prince Legalité".

There was no sign of Hitler's private life becoming normal. For a time he was occasionally seen in the company of Henny, the pretty little blonde daughter of Heinrich Hoffmann. He always used to call her *'mein Sonnenschein'*, but I never heard it seriously maintained that they were having an affair. Apparently he had also taken advantage of Hermann Esser's absence on one occasion to make passionate declarations to his by no means unattractive first wife. Again it was all rhetoric and was followed by a flaming row with the husband, as a result of which Esser was never offered a position of importance when ultimate Nazi success brought the distribution of lucrative jobs for the boys.

It was not until the end of 1927 that I started getting slightly more involved again with the Nazis' affairs, and the occasion for it was the return to Germany of Goering. A general amnesty had been declared in the autumn and he came back first to Berlin, where as far as I could make out he was living on his wits and making a certain amount of money representing a couple of Swedish firms making aircraft components and parachutes. He soon turned up in Munich and I was genuinely pleased to see him. In fact I am not at all sure that he did not come and stay with us. He certainly did so frequently over the next few months and if he was not with us he lived with Captain Streck, who had been Ludendorff's adjutant at the time of the Putsch and was now successfully established in, of all professions, that of a music teacher. Goering was fatter, more business-like and materialistic and concerned chiefly with the Babbitt aim of life.

It seemed to me an entirely good thing that his wider knowledge of the world should be brought to bear on Hitler again, but he did not find the going at all easy. We had corresponded while he was in exile and in the early stages I had helped him from time to time with money, so he rather turned to me as a confidant. The Party hacks were still suspicious of him and Hitler's reception was distinctly cool. General elections were due in the spring of 1928 and Goering wanted to stand high up on the Party list as one of the candidates, partly from ulterior motives I suspect, as it would not only give him a position and a useful income in Berlin but also the protection of parliamentary immunity should opponents in the Government care to rake up any of his past misdeeds. Hitler put him off and sought excuses and in the end Goering lost his temper. It was in February or March. I remember there was snow on the ground as we walked together to the Thierschstrasse, where Hitler still maintained his little flat, for the crucial talk. Goering kept asking me to go up with him, but I preferred not to. I only heard afterwards that the two had had a shouting match, with Goering delivering an ultimatum: "This is no way to treat a man who got two bullets in his stomach at the Feldherrnhalle. Either you put me up for the *Reichstag* or we shall part for ever as enemies." It worked, and Hitler gave way, although it caused much bad blood in the Party and a lot of them went round saying Goering had blackmailed Hitler.

The election results gave little cause for rejoicing. The Nazis obtained twelve seats in the *Reichstag* and considerably less than a million votes. Goering, as I recall, was number seven on the list and just above him was General von Epp, who had now reconciled himself with Hitler and resigned from the Army to stand. In spite of nearly four years' work, the movement had made little headway and was still local in its appeal, only attracting the support of the ultra-nationalist fringe in most of Germany. In spite of Goering's blandishments I had taken no part. His own position in the Party was shaky for quite a time. He had grown enormously fat during his years of exile and the old hands considered that this was no advertisement for a working-class party. Even Hitler expressed doubts about his capacity. "I don't know whether Goering is going to make it," he used to say to me. But Goering fooled them all, developing as a speaker, although all he did was to ape Hitler's style and phrases. For some reason Hitler took this as a compliment, a sign of fidelity, in contradistinction to his attitude to Esser, who did exactly the same, but with more intelligence and independence.

Goering, of course, was delighted with his new-found eminence. I saw him off at the station after the election and he had fitted himself out with a showy great aviation overcoat, made out of leather, with one of those mountaineers' hats, covered with edelweiss and enamel tokens and a great shaving-brush stuck at the back. Having been elected in Bavaria, perhaps he thought he should play the part. "Why don't you make it up with Hitler?" he asked me. "We shall win through in the end and he would certainly put you on the Party list next time. As an M.d.R. you would travel everywhere first-class like me"—waving his free ticket in my face. "What is an M.d.R.?" I asked foolishly. *"Mitglied des Reichstags* [Member of the Reichstag]," he said. "Surely you know that." He kept up his business interests and became known as the wonder of the Nazi Party—the only man who had risen by means of a parachute.

I was far more pleased with a private triumph which had resulted from a second visit to Paris before the elections, where I had gone to stay with an old college-friend, Seymour Blair. I had sent in my card at the Louvre to the director, Henri Verne, who I found was a nephew of the famous novelist. He greeted me with open arms— he knew the name of the family firm well—and when I asked, rather diffidently whether it would be possible to photograph part of the collection for reproduction purposes he immediately promised his full co-operation. I almost fell out of the chair. In my grandfather's day, under Napoleon III, the French authorities had flatly refused such facilities and we had always assumed the request was hopeless. Now not only could I pick whatever I chose, but I was permitted to use our own photographer in a studio at the top of the museum and was promised further facilities in every museum in France. It was a major coup and for some months my time was taken up with little else. I spent two or three lengthy periods in Paris supervising the work and through Verne and his friends met several of the leading French artists—Picasso, Derain, Marie Laurencin and others.

Hitler's, and even Germany's, problems seemed far away, although they were brought home to me once by the odd behaviour of the French workmen who were helping me move the massive canvases from their place on the walls up to the studio where I was working. They were splendid fellows, most of them ex-soldiers. I always had my pocket full of good cigars and we got on famously. One day I felt they were dragging their heels and not displaying their usual cheerful energy, so in the end I ventured to ask if anything was wrong. One of them produced a crumpled copy of a French newspaper from his pocket with the headline, *'Docteur Schacht dit non'*, with a furious story about how Schacht, in an interview in the Hotel Georges V, had said that Germany was unable to continue making any reparations payments. It was around the time of the negotiations on the Young Plan. So I had to double my cigar ration and order up a crate of Munich Spaten beer before personal relations were re-established. At home, of course, the Nazis were in full cry with the same slogan and I could not help feeling what a good thing it would have been if they had seen the effect of this sort of propaganda abroad.

I still saw Hitler occasionally in his café when I was back in Munich and tried to interest him in my accounts of France. He had developed a habit of dropping his voice and changing the subject when he saw me approaching his table, but I did not take it too ill. "I am no longer really in his confidence," I thought, "and he is entitled to keep some things to himself." When we had a few minutes together he was always perfectly pleasant, listening to my Paris gossip, and on one occasion pulled his little trick of drawing public buildings there he had seen illustrated. In ten minutes he had sketched the Opéra, Notre-Dame and the Eiffel Tower, which he pushed over for my approbation with an air as if to prove that he was also a man of the world, and in fact they were perfectly well done. It was an odd, childish quirk. He was always doodling on the back of menu-cards, with squares and circles and swastikas and fancy borders, or scenes out of the Wagner operas. Heinrich Hoffmann usually used to collect them, but I picked up three or four once, only to have them stolen later by a maid.

We got talking once about the Party flag, which he had taken great care to design himself. I told him I did not like the use of black for the swastika, which was a sun symbol and should be in red. "If we did that I could not use red for the background," he said. "I was in the Berlin Lustgarten years ago at a big Socialist demonstration, I tell you there is only one colour with which to attract the masses and that is red." I then suggested that it might be better to put the swastika in the corner of the old black, white and red flag and that even if we used the red background as a war ensign, we should have a peace flag with a white background. "If I put the swastika against a white background we are going to look like a charitable organization," he said. "This is the right thing and I am not going to change it."

I also had occasion to go up to Berlin later in 1928 and went along to have lunch with Goering in the *Reichstag*. He introduced me to Goebbels, whom I met for the first time. I had heard a lot about him; how he had started as a secretary to Gregor Strasser and then switched to profuse support of Hitler when Strasser had tried to make his North German Nazi group too independent. In fact, Strasser was also in the restaurant, but sitting at another table. Goebbels always had a fine nose for which way the wind was blowing and in two or three further Party splits always switched at the last moment to Hitler's side, which, as it turned out, was a great pity.

Goebbels was an odd little narrow-gutted fellow, with his club-footed limp, but he had a beautiful articulate voice and very large brown, intelligent, almost doe-like eyes. He remained a Strasser radical in his political views and talked a lot about the *Bonzen* and the need for helping the unemployed and badly paid. I started on my hobby-horse about soup kitchens *à la* Count Rumford and he said yes, not only for the poorer people, but for everybody. "When we get to power they will all get Spartan soup, for young and old, high and low. We will show them that the German people is really unified in its needs and happiness. We will give our ministers 1,000 marks a month, and if anyone in the country thinks he has a right to make more we will deal with him." That from a man who thought nothing when he came to power of spending 100,000 marks on some Byzantian bacchanal in his Schwanenwerder house on the Wannsee.

My connexion with Hitler and the Party remained vicarious. I had started writing a book on the eighteenth century, which I finally called *From Marlborough to Mirabeau*, and paid, I think, one more visit to Paris to round off the colour photographs for the firm. In fact I was there again at the end of July 1929 and was just returning home when a telegram was handed on board the train at Baden-Baden, to say that our daughter Hertha had died. It was a merciful release; she was five years old and weighed 21 lb. It was probably only superstition on our part, but we felt that we had been partly responsible for her death by giving her a name beginning with an 'H'. There was an old story in the family dating back to my grandfather's time that a gipsy woman in Coburg had told him that any member of the family whose Christian name did not begin with 'E' would have bad luck. With this one exception, we had always kept to it – we were Edgar, Egon, Ernst, Erna, and certainly there was never anything wrong with our health.

I sent my wife up to her relatives in Pomerania for a long holiday and when I had got over the misfortune a little I decided to go and have a look at the annual Party rally in Nuremberg, which had been instituted two years earlier. The first one had coincided with the lifting of the ban on Hitler making public speeches in Bavaria, and for a year he had been free to speak anywhere in Germany. The pulse of the movement was quickening again and I felt under something of an obligation to keep an eye on developments. I travelled on my own in civilian clothes and there on the station platform were Hitler and Goebbels to greet the mass of brown-shirted delegates on their arrival. I got a fairly perfunctory welcome, and Goebbels, who was already engaged in his long campaign to become Hitler's right-hand man and shared, like his rivals, a cankerous jealousy of anyone who seemed to have an unusual *entrée* to him, made one of his typical half-malicious remarks about how glum I was looking. He had a phenomenal memory for small faults of behaviour and attitude in people, on which he would then enlarge to Hitler, and I was astonished years later when he referred again to the incident, suggesting that I had shown little enthusiasm for the Party rally. It was only then that I told him I had just come from the cremation of my daughter, which at least shut him up. I remember being quite impressed with the marching and the bands at the rally, but of course it had not in any way acquired the mammoth, Hollywoodian proportions which were soon to make it such an effective propaganda weapon.

It was, I think, at Nuremburg that I first met Prince August Wilhelm of Prussia—'Auwi'. We came to like each other very well. He was taking an interest in the Nazi Party's activities on behalf of the Hohenzollerns and it was largely through him that I became reconciled again with the movement. I felt that if a member of the former royal family was prepared to identify himself with it, there was more hope of keeping it within bounds. From the end of 1929 Auwi started to use my home as his Munich headquarters and he had a brief meeting with Hitler there at the end of November, although I remember nothing of the details.

At this time also, the Nazis made considerable gains in the provincial elections, especially in Thuringia, where Frick even became the
Minister of the Interior. This had largely been the result of a temporary alliance between Hitler and Hugenberg, who had taken over
the leadership of the German Nationalist Party, in a campaign to
defeat the continuation of reparations and the German signature of
the Young Plan. Although the agitation, which had included a
national plebiscite, was totally unsuccessful, Hitler had succeeded in
impressing his abilities as propagandist and politician on several of
the Ruhr magnates, who had previously confined their support to
Hugenberg. Through a young man named Otto Dietrich, who had
family connexions in the Ruhr and had become Hitler's press relations officer, Hitler met Emil Kirdorf, who, with Fritz Thyssen,
started paying the Nazis quite large subsidies. It was certainly a
larger and more regular income than they had ever had, but as
I have no intimate knowledge of these transactions there is no point
in my enlarging on them.

Needless to say, this gave a great fillip to the Party organization,
and, with political success and an appeal which was now for the first
time national rather than regional, Hitler and his supporters started
to blossom visibly. A large mansion on the Briennerstrasse was
purchased as Party headquarters and became the famous Brown
House. It was the turning-point, and with the spread to Europe in
general and Germany in particular of the consequences of the
economic crash in America, Hitler once more had fertile ground in
which to sow his seeds. I was still bound up in my literary and
artistic work, but recognized that things were on the move again and
that Hitler had not only re-emerged as the man to be watched, but
that unless influences other than those of his immediate entourage
were brought to bear on him anything might happen. This was
something I felt more or less subconsciously, and for some time yet
did nothing really practical about it.

It was only at the beginning of 1930 that I really found myself
being sucked in to the Nazi maelstrom again. Both Auwi and
Goering found my house a convenient centre, Auwi because he
wished to keep a reasonable distance between himself and the Party
offices, and Goering because he had by no means rehabilitated

himself as yet with the old stalwarts. This is an entry in my guest-book for February 24, the day after the murder in a Berlin street brawl of Horst Wessel, which shows that both Auwi and Goering were in the Pienzenauerstrasse with Hitler and Goebbels to discuss the event. The leadership was divided on what action should be taken, and, on the initiative of Goering as I remember, they all met at my house to thrash things out.

The argument was about whether Hitler should go and make a funeral oration at the service in Berlin. Goebbels was wanting him to do it, but Goering said no, the situation was already tense enough and the Party could not guarantee Hitler's safety. "If anything goes wrong it would be a catastrophe," I remember him saying. "After all, there are still only twelve of us in the *Reichstag*, and we simply haven't enough strength to make capital out of this. If Hitler comes to Berlin it will be a red rag to the Communist bulls and we cannot afford to take the consequences." That was conclusive and Hitler did not go in the end, but it certainly did not detract from my opinion of Goering as a moderating influence.

It is probably not generally known that the famous *Horst Wessel Lied*, which became the Nazi anthem and had been composed by the victim, was not original at all. The tune is exactly that of a Vienna cabaret song at the turn of the century, from the Franz Wedekind *Überbrettl* period, although I do not think that Wedekind wrote it himself, to which the words originally ran more or less like this:

> Und als dein Aug' das meine einst erblicket
> Und als mein Mund den deinen einst geküsst
> Da hat die Liebe uns umstricket . . .

which became '*Marschieren im Geist in unseren Reihen mit.*'*

Wessel certainly wrote the new words and hotted up the tune to march time, but that is where it comes from.

My main interest still lay in my book, which finally came out in September 1930. The chief reward was the nicest possible letter

---

* And as your eye met mine
And as my lips kissed yours
Then did love enshroud us . . .
[which became] Walk in spirit within our ranks.

from Oswald Spengler, whom I had recently met in Munich and for whom I had a great admiration. He was a very unprofessorial type, at least for a German, and laid about him in all directions in his tremendous Berlin accent. Yet even he, with his incredible knowledge of world history, had a lot of blind spots about England and America. He had mastered to the smallest detail the sort of history which is taught in German universities, but even his mind had not fully grasped the rôle of the maritime powers.

I had sent him a proof copy of my book and one day on the hall table I found a grubby envelope, which I thought at first was a dentist's bill, in a cheap green cover. I opened it only later in the day and it was from Spengler. He said some very flattering things about it being the most profound and far-reaching study he had ever seen concerning the particular period, the eighteenth century, all in one long sentence right down the page. I think it was the happiest moment of my life. Even my success at the Louvre had been accomplished by and in the name of the Hanfstaengl family, but here was the world's greatest historian praising something which was entirely my own work. A whole new set of perspectives opened up and I thought, ah! now at last with this backing I can really set to work on Count Rumford and Ludwig II of Bavaria and make my reputation as an historian.

In these circumstances it is hardly surprising that the political events of the month found me miles away in another world. New national elections were on the point of being held. The measures necessary to combat the economic crisis had riven the *Reichstag* with faction, but when the members challenged the emergency powers which Chancellor Brüning had obtained from President Hindenburg to meet the situation, he had dissolved the chamber. It was, in fact, the beginning of the death throes of parliamentary Government in the Weimar Republic which were to bring Hitler to power. The Nazis, and indeed every other party, were throwing every ounce of their energy into the campaign.

I tried in a desultory way to gauge which way the wind was blowing and remember one lunch with Seymour Blair, who had come to Munich to see me, and a mutual friend, Anton Pfeiffer, who was one of the leaders of the Bavarian People's Party, at the

Four Seasons Hotel. Pfeiffer was quite a figure and one of his interests was a big German-American boys' school at Nymphenburg. I had told Blair that I would find some excuse to leave the table for a few minutes and go and telephone, and wanted him to ask Pfeiffer, as a foreigner, which way he thought the elections would go. Goering had been on at me to make it up with Hitler and get my name put on the Party list, but I had done nothing about it. Blair told me later that Pfeiffer had said the Nazis would be lucky to get six people in the *Reichstag*, half their 1928 representation. This I felt was unduly pessimistic, or optimistic, depending on which way you looked at it, and thought that in the situation the Nazis might conceivably win thirty to forty seats, but nobody was more staggered than I was to learn that they had obtained nearly 6½ million votes and increased their representation to 107.

This, of course, was a political sensation of the first order, and we were all still digesting its implications when, a day or two later, the telephone rang at my home and there was Rudolf Hess on the line: "Herr Hanfstaengl, the Führer is very anxious to talk to you. When would it be convenient for us to call on you?" All very polite and courteous. 'What can I lose?' I thought, and said, "Yes, certainly, come along whenever you like." In half an hour they were knocking at the door, Hitler very authoritative and staccato and Hess providing silent support. I sat them down and said how pleased I was to see them and what an astonishing success it had been, which Hitler all regarded as self-evident and promptly came to the point: "Herr Hanfstaengl, I have come to ask you to take over the post of foreign press chief of the Party. Great things are before us. In a few months, or at the most in a couple of years, we must irresistibly sweep to power. You have all the connexions and could render us a great service."

I knew what was in his mind. Munich was being flooded with foreign correspondents who had come down to interview this renascent phenomenon and he simply did not know how to deal with them or talk to them. He never had, and in spite of our years of semi-estrangement I was the only person he knew who had the whole background of the Party in his mind and could deal with the problem. In a way I was flattered, but not to be hustled. At least it would give me a position, I hoped of influence, near him, but I had serious reservations. My arch-allergy, Rosenberg, had, of course, also been swept into the *Reichstag* on Hitler's coat-tails, and I felt this would give him an even bigger field for his nefarious theories. I produced all my standing objections, which Hitler tried to counter by saying that if the Party really came to power, Rosenberg and the *Beobachter* would have much less importance.

Then he tried to bribe me by saying that at the next elections he would certainly put me up for the Bavarian *Landtag* or the *Reichstag*, whichever I preferred, and that I could look forward to an important position in the Foreign Office and that now was my chance. It was certainly clear that this was my best opportunity of entering on the ground floor on equal terms with the wild men of the Party whose influence I had always feared, so in the end I agreed. I told him that I had developed a great many other interests, but that I would undertake this liaison work in a voluntary capacity and we would see how it worked out. He left with profuse thanks and spacious phrases: "Hanfstaengl, *Sie gehören in meine nächste Umgebung*" ["You will form part of my immediate entourage"]. But, of course, with no hint of practical arrangements, or where I was to have an office, or how I was to work. Those were the details he could never be bothered with.

If I was to be closely identified with him again, the best thing seemed to collect a small group of advisers with whom I could work out arguments to counteract the wilder aberrations of the Party extremists. I held a whole series of meetings and conferences and dinners at my house in the Pienzenauerstrasse. There was a Major Gramaccini, who had been for many years the Italian member of the Disarmament Commission resident in Munich, who not only briefed me about what was still the relatively moderate Fascist régime in Italy under Mussolini, but reinforced my anti-Rosenberg arguments of the potential danger of offending Catholic opinion and allowing illegal methods to gain the upper hand in the Party. He also warned me that if Hitler thought that future friendship between the two régimes was going to be automatic he was going to be severely disillusioned.

I also called in General von Biskupsky, who was a very presentable former Czarist officer and had at one time formed a brief friendship with Rosenberg, but had fallen out with him. I relied on him for convincing arguments of the necessity of friendly relations with Poland and Russia. I even went as far as inviting General Haushofer to the house and when I found it was impossible to shake his nippomania, turned to a Munich physician named Dr. von Schab, who had spent long years in the Far East in senior medical posts and had a much more balanced view of the Asian people than this geopolitical *fantaisiste*. The trouble was I could never really get Hitler to listen to him. In an attempt to revive the old, more conservative wing of the Party I started to see a lot again of Toni Drexler. He was still very much alive and in fact did not die until 1943 and remained true to his solid trade union background.

My first official appearance with Hitler came almost immediately, when he asked me to travel to Leipzig with him for the trial of two young officers who stood accused of spreading Nazi propaganda in the Army. Hitler had been called as a witness and if I needed any further indication of his ability to rise to an occasion and his extraordinary hold over a growing section of public opinion this provided it. He finished by turning the court into a political forum and gave a two-hour speech which was not only cunningly devised to enlist the sympathies of the Army but constituted a complete summary of the National-Socialist programme, which was, of course, printed under tremendous headlines in every German newspaper. He used one phrase to which I must say I did not attach more than rhetorical value at the time, which was that when he came to power 'heads would roll'. 'Yes,' I thought, 'anyone who has been a traitor to Germany's interests must obviously be dismissed from office and stand trial if necessary', but to Hitler the phrase had a physical meaning, and it was to take years for a lot of people to realize that he meant exactly what he said.

The effect on the audience was, of course, enormous and the press representatives galloped out in a body to send full reports of his speech. One of the correspondents there was Karl von Wiegand, who was the chief European representative of the Hearst group. He wanted Hitler to write two or three articles for the chain for a handsome sum, three or four thousand marks each, which in due course

I arranged. Hitler gave me a 30 per cent cut, which I must say was by no means unwelcome. However, the arrangement leaked out to the Party and the radicals took a very displeased view of this surrender of Hitler to the mighty dollar.

He was certainly beginning to give himself airs in financial matters at the time, and at the Hotel Hauffe, where we were staying, when I thought I was being particularly generous in giving the maidservant a 20 per cent tip of about three marks, I saw him giving her ten marks. In my travels with him he always gave three or four times the amount that was necessary, and claimed that it had a very good effect, as the staff showed the notes around in the kitchen and sometimes even got him to autograph them. It was also at Leipzig that I realized for the first time that he had acquired quite a following among the German aristocracy. If I remember correctly, Prince zu Wied and his charming wife were there, together with several others, for the late-evening conversation sessions, and in this I saw nothing but good. These were people from the right sort of society, and if the political situation developed they would provide a useful restraining influence.

With his power and position suddenly increased beyond measure, Hitler was picking his first team for the struggle that lay ahead. For two or three years the S.A. had been under the command of a Captain Pfeffer, but Hitler was not satisfied with the way in which it was being run. In all conscience it was military enough, with the old *Freikorps* hands in the subordinate ranks still thinking that all they had to do was to keep alive the spirit and comradeship they had developed in the trenches. There had even been a movement at one time to replace their Austrian ski-cap with the round Prussian soldiers' headgear, but this had been turned down for the curious compromise of something which looked uncommonly like a French Army *képi*. Pfeffer had been a soldier in Alsace-Lorraine and this was his idea. However, Hitler wanted the S.A. developed on a national scale as a political weapon, and turned again to one of the best organizers he had, Ernst Roehm, by then serving as a mercenary in the Bolivian army.

By this time his sexual perversion was complete, although to what extent Hitler was aware of this when he sent for him I do not know.

Fellow-officers who had known Roehm during the war always main-tained that he had been completely normal and even described orgies in which he had taken part in the Army brothels. He had certainly acquired a syphilitic infection during this period and this may have had some effect on his subsequent development. The scandal started soon after he had returned in October 1930. Letters from his male companions in Bolivia somehow came into the hands of third parties and the accusations started. General von Epp, who had held a high opinion of Roehm's organizational abilities before the Ludendorff Putsch, even taxed him with the rumours at quite an early stage and received Roehm's completely false word of honour that they were not true. Later, about 1932, the scandal became public, and although it was somehow glossed over, Roehm quite openly admitted his aberration to Toni Drexler, because he passed it on to me. Hitler can have had no illusions at any time and his mock horror when he found it necessary to shoot Roehm in 1934 was, of course, pure invention.

On January 1, 1931, the Brown House was formally opened as Party headquarters. A tiny room had been reserved for me on the third floor, which seemed a very unsatisfactory arrangement, as it meant that the foreign correspondents who came to visit us could wander all over the building on the pretence of trying to find me. My immediate neighbour was Heinrich Himmler. Until the 'thirties he had only been a shadowy hanger-on of the inner group of the Nazi Party, but Hitler had at last found him a niche and had entrusted him with the formation of a special bodyguard responsible for the protection of Hitler's person. Its growth was slow and it was some time before the membership even reached three figures, yet, in the end, it staffed the concentration camps and provided thirty-five Waffen S.S. divisions. But if anyone had asked me to foresee that I would have sent them to have their head examined.

It was in Himmler's office that I saw young Baldur von Schirach for the first time. What persuaded his parents to give him such an operatic name I cannot think. It was enough to give him a knock on the head to last a lifetime. He spoke really quite good English and lounged into my office one day to see if I would take him on as my secretary, or adjutant, as the Nazi phraseology had it. He

slouched on the other side of the desk and picked up a pen and
played with it and shifted other things around as he talked, so that
I got pretty sharp with him and asked where he had learnt his
manners. This was a bad start to our relationship and he never liked
me, but he ended by marrying Henny Hoffmann and at one time
was regarded as the golden boy of the Party and almost the crown
prince.

As far as my nominal duties were concerned, I derived little
satisfaction. Hitler had never grown out of his café habits and his
congenital inability to keep to an orderly daily time-table. I would
make appointments with journalists and he would never keep them,
or have to spend the whole day hunting him down in one of his
public haunts. His whole life was lived in this impromptu Bohemian
style. He would turn up at the Brown House at eleven or at twelve
as it suited him. He would come announced and unannounced and
would keep people waiting for hours.

The only place where you could be reasonably sure of catching
him was still the Café Heck, where he used to hold court from about
four o'clock in the afternoon onwards. He hated any sort of gathering where he could be pinned down, and preferred his informal
Stammtisch which gave him unlimited occasion to talk and expatiate
without being contradicted. He usually had people listening to him
spellbound and it was very hard to get anything out of him, as
everyone there hung on his words and it took hours to get him alone.
In due course he realized that I had not come to hear the same
repeated stories of the Party's history for the fiftieth time and that
I had something particular to say to him, but that time was not yet.

I did what I could. There was a not unfriendly journalist in Paris
named Gustave Hervé, who was the editor of *La Victoire*, with
whom I arranged an exchange of open letters advocating Franco-
German understanding. Then there was old Hermann Bahr, the
very respectable Austrian feuilletonist and author. He was a staunch
Catholic, but had written an article somewhere not unfavourable to
the Nazi movement and I persuaded Hitler to take advantage of his
prestige and print an article by him in the illustrated *Beobachter*.
Rosenberg slashed it to pieces and Bahr, very put out, would have
nothing further to do with us. There was a Portuguese journalist

from *Diario de Noticias* in Lisbon. I tried to get Hitler to have a few words with him in the Café Heck, but the trouble was he had no idea what to talk to foreign journalists about. He either wanted them to be converted to Nazism in advance or expected them to become passionate admirers. He had no command of the amiable banalities with which a true politician can fob off the press. In this case our Portuguese visitor was very annoyed. He had spent several days at the expensive Regina Hotel to no purpose and, of course, wrote a very unfavourable article. This came back into the hands of Philip Bouhler, one of Hitler's adjutants, who spoke excellent Portuguese as a result of long residing in Brazil. So of course they all rounded on me for not doing my job properly.

I see from a letter I wrote on February 9, 1931, that all my reservations were being reinforced. Someone named Maximilian von Hamm had approached me through my friend Karl Oskar Bertling in Berlin to ask if some employment could be found for him in the Party organization. He cannot have found my advice encouraging: "The foreign and internal policies of the N.S.D.A.P. under that Russified German Alfred Rosenberg are so incredibly clumsy, not to say criminal, that at the moment I can only see a second disaster looming for the Party. The anti-clerical agitation furthered by this Mythos of his can only lead to national Bolshevism. . . . Most of the people in the Party leadership are second-raters and nothing good can come from their continued influence. . . . You will have cause to be grateful if I dissuade you from joining us. . . . It is very sad to have to write you this, but unless he mends his ways, Hitler, for all his incredible powers as an orator, will never be more than the drummer-boy for the rest. As things are he simply does not possess the qualities for a leader of Germany."

Nevertheless, I still found myself being caught up willy-nilly in the Party's internal squabbles. I was dragged up to Berlin by Hitler in April 1931, when the S.A. formations there revolted against the leadership. They had not been paid and thought they were being prevented from playing their true part in the political struggle. Hitler had to go round from suburb to suburb and beseech them with tears in his eyes to rely on him to see that their interests were protected. He managed to restore order and we all sat around the next day in a sort of commercial travellers' hotel called the Herzog von Coburg, opposite the Anhalter Station, Goebbels, Hitler and Walter Stennes, who was usually referred to as the leader of the revolt, but was in fact much more the victim. I found him a very decent fellow, a nephew of Cardinal Schulte of Cologne, and he took me over to one of the open windows, where our conversation was drowned by the noise of traffic, and said: "Does Hitler realize that the real instigator of this revolt is standing by him?" – and that was Goebbels. "He has been egging them on to demonstrate in the streets in spite of Hitler's orders that we were not to get into fights, and now they blame it all on me." Part of the trouble was that some of the money they should have been receiving had been pocketed by Goebbels to set himself up in luxury. He was in the middle of his affair with his future wife Magda, who at that time was still married to a Herr Quandt, and needed presumably to impress her with his power and affluence. Stennes, in fact, came to no harm and eventually made his way to China, where he became an adviser to Chang Kai-shek.

A much more significant meeting occurred shortly after our return to Munich, when Auwi was again my guest with Goering and brought a letter from his father, the Kaiser, to Hitler, which, although phrased in very general terms, more or less formally appointed Auwi as his representative with the Nazi movement and promising support and benevolent interest. I did not see the text myself. I was standing two or three yards away when the letter was handed over and Hitler read it through silently and folded it away in his pocket with an approving grunt. Afterwards Auwi said to me: "Hitler ought to be very pleased with that. My father has given him a pretty open undertaking to give what help he can and I shall make a point of keeping in with Hitler as much as possible myself." And then with the possibility of a restoration running through his mind, he added: "After all, I am the best horse in the Hohenzollern stable."

In fact Auwi stayed on for several weeks as my guest and the telephone was always humming to Doorn and Potsdam. It cost me a fortune. Hitler was shrewd enough to realize that monarchist support could be a very important factor and, in fact, he played on the German royal families' hopes of a restoration for years, at least as long as it suited him. "I consider a monarchy a very suitable form of State organization, particularly in Germany," he said to me once, and, of course, he talked in similar terms to whoever wanted to believe it. "The problem has to be studied very carefully. I would accept the Hohenzollerns again at any time, but in the other States we would probably have to put in a regent until we found a suitable prince." When the time came he maintained the illusion by appointing a number of people as *Reichstatthalter*, of whom General von Epp in Bavaria was the best known. Hitler had a very low opinion of the Crown Prince, whom he regarded as a light-weight interested only in horses and women, and although he had a certain affection for his brother Auwi, he had no illusions about his capacity. "Perhaps the next Kaiser is already marching in our ranks as a simple S.A. man," he once said to me, and I knew that the prince he had in mind was Alexander, who was Auwi's son by his first marriage.

It was Auwi as much as anybody who revived my hope in the Party's future. He took a much more optimistic view than I did and it was largely his example which prompted me to accept formal membership. Sometime about August of 1931 he resigned from the *Stahlhelm* and joined the N.S.D.A.P. We registered the same day and, as a result of one of the many reclassifications of membership which were always going on, we received the adjacent membership numbers of 68 and 69.

Another factor had also intervened to cement my relationship with Hitler. The economic crisis was by now affecting every facet of German life and our family firm was not spared. I had a long talk with my brother Edgar to see if he was prepared to take me in as a whole-time working director, but he told me that we were in quite serious trouble and there was no question of it. I was in something of a cleft stick. I could certainly not go on working for Hitler for nothing if that was the case. I was trying to sort out in my mind what should best be done and was having lunch at the Café Heck one day when Hitler came in.

I was sitting with Otto Gebühr, the actor, who had never met Hitler, so I introduced them. I remember how Hitler had admired his portrayal of Frederick the Great, so I introduced him as 'His Majesty the King of Prussia'. This amused Hitler and they got on very well, which put Hitler in a good mood by the time that Gebühr had to leave us. We chatted vaguely about the job he had asked me to do and I told him I was finding it very frustrating and that I really could not go on unless some of my expenses were paid. "How much do you need?" Hitler asked. "Would a thousand marks a month help?" "Well, it would certainly do as a start," I said, but that was, in fact, all I ever got from them, even after they had come to power. In spite of all my misgivings, I was now attached to the Hitler chariot at the psychological turning-point of his life.

CHAPTER IX

GELI RAUBAL

*Hitler takes a luxury flat – The amours of his niece – Porno-
graphic drawings and blackmail – Soprano without talent –
The unwilling sub-tenant – Suicide – Corpse without inquest –
Hara-kiri and a pregnancy – The impotent Herostratus.*

WITH THE advent of money from the Ruhr, Hitler had at long last
given up his little flat in the Thierschstrasse and abandoned his pre-
tension of being the leader of a working-class party. Some time
before the end of 1929 he had moved into a handsome nine-roomed
apartment at 16 Prinz Regentenplatz, in one of the most expensive
parts of the city. He took with him Frau Reichert, his landlady in
the Thierschstrasse, together with her mother, Frau Dachs. He then
took into his employment as manservant a former non-commissioned
officer named Winter, who had been the valet of General von Epp.
In due course Winter married the lady's maid of Countess Toerring,
and the pair became the principal servants in the flat. Angela
Raubal, the half-sister Hitler had brought from Vienna, remained
in charge of his house at Berchtesgaden.

Her daughter Geli was by then a buxom young woman of twenty-
one. A couple of years earlier she had taken a bed-sitting-room in
Munich not far from Hitler's old flat, and had, I think, made a
pretence of starting some course of study at the university. She
completed one aspect of her education pretty quickly, and was soon
having an affair with Emil Maurice, Hitler's driver. Nor did she
keep her sentiments exclusive. Maurice was furious one day to find
her *flagrante delicto* with a student, whom he threw out of the
room neck and crop.

Hitler came to hear of this liaison, but at first his reaction did not
seem to go beyond anger with Maurice. In his usual fashion he did
not sack him directly, the man was an old faithful Party hack, but
he gradually started to freeze him out, fell behind in paying his

wages, and in the end Maurice himself made the break. There was, I believe, a minor lawsuit about money, and his job was taken over by Julius Schreck.

Geli went to live with the Bruckmanns for a while to keep her out of temptation's way, but as soon as Hitler moved into his new apartment, she was given a room there. She and her mother were, of course, completely dependent on Hitler, but what particular combination of arguments her uncle used to bend her to his will, presumably with the tacit acquiescence of his half-sister, we shall probably never know. Whether he assumed that a young woman who was already no saint might be brought fairly easily to submit to his peculiar tastes, or whether in fact she was the one woman in his life who went some way towards curing his impotence and half making a man out of him, again we shall never know with certainty. On the evidence available I incline to the former view. What is certain is that the services she was prepared to render had the effect of making him behave like a man in love. She went round very well dressed at his expense, or, more probably, at the Party's expense, as a lot of resentment was expressed, and he hovered at her elbow with a moon-calf look in his eyes in a very plausible imitation of adolescent infatuation.

She was an empty-headed little slut, with the coarse bloom of a servant-girl, without either brains or character. She was perfectly content to preen herself in her fine clothes, and certainly never gave any impression of reciprocating Hitler's twisted tendernesses. I only got the story at third hand, it was not the sort of thing you could expect a young woman to talk to a man about, but she is supposed to have remarked to a girl friend, who passed it on to one of the wives in the Party, that her uncle was a "monster. You would never believe the things he makes me do." In addition, there was, of course, an unpleasant suggestion of incest about the affair, which I can only assume harked back to their in-bred peasant family. Hitler's parents were cousins, and if you look at his genealogical tree there are several marriages between blood relations. It was yet another facet of the darker side of his character.

My first indication that there was something wrong with the relationship came, as I recall, fairly early in 1930 from Franz Xaver

Schwarz, who was the Party treasurer. I had known him for years. He was a qualified accountant and had been a senior official of the finance section of the City Council. He may even have run it. When he told me the Nazis wanted him to take over their book-keeping, I encouraged him. Their financial affairs were obviously in hopeless disorder, with everyone making pickings wherever they could find them and it seemed to me he would introduce a measure of integrity and stability.

I met him on the street one day, and he looked very down-in-the-mouth. I was pretty pessimistic about the Party outlook myself, so we exchanged our woes and Schwarz said, "Come up and have a cup of coffee with us. My wife would like to see you again and we can have a talk." He had a little flat in the shabbier part of Schwabing. His wife greeted me, gave us our coffee, retired to the kitchen again, and Schwarz poured out what was on his mind. He had just had to buy off someone who had been trying to blackmail Hitler, but the worst part of the story was the reason for it. This man had somehow come into the possession of a folio of pornographic drawings Hitler had made. How he came by them I never heard. Perhaps they were stolen out of Hitler's car. They were depraved, intimate sketches of Geli Raubal, with every anatomical detail, the sort of thing only a perverted *voyeur* would commit to paper, much less oblige a woman to model for. Schwarz had bought them back. "Heaven help us, man," I said, "why don't you tear the filth up?" "No," said Schwarz, "Hitler wants them back. He wants me to keep them in the Brown House safe." So this is the man, I thought, who prates about cleaning up Germany, the dignity of conjugal life, *die deutsche Frau* and all that. Anyone who thought he was going to reform Hitler carried a lot of millstones round his neck.

At some time during 1930 Geli started to take singing-lessons. Hitler had some idea she might develop into a Wagner heroine and sent her first to an early Party member named Adolf Vogel. He dated back to the Café Neumaier days in the 'twenties and one of his early pupils became a well-known opera singer under the name of Bertha Morena. In fact her real name was Meyer and she was a full Jewess. Hitler had admired her voice and simply would not believe it when I told him about her background. I did it only to make his anti-Semitic prejudices look foolish, and it goes to show how skin-deep they were.

Vogel did not find Geli a very apt pupil. Her voice was indifferent, her theatrical gifts precisely nil, and the possibilities of an operatic career began to fade. Hitler was going to be compelled to fulfil his Lohengrin rôle in real life only. The next teacher appointed was Hans Streck, the Ludendorff adjutant of the Putsch days, who persuaded Hitler that perhaps the girl could be taught to sing *Lieder*. Streck had built up quite a clientele and had a studio in the Gedonstrasse, near the English Garden. It was arranged that he would give Geli twelve lessons a month and be paid 100 marks. "Geli is the laziest pupil I have ever had," he used to complain. "Half the time she rings up to say that she can't come and she learns very little when she does." She never practised at home and the main impression Streck derived was of Hitler's boundless tolerance of the waste of his money. He used sometimes to come and call for her before the lesson was over, and would creep in and listen from the hall.

My wife also used to keep her voice in trim with Streck and occasionally used to see Geli there, although our contact with her was very limited. We saw her on one occasion with Hitler at the Residenz Theatre, where we had gone to see a Bavarian piece by Ludwig Thoma. They were standing in one of the side galleries during an interval, with Hitler mooning at her, thinking he was unobserved, but as soon as he saw me he switched his face to the Napoleonic look. However, he was perfectly friendly and when we suggested that they should join us for supper at the Schwarzwälder Café he agreed. We got a quiet table up on the first floor and chatted amiably about the play we had just seen. I was furious because three of the actors had Berlin accents, which for me had completely spoilt its regional character, but Hitler couldn't see this, which surprised me in a man who in politics and music had such a highly developed sensitivity.

When we left we walked part of the way together, by which time Hitler was back on to politics again and emphasized some threat against his opponents by cracking the heavy dog whip he still affected. I happened to catch a glimpse of Geli's face as he did it and there was on it such a mixture of fear and contempt that I almost caught my breath. Whips as well, I thought, and really felt sorry for the girl. She had displayed no sign of affection for him in the restaurant and seemed bored, looking over her shoulder at the other tables and I could not help feeling that her share in the relationship was under compulsion.

On the evening of September 18, 1931, she shot herself in Hitler's flat. Winter found the door of Geli's room locked from the inside the next morning, burst it open and discovered the girl lying on the couch in a beige dress with a bullet in her lung. In her hand was Hitler's revolver. They had heard nothing the evening before. The shot had probably gone unnoticed amid the general tumult in the streets of Munich which precedes the famous *Oktober Fest*.

Hitler was away. He had left in the afternoon of the 18th on some Party tour to Nuremberg and points north. After Frau Winter had rung up the Brown House with the news of the tragedy, Hess tried to get Hitler on the telephone at his Nuremberg hotel, but he had already left and a hotel page had to chase the column in a taxi. Schreck drove him back at breakneck speed and he arrived to find that Gregor Strasser and Schwarz had been in the flat and had the situation under control. Hitler was in a state of hysteria, and left the same day to stay with the Müllers, the *Beobachter* printer, on the Tegern Lake. Not, it will be noted, with his bereaved half-sister at Berchtesgaden.

The whole affair was hushed up and glossed over as much as possible. At first an attempt was made to suggest that there had been an accident. During the day of Saturday, the 19th, Baldur von Schirach got on to the Brown House from the apartment to tell Dr. Adolf Dresler in the press department to issue a communiqué about Hitler having gone into deep mourning after the suicide of his niece. Then the group at the flat must have got into a panic, because twenty-five minutes later von Schirach was on the phone again asking if the communiqué had gone out and that it was the wrong wording. They should announce that there had been a lamentable accident. But by then it was too late. The word was out, and by Monday, the 21st, all the opposition papers carried the news.

The *Münchener Post*, a Socialist daily, was the most explicit. Its long account was full of circumstantial detail and alleged that Hitler and his niece had been having frequent arguments of late, culminating in a final row over the breakfast table on the morning of the 18th. Geli had long expressed the wish to return to Austria, where she intended to become engaged. An unposted letter to a girl friend in Vienna had been found in the flat saying that she hoped to leave soon. The report also alleged that when the corpse was found, the bridge of the nose was broken and the body showed other signs of maltreatment.

Two days later, on the Wednesday, the *Völkische Beobachter* carried on an inside page a denial by Hitler of all these allegations, threatening the *Münchener Post* with legal proceedings if it did not publish a withdrawal. In the meantime, so I learnt from acquaintances in the Party, the corpse had been smuggled down the back stairs of the block of flats and placed in a lead coffin in the mortuary of the Munich East Cemetery. After that a veil was drawn over the whole affair, and apart from one further broadside in the *Münchener Post,* disappeared from the newspapers for sheer lack of further information. The opposition paper made the telling point that the death of a Nazi street fighter would be made the basis in the *Völkische Beobachter* of leading articles and a campaign lasting several days, while the death in the cause of Hitler's niece was passed over in silence.

After that no further details were announced. The Party high-ups had got hold of Gürtner, who was still Bavarian Minister of Justice, and persuaded him to dispense with the formalities of an inquest and a coroner's verdict. This was of course highly improper, but Gürtner had long been a sympathizer and may have thought it worth his while to keep his political fences in repair. If so he was handsomely paid off, as within a year they had lobbied his appointment as Reich Minister of Justice in the von Papen cabinet, even before they came to power and he retained the post well into the 'thirties. Gürtner also gave authority for her body to be transported to Vienna, where she was buried in the Central Cemetery. Himmler and Roehm were there to represent Hitler. Perhaps he thought the scandal would die down more quickly if there was no grave in Munich to remind people of what had happened.

Apart from the fact that Hitler was prostrate with grief or frustration or some darker emotion, exactly what had happened? There are few facts, but much room for conjecture. One of the few surviving eye-witnesses of the scene is Frau Winter and I strongly suspect it was made worth her while for the rest of her life to adhere to the official version of an inexplicable accident. Goering came to see us a fortnight later but gave us a purely romanticized version of the affair. Hitler was apparently furious at Strasser for maintaining and publishing the fact that it was a suicide and had fallen on Goering's neck weeping with gratitude when Hermann suggested that it was just as likely to have been an accident. "Now I know who is my real friend," Hitler had sobbed. I think it was pure opportunism on Goering's part. He wanted to eliminate Strasser as a rival in Hitler's favour. Circumstances never healed these eternal jealousies in the Party.

It was months before I learnt from Streck that Geli had rung up two days before she died to say that she would be taking no more lessons in September, was leaving for Vienna and would let him know when she returned. The story gained currency in Party circles that Hitler and his niece had had a flaming row at breakfast on the 18th. Even Frau Winter admits that they were having an argument of some sort, but tries to minimize it. Clearly there was an emotional crisis of some sort. I talked at some later period to Karl Anton Reichel, one of the closest intimates at the Café Heck *Stammtisch*. He told me that Hitler had shown him a letter he had written to Geli at Berchtesgaden. It was couched in romantic, even anatomical terms and could only be read in the context of a farewell letter of some sort. Its most extraordinary aspect was a pornographic drawing which Reichel could only describe as a symbol of impotence. Why on earth he should have been shown this letter I cannot imagine, but he was not the man to make up such a story.

It was not until the autumn of 1937, when I was in exile in London, that I was given another leading clue which might explain the change in Hitler's attitude between the time he wrote that letter and the morning row on the day that Geli Raubal died. I was visited by Mrs. Brigid Hitler, an Irish woman, who had met Hitler's half-brother Alois, the full brother of Angela Raubal, in Dublin in 1909, when he was studying the hotel business as a waiter. She married him and they had a son, Patrick, although Alois subsequently deserted her. She maintains that the immediate family knew very well that the cause of Geli's suicide was the fact that she was pregnant by a young Jewish art teacher in Linz, whom she had met in 1928 and wanted to marry at the time of her death.

Geli had been circulating the story that she wished to return to Vienna to consult another singing professor concerning the training of her voice. She had even asked Hans Streck for the name of his own teacher there, who was Professor Otto Ro. It may well be that Hitler extracted from her the real purpose of her visit. It is not too difficult to reconstruct the reaction of that tortured mind and body. His anti-Semitism would have caused him to accuse her of dishonouring them both and to tell her that the best thing she could do was to shoot herself. Perhaps he threatened to cut off all support from her mother. He had swallowed for so long the Haushofer line about the samurai and bushido and the necessity in given circumstances of committing the ritual suicide of hara-kari that he may have overwhelmed the wretched girl to take just that step. If so, it would be the first example of many similar instances to follow. Gregor Strasser was invited to do the same when he tried to split the Party at the end of 1932. There is ample evidence that Roehm was provided with a pistol for the same purpose in the 1934 purge. Not the least reason for Strasser's death at the same time was the too intimate knowledge he gained of Geli Raubal's death.

Hitler's only visible reaction at the time of his niece's death was to close up her room and have a not particularly good Munich sculptor named Ziegler, who was a Party friend, make a bust of Geli, which was installed in the room and always surrounded by flowers. On each anniversary of the tragedy he used to shut himself in there for hours.

I am sure that the death of Geli Raubal marked a turning-point in the development of Hitler's character. This relationship, whatever form it took in their intimacy, had provided him for the first and only time in his life with a release to his nervous energy which only too soon was to find its final expression in ruthlessness and savagery. His long connexion with Eva Braun never produced the moon-calf interludes he had enjoyed with Geli and which might in due course, perhaps, have made a normal man out of him. With her death the way was clear for his final development into a demon, with his sex life deteriorating again into a sort of bi-sexual narcissus-like vanity, with Eva Braun little more than a vague domestic adjunct.

He certainly had an eye for good-looking women and two or three more are sometimes named as having enjoyed his special favour. But in my experience none of them went beyond an expressive shrug and sigh and an upward hopeless lift of the eyes to describe how far the relationship had led. He would call them 'his princess' or 'his little countess' and was never chary of making passionate declarations of affection. He was perfectly prepared to indulge in the physical preliminaries, but when it came to carrying matters to a conclusion, or even worse, when he had succeeded in awakening the woman's interest and acquiescence in the idea of consummation, there was nothing he could do about it.

Psychologists could fill a whole text-book about Hitler, starting with his own description of himself in *Mein Kampf* as a *Muttersöhnchen* – a mother's boy. Hitler claims that this was a stage he grew out of, but many of them do not and neither did he. Germany and the world were yet to suffer from the fact that he had all the psychological faults of the type magnified to a daemonic degree. His over-compensation for the inferiority complex of an impotent masturbator was the driving force of his lust for power. Uneasily aware that he was incapable of perpetuating himself as a father, he developed a substitute-obsession to make his name known – and feared – throughout the ages, whatever monstrous deeds such a mania involved. He became the modern counterpart of Herostratus, who, desirous of acquiring eternal fame, if only by a great crime, burnt down the Temple of Diana at Ephesus.

CHAPTER X

LOHENGRIN PREVAILS

Poacher and gamekeeper — Prejudices strengthened — The Prussians of Asia — Peripatetic boredom — The court minstrel — Assertion at arm's length — Encounter with Churchill — A message from Roosevelt — Split with Strasser — Buskers in the Kaiserhof — Two organized disappointments — No mate for the glow-worm.

It would be reasonable to ask why, in view of all my misgivings about the character and intentions of Hitler and his circle, I continued for so long in close association with them. It is a question which could be put in one form or another to many other people: the industrialists who supplied him with funds; the many perfectly respectable and orthodox Conservative politicians who, when the time came, entered into coalition with him; the members of families with impeccable pedigrees, from the Hohenzollerns downwards who associated themselves with his movement; the millions of unemployed workers and members of the proletarianized middle class who came to believe he provided the only alternative to the Communists as a solution to the ghastly depression of the early 1930's, and, last but not least, the 43.9 per cent of the population which voted his confirmation in power.

I was an idealistic National-Socialist, I make no bones about it. It is a term which meant many things to different men, and I was no politician, but a piano player and art lover with ambitions to become a historian. I had a better eye for effects than causes. I had seen Germany degraded and destituted, and wanted to see the return of the comfortable and traditional values of my youth, combined with an honoured and respected position for what were then still called the working classes. Behind a cloud of words and threats and exaggerations, I thought this was what Hitler wanted. Above all, in his second surge of political activity, I was convinced again that nothing was going to prevent him from reaching the top. If only the radicals like Strasser and Goebbels and the crackpots like Rosenberg and Hess could be off-set by people of more cosmopolitan views, in which I included myself, I believed the social revolution he preached would be orderly and beneficial. I was convinced, to use the old phrase, that there was every possibility of this poacher becoming a reliable gamekeeper.

Too many of us, the monarchists, industrial leaders, the Papens and Schachts and Neuraths, thought we could tame him. There never will be a limit to wishful thinking. We all hoped to be the sage advisers of an unruly but irreplaceable genius. Instead we had a tiger by the tail. I pulled it once too often, let go and paid the consequences with ten years of exile. I am not trying to make excuses, and do not need to rely on my own account for the evidence that I tried to fight the Nazis' excesses when they came to power. I criticized them to their faces, Hitler, Goering, Goebbels, all of them. For quite a time I got away with it, partly because I had been around a long time and still played the piano for Hitler and entertained him with my jokes, partly because I shared the Bavarian background of some of the leaders, was uninhibited, outspoken and emotional anyway, and partly, I suppose, because I controlled no faction, was no orator, and although a lot of people thought as I did, we could not combine and therefore represented no real threat.

I became a member of the inner circle again largely on personal grounds. After the crisis of Geli Raubal's suicide, Hitler seemed to suffer a temporary fit of nostalgia for the old days. His infatuation for my wife, which had never been entirely stilled, brought him increasingly into our lives again. Nor was he the only Party leader in the throes of a domestic loss. Goering's wife Karin died in the middle of October 1931. She and Helene had revived their friendship and Goering sought solace for his personal isolation with us. He was still not entirely accepted in the Party and our house continued to offer him a useful retreat. So it was that at the beginning of the fifteen months which were to bring them to power they both, if for dissimilar reasons, sought our company.

Hitler emerged from the shadow cast by his niece's death, to find a political situation tailored to his order. The Nazi's position as the

second largest party in the *Reichstag* had not, in spite of all their
agitation and accretion of strength, brought them any nearer to
power. But the defences of the established forces were breaking up.
No stable coalition could be found to deal with the economic collapse and the four million and more unemployed, and neither
Hindenburg nor General Schleicher, who had emerged as his and
the Army's political adviser, was convinced that the emergency
powers accorded Chancellor Brüning provided any long-term solution. Their increasing weakness coincided with the growing surge of
political radicalism and the final hardening of Hitler's character into
the savage urge to impose himself on all those with whom he came
in contact, which was the only outlet to his repressions and super-
human energy.

He was still making a virtue of legality. That was one of his many
postscripts to Machiavelli. He did not make a revolution to acquire
power, but acquired power in order to make a revolution. It was a
process which very few people foresaw. His great catch-phrase at the
time concerned the necessity to *umorganisieren* – to reorganize the
State – a seemingly acceptable necessity in view of the Weimar
Republic's increasing decrepitude. But then he gave his own meaning to the words he used. Careful though he was to disguise his
thoughts and intentions, I found it, in my renewed association with
him, more and more difficult to penetrate his mind and put over my
own ideas. His personal manner in a room had not noticeably
changed. He could still relax and look back on earlier stages of his
struggle and talk about them with charm and humour. But in his
view of the future he had become more abrupt, the underlying
extremism and radicalism had tightened up, the old Hess and Rosenberg prejudices had become sharpened. Here the new influence was
Goebbels, and the nearer we got to Berlin and power, and Goebbels
and his Sportpalast tirades, the more Hitler was lost to me.

The first personal recognition of Hitler's importance on the
national front came towards the end of 1931, when, after preliminary talks between Schleicher and Roehm, who still eagerly
fostered his Army contacts, Hitler was granted interviews with
Hindenburg and Brüning. The only positive result was a violent outburst of jealousy on the part of Goering, who could not bear to think

that his Bavarian rival had provided the sort of contact he regarded as his exclusive right. Hitler made a bad impression and received a worse one: "They are all bourgeois. They consider us as trouble-makers and disturbers of order, to be treated in the same way as the Communists," he told me. "They have got it into their heads that we are all equal before the law. If they cannot see that the Com-munists are out to destroy the State entirely and that we wish to give it a new content on a German patriotic basis then there is nothing to be done with them. *"Hanfstaengl, Sie hätten dabei sein sollen"* – "Hanfstaengl, you ought to have been there," which is what he usually said when something had gone badly wrong.

My own position was somewhat anomalous. I was never a member of the Party organization, but had a purely advisory capacity as foreign press chief directly under Hitler. I had a constant battle to hold my own, as not only did Hitler until the end of my days with him have a total incomprehension of the ways of the press abroad, but everyone else in the Party within striking distance wanted a piece of my job. Otto Dietrich wanted a share in it as home press chief, although he was small fry and easy to deal with, and Goebbels thought it ought to be part of his propaganda organization, and he of course was a very different proposition. Baldur von Schirach also had ambitions, with a certain amount of tacit encouragement from Hitler, who used him as interpreter at some of his interviews. This was typical of Hitler's divide and rule methods. He did it with everyone. He would never delegate clear functions and they all overlapped, so that he was able to maintain final control as arbiter.

Schirach was a great trial to me. He used to insinuate himself into conversations with visitors whenever he could. When I would try and tone down some of Hitler's more radical pronouncements, in the hope of avoiding too much china being broken, Schirach used to tattle this to Hitler afterwards. There was one occasion when Hitler was talking about the Jews to a visiting British M.P., whose name I forget, and I was being very careful to emphasize that the Nazis only demanded the reduction of their representation in the professions to the same proportion as their strength in the population – which was the accepted party *numerus clausus* policy – when Schirach broke in on his own account: "We students don't wish to have any Jewish professors at all."

Fortunately one of my early interventions stood me in good stead for a long time. In November 1931 the State authorities in Hesse seized a series of documents drawn up by the local Party headquarters which threatened an armed *coup d'état* by the S.A. They became known as the Boxheim Papers and caused a political scandal of the first magnitude. In view of Hitler's very clear instructions to the S.A. at the time to refrain from violence, this is one of the few instances when I think his disclaimer was probably genuine. The Party press was still insignificant and all the other papers were howling for the Nazis' blood. We were in Berlin at the time and I called the foreign press to the Kaiserhof Hotel, which Hitler was already starting to use as his headquarters, for a conference. He came in and talked brilliantly, lucidly, rationally and with complete conviction. Their stories went out with such effect that the German opposition papers were obliged to reproduce them on the rebound with banner headlines. It was a complete break through of their normal policy of either denigration or silence concerning Hitler and he was of course ecstatic at this success: *"Das war sehr gut, Hanfstaengl, das haben Sie wirklich fein gemacht."* The trouble was that that was the sort of effect he expected me to produce every time.

The next major interview set me right back on my heels. We were in Munich again and Hitler rang for me to come and interpret at an interview in his flat with a Japanese professor named Momo, whose visit had been sponsored by his embassy. "But I don't speak Japanese," I complained. – "He talks English and this is very important," Hitler countered, so I went along and this little character came in, hoicking and hissing like something out of the *Mikado,* and they started a dreadful mutual admiration session. "I have come to discuss your movement, the heroic spirit of which we Japanese admire so much," said Momo. So Hitler went into a brazen eulogy of Japanese culture and samurai swords, warrior codes and the Shinto religion, all the drivel he had picked up from Haushofer and Hess. Momo needed little encouragement. "We are both the victims of democracy, we both need living space and colonies, we must have raw materials to ensure our future. It is Japan's destiny to lead all

Asia. . . ." This was awful and I tried to persuade Hitler to be more reticent, but he was in full flood: "Asia and the Pacific Ocean is a sphere in which we Germans have no demands," he ranted. "When we come to power we shall respect Japan's legitimate aspirations there." This of course was meat and drink to Momo, who fired off a great report. He was, needless to state, a Government emissary disguised as a newspaperman, and at the time of the anti-Comintern Pact in 1936 he turned up again. I had, of course, been appalled. Here were my worse fears taking shape, but in my protestations to Hitler I might just as well have been talking in Hindustani. My expostulations that such a policy would finally alienate American sympathy fell on deaf ears. Hitler brushed them all aside: "Hanfstaengl, today we have made history," he said fatuously.

As an antidote I tried to farm in as many American correspondents as I could. There was Harold Callender of the *New York Times,* who came at the end of November 1931, and of course Knickerbocker, probably the best informed, most conscientious and expert journalist of his day. I got Hitler to see him for the first time on the basis of a typewritten list of questions and the interview went very well. Knickerbocker spoke excellent German, and Hitler liked his lively way and red hair. The only back-lash I had was over photographs. Knickerbocker had James Edward Abbé with him, one of the best photographers I have ever known. I had long since wanted to have something else available, other than the dreadful things often taken by Heinrich Hoffman, which showed Hitler with a clenched fist and a distorted mouth and flaming eyes, looking like a madman.

I had told Hitler in one of his quieter moments that he must have some pictures taken which made him look like a statesman, the sort of man with whom foreign diplomats felt they could do business, and in the end we got them by a trick. Abbé pretended that he was taking the photographs of Hitler talking quietly to Knickerbocker, but aimed most of the time at Hitler alone, and I thought the results were first class. He looked normal, intelligent and interesting. What happened? I was called round when the prints arrived and found Hitler furious. "I don't look like that," he shouted. "What is this?" — "Of course you look like that," I told him. "They are much better

than those things that make you look like a fakir." The reason of
course was that Heinrich Hoffmann had been enraged at this breaking of his monopoly and Hitler was taking it out on me. More to the
point was the fact that Hitler apparently had an arrangement with
Hoffmann to share in the proceeds of his work and this in due course
was to provide a very handsome side income.

The tempo of the year 1932 was determined by its four national
elections, two rounds for the Presidency, and two for the *Reichstag,*
plus voting in the individual States. By train, by car and for the first
time by plane, Hitler conducted a series of campaigns which rocked
the rival Parties and exhausted companions and opponents alike. I
accompanied him almost everywhere as a sort of right interference
guard for the foreign press.

The first step he took was to make himself a German citizen. He
disappeared from the Kaiserhof on February 22, 1932, and spent
part of the afternoon at the representation in Berlin of the State of
Brunswick, where the Nazis wielded sufficient power to have him
appointed an *Oberregierungsrat* in the local civil service, an established post which carried with it the automatic grant of citizenship.
The original plan had been to give him a nominal post as professor
of arts in the Brunswick education service. However, when I
threatened to greet him with 'Heil, Herr Professor', after all the years
he had spent making fun of academicians, the idea was modified. He
displayed his warrant when he returned in the evening, and from
that time on I sometimes addressed him by his new title as a joke.
I must have been the only person to get away with it. "Now at last
you can stop singing the *Blue Danube* and learn the *Wacht am
Rhein,*" I told him, which put him such good humour that he signed
a photograph for my son which I still have. It says: 'For my young
friend Egon Hanfstaengl, with my best wishes.'

The boredom and confusion of the election tours was such that I
can no longer sort them out in my mind. The team, with occasional
additions and subtractions, was Brückner and Schaub, the adjutants,
Sepp Dietrich, the later S.S. General, as bodyguard, Otto Dietrich,
Heinrich Hoffmann, Bauer the pilot and myself. We must have
visited every city in Germany several times, and it was always
claimed afterwards that Hitler was the first politician to come to

power who knew the country inside out. Of course he knew nothing
of the sort. – It might just as well have been the Bürgerbräu or the
Sportpalast wherever we went, whipping up mass hysteria within
the confines of four walls and travelling and sleeping in between.
When he was not speaking he was in the hotel behind closed doors
trying to iron out quarrels in the local Party organizations.

Like the leadership itself they were all split into nationalist and
socialist wings – it is very necessary to bear in mind that hyphen in
the name of the party, because the two groups were intrinsically
quite separate and only combined out of self-interest. The hyphen
of course was Hitler. The regional leaders used to drive him mad,
and more than once he would say to me: "I know why these
Gauleiters are always harrying me to speak for them. They take the
biggest hall in town which they could never fill themselves. I cram
it to the roof for them and they pocket the proceeds. They are all at
their wits' end for money and I have to tear round Germany like a
maniac to see that they don't go bankrupt."

I think it was probably only in the later elections that we travelled
everywhere by plane. Often in the early stages we went in a great
convoy of cars, which was usually met at the outskirts of a town by
a pilot to take us through back streets to the meeting hall. Hitler left
nothing to chance and always had a street plan on his knee ready
for use. The precaution was probably not exaggerated as the Communists were always waiting to attack us and on two occasions, in
Breslau and Cologne, wrong turnings took us into red beflagged
streets which we got through in the midst of fisticuffs and uproar.
It should not be forgotten how strong the Communists were in these
years. In 'red' cities like Chemnitz, people did not even dare to
display Christmas trees for fear of being attacked by fanatics.

In Nuremberg a bomb was thrown from the roof of a house and
hit Streicher's car, which only had the driver in it, and once in
Bamberg late at night we had a couple of windscreens shattered with
revolver shots. On these occasions Hitler would berate the local
Gauleiter at the top of his voice. His use of a map was of long
standing and I can remember when we arrived at Brunswick, while
Emil Maurice was still the driver and there was no map. Hitler
began to yell imprecations but Maurice, who was an old hand and

allowed himself a number of liberties, said: "Herr Hitler, what are you getting so excited about. Just remember Christopher Columbus." Hitler stopped in full spout. "What do you mean Columbus?" – "Well, Columbus had no map but that did not stop him discovering America."

Sometimes we would still stop *en route* for a picnic. There was one not far from a monastery or theological seminary, with a couple of teams of young clerics playing football in long habits. I think it was near Eichstätt. I pointed them out to Hitler but he refused to be entertained. "We'll teach them asceticism if we come to power," he said. "I am not going to have a lot of fat monks loafing around looking like characters out of a Grützner picture. They can keep up their social service if they like or work in the hospitals as practical Christians. But I am not going to have them holing themselves up in abbeys pretending they are superior to the rest of us, and they are going to be kept away from the new generation. We Nazis will see to their education. Of course the finest propaganda of all would be if the Pope were to excommunicate me." I looked at him astonished, but it was a phrase I was often to hear him use later. "If you feel like that why don't you announce officially that you have withdrawn from the Church?" I asked. "Why should I deprive him of the pleasure?" Hitler answered, "let him do it." What he meant was that if he proclaimed himself an atheist he would lose Catholic votes, but that as a mere heretic he might get away with it.

The plane journeys were misery. There were always protracted security precautions to ensure that the machine had not been tampered with. That was Bauer's responsibility and when he slept I do not know. Hitler used to sit in the left- or right-hand front seat and either doze or pretend to doze, look out of the window or back at his map and hardly talk at all. The others would sometimes try and attract his attention with a letter or a photograph to push their pet peeve, but then he would retire behind a newspaper or some document or other. The most extraordinary thing about him was that he never had a notebook. He never wrote a thing, never took notes, never had a pencil and only occasionally a fountain-pen to sign his autograph with. His notebook was Schaub – Schaub make a note of this or that – he never wrote it down himself. I got used to the requirement and always had six or seven pens or pencils in my pocket.

The atmosphere used to get on my nerves. It smacked of a low-grade orderly-room, with this stupid, inartistic, inarticulate bunch. We were in all these towns and never went to a museum or historical house. I used to carry two picture postcards with me of Goethe's workroom in Weimar and when I could stand the boredom no longer take them out and look at them for minutes at a time to relax in their mood of classical repose, while this rattle-trap of an aircraft plugged on. Of course the others used to jeer at me. At first I sprinkled Yardley's Lavender on my handkerchief to keep out the smell of petrol, but even Hitler objected to this, so in the end I resorted to smelling-salts. The others were not above a sniff at the bottle too, as it would of course have been very *infra dig* and very un-National-Socialistic to be airsick.

One incident which I think has never been recorded is how we nearly crashed in the Baltic on the way back from Königsberg. We had made a brief stop at Danzig and were, as I recall, bound for Kiel. The weather was very bad and overcast, but Bauer got above the clouds and we flew along in bright sunshine. What had not been taken into account was the increasing headwind and when we finally came down again we could see nothing but rain-lashed water. Bauer had the direction-finding apparatus on, but for some reason the Berlin station had failed and Bremen and Lübeck were badly inter-rupted and kept giving us different readings. Fuel was starting to run low and the atmosphere got very tense. I was sitting up ahead by Hitler, and although he said very little I could see his jaw muscles working. "That is the North Sea," he exclaimed. His left hand on the little folding table was clenching and unclenching in spasm and then I remembered that he couldn't swim and realized the sup-pressed agony he must be going through. I tried to make a bad joke by suggesting that we would soon be in England and might at last get a decent cup of tea, but Hitler was in no way amused.

In the end he could stand it no longer, jumped forward and yelled at Bauer: "You must turn south, it is the only way to hit land," which of course was quite right. I had not taken the headwind into account and also thought we had crossed Schleswig-Holstein above the clouds and were out over the North Sea. The situation was now really serious. The petrol tanks were as good as empty but at the last moment we hit the coast over a small medieval town which none of us could recognize. It was Heinrich Hoffmann who got our bearings. "It is Wismar," he suddenly shouted. He had remembered a photograph he had seen years before. Bauer, who had made us fasten our safety-belts and was about to bring the big plane down in a field in a forced landing, calculated quickly that he could just make the airfield at Travemünde, which he did literally with not more than a few pints of fuel to spare. Hitler was quite groggy, and it was one of the few occasions when I saw him in a physical fright.

These trips naturally attracted a lot of attention from the foreign press and from time to time one or other of the correspondents would accompany us part of the way. Sefton Delmer of the London *Daily Express* took a great interest in our campaign and became very much *persona grata* with the Nazi leadership. I was with him on one occasion when he went off to interview Dr. Georg Heim, the leader of the Bavarian Peasant Party, at Regensburg. Some of Heim's remarks harked back to Bavarian ideas of separatism, and as this seemed to me a valid point for the Nazis to refute, I persuaded Delmer to drive all the way down to Berchtesgaden and give Hitler a full résumé of his talk. Hitler, of course, was delighted: "That is worth two million votes to us," he shouted, slapping his thigh. He was really very partial to Delmer and, when he became Chancellor, willingly agreed that the *Express* man should be given the first exclusive interview.

It was towards midnight that I was usually called upon to play my rôle of court minstrel. Hitler would loll in the corner of his suite or the hotel lounge, exhausted with speeches and Gauleiters and say, "Hanfstaengl, play me something." It was not easy, as I never had any time to practise and had to cobble some of the passages, so I would start off with a little Bach or Chopin or some of the marches to get my fingers warm, but in the end it always had to be *Tristan* and *Meistersinger* and Hitler would sit there in a half doze and gurgle with delight. It would usually go on for an hour or more, often with repeats of his favourite pieces, but it gave him a respite as the Chauffeureska did not dare to interrupt or talk to him and just lumbered round the other rooms drinking and smoking cigars. There were never any women around. In that dark corner of his life there was a great hiatus.

People often ask me how Hitler reacted to the political events of this fateful year that brought him to power. The question begs the simple fact that he was not a politician in the ordinary sense. He did not concern himself with the day-to-day kaleidoscope of the political scene. He was not looking for alliances or coalitions or temporary tactical advantage. He wanted power, supreme and complete, and was convinced that if he talked often enough and aroused the masses sufficiently he must, in due course, be swept into office. Of course his intention was brought, by the members of the entourage or the local Gauleiters, to specific developments and regional issues. Although the general content of all his speeches was more or less the same, he would work in such points as reinforced his arguments or gave him the opportunity for new attacks and abuse of the Government and rival parties.

Otherwise it was just like accompanying a musical artist on a concert tour. He would give his performance, have his bags packed, and be off to the next town. There was little time in between for anything but recuperation. We were reduced to the status of boxers' seconds, sponging him off between rounds, while he gasped for air and gathered his wits. If the necessity arose for an important talk at any of the stops with some prominent personality who might be won over or made use of, Hitler would shut himself up in his room alone or walk out in the garden with them. No one was ever vouchsafed an account of these interviews. He stored up the information he needed and that was that. Nor was there anything in the nature of a conference to plan campaign strategy. The committee idea was absolutely foreign to Hitler. He would pick one man's brains and then bounce these ideas off the head of someone else. By the time their propositions had cancelled each other out he had made up his mind which line to adopt. His habit of keeping people in separate compartments was one of the first quirks I had noticed in him and he retained it to the end.

He even kept his senior partners at arm's length. There was no warmth in his opinions of them. He regarded Goering as little more than a useful muscle-man, wielding a great claymore at their opponents: "Give him a full belly and he really goes for them," Hitler once commented to me approvingly. This was the kind of man he could use. In picking his Gauleiters, he always looked for the bawling sergeant-major type, ready to use their fists if need be. The Gau-bulls, some of us used to call them. Hitler only really had time for people who could sway an audience. This reconciled him to Hermann Esser, although he was secretly jealous of him, as Esser was quite a ladies' man in a raffish sort of way. Esser had one extraordinary quality: he had joined the party so young and so early and had come under the influence of Hitler for so long that he could speak exactly like him. Every phrase, every nuance, plus more of a sense of humour and a quicker appeal for the women in the audience. He could always fill a hall anywhere, and with the Nazi oratorical strength spread thin, this made him extremely valuable.

There was another senior Nazi for whom Hitler's jealousy had deeper roots, and that was Gregor Strasser. He was the one potential, indeed actual rival within the party. He had made the Rhineland his fief. I remember during one tour through the Ruhr towns seeing Strasser's name plastered up against the wall of every railway underpass. He was obviously quite a figure in the land. Hitler looked away. There was no comment about 'Strasser seems to be doing well', or any approving sign. In Berlin, Strasser had been superseded by Goebbels, for whose golden voice Hitler had genuine admiration: "I have heard them all," Hitler said once, "but the only speaker I can listen to without going to sleep is Goebbels. He really can put it over."

Another, more ominous, characteristic was the distance he was starting to keep between himself and his immediate collaborators and entourage. He had always been a lone wolf all the years I had known him, and although he dominated most groups by the sheer force of his rhetoric, this was instinctive rather than deliberate behaviour. Now there was a new harshness in his tone, a conscious attitude of speaking from a higher level and keeping people in their place. He did not seem to mind what liberties he took. One day there was an article in the *Völkische Beobachter* to which he took exception, and he rang up Rosenberg to find out who had written it. It was the work of some other Baltic crony, but instead of berating Rosenberg he turned on poor little Otto Dietrich, who had no jurisdiction over the paper, and called him down in my presence like a dog, overwhelming all Dietrich's protestations that he had no responsibility. "What do you think of that?" the victim said to me afterwards. "For two pins I would have thrown my job in his face." But, of course, he did not do so, and there was another collaborator taken down a notch.

Hitler did it to all of them in turn. At table one day he rounded on Heinrich Hoffman, criticizing his photographs, telling him that he drank and smoked too much, that he would kill himself if he continued that way, and so on. Then, when the victim was out of the room, he would praise him behind his back to keep the rest of us in our place. Hitler would also say things which later proved to be sheer duplicity. We were staying in Mecklenburg on a big estate, which I believe belonged to Magda Goebbels' divorced husband. The bailiff, Walter Granzow, was a Party member. I found that his and several of the farms around were being worked by unemployed students who had founded what they called the Artamanen Society. They received no pay, just their keep, and their chief purpose was to keep Polish workers from coming over and settling on the land. Their idealism impressed me and I told Hitler he ought to address them. So they were called together and he made a very pleasant half-hour's speech, praising their efforts and particularly commending them for preventing foreign blood being introduced into Germany. What pleased me most was his statement that "in the Third Reich of the National-Socialists, we Germans will never attempt to infiltrate or subject other nations to our will. That would be to repeat the fault of Roman imperialism." If he believes that, I thought, then there will be no danger of war if he comes to power, but I underrated Hitler's ability to tell people what they wanted to hear and still reserve his own intentions.

At the first Presidential election on March 13, Hitler polled 11·4 million votes to Hindenburg's 18·6, leaving the old President just short of his necessary absolute majority. The Nazi vote had increased in eighteen months by 86 per cent, but many of them were in despair at the result. They seemed as far away from power as ever. Goebbels was literally weeping with defeatism, although Goering managed to keep a cooler head. At one moment there was a move to abandon the second round of voting four weeks later, but I felt there was no stopping now. Where the radicals only saw a solution in an armed uprising of the S.A., I argued with Hitler that he must stand again. A third of the population had shown themselves ready to accept him as presidential timber. "You must give the world time to adjust itself to the idea that Adolf Hitler can follow in the steps of Hindenburg. Up till now they have only known you as the Opposition leader," I told him. "To win you must attract the support of the smaller parties." I thought the necessity of reaching a compromise with other political leaders would help act as a brake on the wild men of the Party. Anyway, Hitler did stand again and got two million more votes. Hindenburg got another million, and that was more than enough.

The emergence of Hitler as a national, and indeed international, figure of the first rank nearly provided one of those confrontations which would have been the delight of historians – with Sir Winston Churchill. Sir Winston refers to the incident in his memoirs, but as he was not at the time in possession of all the facts, the story will bear retelling. I had seen quite a lot of his son Randolph during our election tours. I had even arranged for him to travel once or twice in the plane with us. He had indicated that his father was coming to Germany and that we should arrange a meeting. In April, either during or just after the second presidential campaign, I landed with Hitler at Munich airport to find a telephone message awaiting me from Randolph. His family were staying with a party at the Hotel Continental (not the Regina Palace, Sir Winston's memory plays him false), wanted me to join them for dinner, and hoped that I would be able to bring Hitler along to meet his father. I told him I would do what I could, but that we were tired, dirty and unshaven, and I would ring him back.

I caught up with Hitler at the Brown House and burst into his room. It looked, I might say, like an hotel lounge, early Adlon and late North German Lloyd, but that was his taste. He was trying to catch up on business and in his most unapproachable mood. "Herr Hitler," I said, "Mr. Churchill is in Munich and wants to meet you.

This is a tremendous opportunity. They want me to bring you along to dinner at the Hotel Continental tonight."

I could almost see the asbestos curtain drop down. *"Um Gottes-willen,* Hanfstaengl don't they realize how busy I am? What on earth would I talk to him about?" "But, Herr Hitler," I protested, "this is the easiest man to talk to in the world – art, politics, architecture, anything you choose. This is one of the most influential men in England; you must meet him." But my heart sank. Hitler produced a thousand excuses, as he always did when he was afraid of meeting someone. With a figure whom he knew to be his equal in political ability, the uncertain bourgeois re-emerged again, the man who would not go to a dancing-class for fear of making a fool of himself, the man who only acquired confidence in his manipulation of a yelling audience. I tried one last gambit. "Herr Hitler, I will go to dinner and you arrive afterwards, as if you were calling for me, and stay to coffee." No, he would see, we had to leave the next day early – which was the first I had heard of it, as I thought we had two or three days free: "In any case, they say your Mr. Churchill is a rabid Francophile."

I rang Randolph back and tried to hide my disappointment, pointed out that he had caught us at the worst possible time, but suggested, against my better knowledge, that Hitler might join us for coffee. I turned up myself at the appointed hour. There was Mrs. Churchill, serene, intelligent and enchanting, Lord Camrose, Professor Lindemann, one of the Churchill daughters, and one or two other younger people whose names I forget. We sat down about ten to dinner, with myself on Mrs. Churchill's right and my host on the other side. We talked about this and that, and then Mr. Churchill taxed me about Hitler's anti-Semitic views. I tried to give as mild an account of the subject as I could, saying that the real problem was the influx of eastern European Jews and the excessive representation of their co-religionaries in the professions, to which Churchill listened very carefully, commenting: "Tell your boss from me that anti-Semitism may be a good starter, but it is a bad sticker." I had to get this bit of slang explained, which made the rest of the party laugh.

I had noticed that Lord Camrose, on the other side of the table, was paying very close attention to everything that Churchill said, but over coffee, brandy and cigars, my host and I pushed our chairs back and he became confidential in his tone. I can remember the scene to this day. With his left hand, the one next to me, he held a brandy-glass almost touching his lips, so that his words reached my ears alone, and in the other a fat cigar. "Tell me," he asked, "how does your chief feel about an alliance between your country, France and England?"

I was transfixed. I could feel my toes growing through my shoes into the carpet. Damn Hitler, I thought, here is the one thing which would give him prestige and keep him within bounds and he does not even have the social guts to be here to talk about it. "What about Italy?" I asked in an attempt to assess the full range of Churchill's ideas. "No, no," he said, "we would have to leave them out for the time being. You cannot have everybody joining a club at once." I managed in my desperation to say how interested Hitler would be to discuss such a subject and expatiated excitedly on my own hopes. I must get hold of Hitler, I thought, and turning to Mrs. Churchill made a flimsy excuse about having forgotten to telephone my home to say how late I would be and would she please excuse me while I rang up. "But of course, ask your wife to join us," she said.

I got on to the Brown House. Hitler had left. I rang his apartment. Frau Winter had not seen him. Then I telephoned my wife to say I did not know what time she would see me. She was tired and preferred not to wait up or come out. I lurched out of the call-box into the hall and whom did I see nine or ten steps up the staircase—Hitler, in his dirty white overcoat and green hat, just saying good-bye to a Dutchman, whom I knew was a friend of Goering's and had, I think, channelled money to the Party in his time. I was beside myself.

"Herr Hitler, what are you doing here? Don't you realize the Churchills are sitting in the restaurant? They may well have seen you come in and out? They will certainly learn from the hotel servants that you have been here. They are expecting you for coffee and will think this is a deliberate insult." No, he was still unshaven, which was true. "Then for heaven's sake go home and shave and come back," I said. "I will play the piano for them or something until you get back." "I have too much to do, Hanfstaengl. I have to get up early in the morning," and he evaded me and walked out. I put on the best face I could and went back to the party. Who knows, I thought, perhaps after all he will turn up. I kicked myself for not having been more explicit to Hitler, but the Continental had a narrow little panelled hall, with porters and receptionists every yard. I could not blurt this thing out in front of the Dutchman, and Hitler had been backing away from me the whole time. So I played my football marches, and *Annie Laurie*, and the *Londonderry Air*, and the party was in high fettle. All except me, of course.

Hitler never turned up. He had funked it. The next morning early his car was waiting for me outside my house. We picked him up with his tame thugs and drove off to Nuremberg, where, if you please, he spent the whole morning talking shop with Julius Streicher. On the way there I leant forward in the car and told him all about my talk. He did not really believe it, or if he did I could feel that Hess and Rosenberg had been at him trying to prevent this outside contact at all cost. "In any case, what part does Churchill play?" Hitler complained. "He is in opposition and no one pays any attention to him." "People say the same thing about you," I answered, nettled. But it was no good. He had made up his mind not to expose himself to anyone with the capacity to steal his thunder. I did not even pass on Churchill's comment about his anti-Semitism in case it provided him with the excuse he needed. The Churchills stayed in Munich for two or three more days, I believe, but Hitler kept away until they had gone.

The *Reichstag* elections at the end of July had brought the Nazis yet further towards, but still so far from, their goal. With 230 seats out of 608 they became the strongest single party, and during the first fortnight of August, the new Chancellor, von Papen, talked to Hitler about his entering the Government as Vice-Chancellor. With the possibility of total power looming on the horizon he had become more chary than ever of compromising himself in coalition. "What sort of a fellow is this Papen?" he asked me. "You must have known him during the war in New York." "Socially he is a charmer," I said. "But politically he is a *Luftikus* [a light-weight]." This appealed to him. *"Ein Luftikus,"* he repeated, slapping his thigh, "that just describes him," but he did not entirely dismiss the idea of collaborating with him. "Mind you, if it amuses his vanity to go on living with his wife in the Chancellor's palace and they confide the real power to me, I would not mind," he added. But the time for that was not quite yet. It was late in the evening when we drove out of Berlin after the talks had failed, and quite dark. We all sat very silent in the car. Schreck was at the wheel, the inevitable Schaub, Brückner and Sepp Dietrich in attendance – *"Wir werden schon sehen"* – We shall see," muttered Hitler.

This, of course, was the worst possible time for me to press my American complex on Hitler. Their economy was nearly as shattered as ours, and the only other stories one heard were about gangsters in Chicago and the scandals surrounding Jimmy Walker, the mayor of New York. It all gave Hitler a perfect argument. "Any country which cannot even master its own internal police problems cannot hope to play a part in foreign affairs," he used to say. Schirach and company also never failed to bring to his attention the bad press he was getting, which he ascribed entirely to Jewish influence or to my ineffectiveness, if he was in a bad mood. I would have despaired if I had not received a private emissary from Franklin D. Roosevelt, my old Harvard Club friend, about to be swept into the Presidency. The message was to the effect that it looked as if Hitler would also soon achieve power and that Roosevelt hoped, in view of our long acquaintance, that I would do my best to prevent any rashness and hotheadedness. "Think of your piano-playing and try and use the soft pedal if things get too loud," my visitor quoted. "If things start getting awkward, please get in touch with our ambassador at once." The message heartened me enormously, and in due course I was to do just that.

November brought *Reichstag* elections again, but in spite of a frenzied campaign, the Nazis lost ground. Their representation was reduced to 196, and it was at this point that Schleicher became Chancellor, to exercise the power he had so long controlled from the wings. His plan was to split off the Strasser wing of the Nazi Party in a final effort to find a majority with the Weimar Socialists and Centre. The idea was by no means so ill-conceived and amidst the momentary demoralization and monetary confusion in the Nazi ranks, very nearly came off. With the failure came the final break between Hitler and Strasser, who, two years later, paid for this disloyalty with his head.

I always thought Strasser's reputation undeserved. He was a good organizer, but another of the un-Teutonic figures in the party. He looked like a Levantine business man. But several people had a high opinion of him; one of whom was Spengler. I had often tried to bring Hitler and the great historian together, in the hope that his Olympian acidity would deflate Hitler a little. They did, in fact, meet without my intervention and I learnt of it one Sunday when the subject came up at a luncheon given to Hitler by the Wagners at Bayreuth. I could see Hitler had a bad conscience about it in my company, as he faked a sort of sleepiness, scratching his ear and asserting that Spengler had only talked in terms of compromise, that his whole background was too monarchist and conservative, and that he had no understanding of racial problems. "Hanfstaengl, you should have been there."

I could hardly contain myself, as I had indeed wanted to act as catalyst at the conversation. I rang up Spengler in Munich the next day and he invited me round to coffee and cigars. I found him completely contemptuous. He thought Hitler a fantastic and won my heart with a demolition of the Rosenberg mythos, which Hitler had made the mistake of spouting. "There are no brains in the party, Hanfstaengl," he complained. "They are just a lot of pinheads." I tried to bring up the name of General von Epp, who was being mentioned as the possible next President. "Impossible," snorted Spengler, "he is a man without ideas, without powers of decision, he is just plain stupid. The only man who appeals to me in the whole movement is Gregor Strasser. At least he has a trade union background and a sense of realities."

That, I thought, was a powerful enough recommendation, and when, back in Berlin, Knickerbocker asked me to get an interview with Strasser, I organized it for him. It was a terrible flop. Knickerbocker had got hold of a book on economics published under Strasser's name, of which he had carefully read every word, and came out with a whole list of contradictions. After an hour of this

cross-examination, Strasser had sweated through his second handkerchief and was reduced to retorting: "If you read the book again
you will understand what I mean." As soon as Knickerbocker had
gone he flew into a rage and said that if I ever brought anyone like
that in again he would throw him out. It was only later that a
member of his staff told me that the book had been written by
a subordinate and that Strasser knew less about it than Knickerbocker.

My first indication of Strasser's threatened defection came from
Sefton Delmer—we used to anglicize names when we talked over
the telephone. "Hempstalk," said Delmer, "tell your boss that Mr.
Streeter [Strasser] has been to see Mr. Creeper [Schleicher]." I went
downstairs to Hitler's office in the Brown House with the news. He
just grunted glumly, which was always the worst sign. Many years
later I was to hear from a friend of ours, Dr. H. Martin, a private
banker in Munich, Strasser's story of his final break with Hitler. The
row took place on December 8, 1932, in the Kaiserhof in Berlin.
Goebbels, needless to say, was there in support of Hitler.

For upwards of a year Strasser had espoused the opinion that the
only solution to the chaotic situation in Germany was for the Nazis
to enter the Government in a normal coalition. He knew of Hindenburg's and Schleicher's aversion to Hitler, particularly after the
incident of the Potempa telegram, in which Hitler condoned the
murder of a Communist miner by five Nazi toughs. As a result,
Strasser was prepared to serve under Schleicher as Vice-Chancellor,
leaving the leadership of the Party to Hitler. At the Kaiserhof meeting they could come to no agreement; in fact the split between them
was widened. Hitler told Strasser he was a traitor to the Party and
said his only recourse was to shoot himself. Strasser reciprocated the
invitation.

The next day Dr. Martin happened to call on Strasser at his flat
in the Tengstrasse and received a full account of what had happened. He found Strasser calm and resigned, in spite of his bitter
words: "Dr. Martin, I am a man marked by death. We shall not
be able to go on seeing each other for long and in your own interests
I suggest you do not come here any more. Whatever happens, mark
what I say: From now on Germany is in the hands of an Austrian,

who is a congenital liar, a former officer, who is a pervert, and a clubfoot. And I tell you the last is the worst of them all. This is Satan in human form."

It was also about this time that I first made the acquaintance of Ribbentrop, who was a very late-comer in the Nazi hierarchy. He was a friend of Count Helldorf, the S.A. leader in Berlin, with whom he had ingratiated himself by sending crates of champagne into the gaol when Helldorf was temporarily detained. I took to him because he had some presence, spoke French and English and seemed a cut above most of the mental breast-stroke swimmers near Hitler. At least he was, and continued to be, an antidote to Rosenberg in the field of foreign policy. My first clear recollection of him was in the palace of the *Reichstag* President, which Goering had occupied since the July elections. Hitler was up with Hugenberg in the library on the first floor trying to get more money out of him, without immediate effect, and came down completely worn out. He saw me and, as usual, said: "Hanfstaengl, play me something," so I launched into melodies out of *Tosca* which I had in my head, although I had to start three times to find the right key. When the performance was over, Ribbentrop came over to me and said pompously: "Hanfstaengl, you have brought the Führer through a difficult hour."

The top floor of the Kaiserhof Hotel in the Wilhelmstrasse had by now been taken over more or less completely as the Nazi operational headquarters. I cannot say its atmosphere was thereby improved. Whenever the top echelon were there for meals they behaved like a bunch of old buskers. Each one would boast of his successes in recent meetings and how many bouquets of flowers had been brought him, or his success in dealing with Communist hecklers. It was frightful, like being in the green room of a music-hall. Berlin was also Goebbels' territory. They had a big flat out on the Reichs-kanzlerplatz in the west of the city, and once when Hitler was convinced that the Kaiserhof kitchen staff had been infiltrated by Communists who were putting poison into his food, Magda Goebbels won his heart by preparing delicate little vegetarian dishes which were brought over to the hotel for him in heatproof containers.

This was the period when Goebbels really began to gain ground. Hitler would often ride over and spend the rest of the evening with them and I was usually dragged along for my final piano act. My marches were high in favour and I had a relatively new one called *Deutscher Föhn*, which appealed to Hitler. "This is what we will have the band play when we march into Berlin," he used to proclaim, but the Goebbels were jealous. This ability gave me a special access to Hitler which they resented and they took to having all the radios on at full blast when we arrived, so that I could no longer compete. Goebbels soon found an even better answer. He had taken recordings of some of Hitler's more successful speeches and used to turn these on. Hitler would curl up in a big Morris arm-chair and semi-doze to the sound of this phonetic super-reflection of himself, drowning in his own narcissistic sound-image. They would follow this up with one of the Wagner recordings, just to outsmart me, because they knew that if he listened to my piano-playing it was sometimes a prelude to his listening to me, and that was something to be prevented at all costs.

About the only thing which reconciled me to the Goebbels was their unashamed enthusiasm for finding female companionship for Hitler. I was all in favour of this. I thought if he could find another woman it would be the best way of taming him and making him more human and approachable. One of their offerings was a vivacious blonde named Gretl Slezak, whose father, Leo, was the famous opera singer, and she herself had a very pleasant voice. She was not all that young, probably about 27 or 28 at the time, but she was a professional *ingénue* and asked the most delightfully asinine questions about the Nazis and what Hitler stood for and did he really mean to be beastly to the Jews, and so on. In fact she had a Jewish grandmother, so the question was not entirely without point. Hitler responded very well and tossed back her remarks by telling her not to bother about such matters and that the most important thing was to spend a pleasant evening. The Goebbels deliberately shut off their radio-sets and egged me on to go and strum at the piano. I felt rather like the man must feel who plays incidental music in a brothel. However, I thought this was all in a good cause and if only we could keep him interested, who knew what might come of it.

Hitler and Gretl had gone into the darkened drawing-room next door, and I assumed they were fondling each other, so I kept my foot off the loud pedal and hoped fervently that this would really be the start of a beautiful friendship. After three-quarters of an hour or so we all took our leave of the Goebbels – needless to state, Brückner and company were also along – and left for the Kaiserhof, by which time it was about one o'clock in the morning. "I must take this young lady home," said Hitler. If she brings you round to some sort of normalcy, I thought, she will be doing us all a service. The rest of us had a last drink in the hotel as a sop to our consciences for leaving him unguarded, and when I went to my room, sure enough Hitler's jackboots were the only ones missing from outside his door in the corridor – it was quite near mine. Well, well, I thought, this is really an auspicious beginning. I believe, in fact, that he returned quite late, but there was no clue to be obtained from his behaviour next morning as to what had happened. Gretl Slezak continued to be seen around and I got to know her very well. One day she was in a confidential mood and I asked her what had been going on. She just looked up at the ceiling and shrugged. It was all I needed to know.

Leni Riefenstahl was another of the Goebbels' introductions. She was in their apartment one night for dinner. It was considered, I might say, the acme of luxury, but in fact conformed to the early Pullman taste of all these top Nazis. I do not want to be too malicious, but, after all, these people came from nowhere and the only spacious furnishings they saw were in the hotels in which they stayed, so they came to accept the style as the height of breeding and sophistication, instead of the dreadful *kitsch* it was.

Leni Riefenstahl was a very vital and attractive woman and had little difficulty in persuading the Goebbels and Hitler to go on to her studio after dinner. I was carried along and found it full of mirrors and trick interior decorator effects, but what one would expect, not bad. There was a piano there, so that got rid of me, and the Goebbels, who wanted to leave the field free, leant on it, chatting. This isolated Hitler, who got into a panic. Out of the corner of my eye I could see him ostentatiously studying the titles in the bookcases. Riefenstahl was certainly giving him the works. Every time he straightened up or looked round, there she was dancing to my music at his elbow, a real summer sale of feminine advance. I had to grin myself. I caught the Goebbels' eyes, as if to say, 'If the Riefenstahl can't manage this no one can and we might as well leave.' So we made our excuses, leaving them alone, which was all against his security regulations. But again it was an organized disappointment. The Riefenstahl and I travelled in a plane a day or two later and once more all I got was that hopeless shrug. However, she had made her mark and obtained quite a lot of privileges from Hitler for her film activities.

A third woman also appeared about this time. There is an entry in my guest-book dated January 1, 1933, signed in our Pienzenauer-strasse house by Schaub, Heinrich Hoffmann, his then sweetheart Erna Gröbke, whom he later married, Brückner and his girl friend Sophie Stork, Rudolf Hess and his wife Ilse, Ingeborg Groen, who presents no picture to my memory, Hitler – and Eva Braun. They had all come on for coffee after a performance of *Meistersinger* at the Hof Theatre. We may even have had dinner at the Four Seasons Hotel first. It was not my first sight of Eva Braun. She was a pleasing-looking blonde, the slightly helpless type who appears to need protection, well built, with blue eyes and a modest, diffident manner. I had seen her working behind the counter at Heinrich Hoffmann's shop some months earlier, and had certainly registered the fact. She was friendly and personable and eager to please. We had no sense that evening that she was there in any particular capacity, but rather as a friend of one of the other girls in order to make up the party.

Hitler was in his most benign mood. It took us right back to the 'twenties when we had first met him. The conductor that evening had been Hans Knappertsbusch and Hitler had not liked his *tempi* and interpretation and was expatiating on the subject. He could really do so with good sense and would hum or whistle many of the passages, the words of which he knew by heart, in order to show what he meant. We had refashioned the house by then and the studio he remembered from his early days had lost its height due to the necessity of putting in additional rooms. He thought it was a pity and said we should have built outwards and left it as a lofty room for receptions. I could not help thinking that if I had had my thousand dollars back when I needed them it would have been another thing and that it was all very well for him to talk. But he reminisced charmingly about the old days and it was really a very pleasant party. I think it was almost the last time that I saw him in this mood.

The conversation kept coming back to the *Meistersinger* we had seen. It was probably Hitler's favourite opera and he was, of course, a completely Wagnerian figure himself. It would take three or four of the characters to make up his. There was a lot of Lohengrin, with its German connotations of impotence, something of the Flying Dutchman and a mixture of Hans Sachs and Walter von Stolzing. I could not help thinking, while he talked, of the Hans Sachs line about: *'ein Glühwurm fand sein Weibchen nicht, das hat den Schaden angericht* [a glow-worm did not find his mate and that was the cause of all the trouble].' Hitler never did find his mate. Eva Braun was no answer to the problem.

Before they left, Hitler signed his name with the words, 'on the first day of the New Year'. He looked up at me and said in a tone of suppressed excitement: "This year belongs to us. I will guarantee you that in writing." On January 4 came the famous meeting with von Papen at the house of the Cologne banker, Kurt von Schroeder, the final step in his path to power.

Three weeks later I was back in Berlin trying to get my foreign journalist friends through a police cordon into a Nazi mass meeting in the Lustgarten. It was just after the new Nazi electoral success in the State of Lippe. The policeman would not let us through. "But I am Dr. Hanfstaengl, the foreign press officer of the Nazi Party and these gentlemen have got to see this to file their stories," I told him in exasperation. "My orders are not to let anyone through," he said stubbornly. "But for heaven's sake, man, don't be so difficult. In another week we shall be in power, anyway," I shouted. He was not to be moved. "Come back in a week and I'll let you through then," he said. By that time my statement was true.

CHAPTER XI

DISILLUSIONMENT AT NUREMBERG

Neurath versus Rosenberg – First brush with Goering – Reichstag fire fever – Goebbels at Potsdam – The one-man revolution – Interventions with Himmler – Hostages for a policy – No make-up for the Mitfords – The shape of things to come.

I FELT singularly unmoved by the clamour and hysteria of that January 30 in 1933 when the Nazi Party came to power. Certainly it was an exciting moment, but I had too many reservations concerning the dangerous turbulence of the radicals to feel unduly confident about the possible march of events. We were all standing around in the Kaiserhof while Hitler was with the President. He came back through shouting crowds and up in the lift to the first floor. *"Jetzt sind wir so weit,"* he announced in a state of euphoria. We all crowded round, waiters and maids alike, to shake his hand. "Well, *Herr Reichskanzler,*" I said, "at least I am not going to have to call you *Herr Oberregierungsrat* any more." Ribbentrop was there, already trying to put on Bismarckian airs, and Goering, of course, here, there and everywhere in his most resplendent uniform. I missed most of the junketing because I was pinned in my room by the foreign press and answering telephone calls from scores of acquaintances all over Germany, who suddenly remembered that they had been to school with me or had known my father and wanted to make their number with someone near the centre without delay.

That evening there was a big S.A. parade. They even played my march, *Young Heroes*, as they stamped down the Wilhelmstrasse, but any feeling of identification was rudely shattered the next morning. The offices in the Chancellery were somehow not yet ready for occupation and a wild flurry of discussions was still being carried on in the Kaiserhof. I was sitting down in the corner of one of the big reception-rooms, and diagonally opposite Hitler was in conversation with Frick. As I have found many times in my life, I was, acoustically speaking, strategically placed. Imagine my horror when I heard Hitler say: "The best thing to do with *Parteigenosse* Rosenberg is to put him as State Secretary in the Foreign Office."

I felt as if I had been seared with a red-hot iron. This was how Hitler proposed to implement his countless evasive statements of intention to me concerning Rosenberg. How there would be no place for him in the Government, how his importance as editor of the *Beobachter* would diminish in the national scene. . . . I had to do something immediately. Almost running out of the room, I tore down to the Foreign Office and demanded to see von Neurath. I had never met him in my life, but after a short pause I was accompanied upstairs. "Your Excellency," I said, "I must tell you something of the utmost importance. You know who I am, I hope." "Yes, yes, you are the foreign press chief." "This is a very delicate matter for me and I must ask you to keep our conversation absolutely between ourselves." "Of course," he said, surprised and puzzled. "I have just come from the Kaiserhof, where I heard Hitler say that they are going to put Rosenberg in here as your State Secretary. Of course it is only a step to making him Foreign Minister. I beg you to sound the alarm here. Go and see the President, if necessary. This must be stopped at all costs." Even the phlegmatic Neurath was astonished. "I do not know how to understand you, Herr Hanfstaengl. Surely you are one of the better-known members of the Party?" "Certainly I am," I replied, "but where the good of Germany is concerned there are limits and this I will not stand for." Neurath must have moved fast, because the scheme came to nothing. As a sop, Rosenberg found himself set up in a sumptuous villa in the Tiergarten as head of the foreign policy section of the Party, which mercifully restricted his influence. Neurath was grateful for my intervention and we afterwards became close associates.

It had been a bad start. Hitler had been very difficult to deal with for weeks. With power almost within his grasp, he listened only to suggestions which fed his mounting exaltation and swept aside any ideas of mine to give his coming assumption of office a more propitiatory air. There had been a very influential French journalist

named Drach, a Jew in fact, who had proposed to signalize the event
with an article in *Je sais tout*, suggesting that French and German
ex-service men should meet somewhere on their common border for
a solemn ceremony of reconciliation to bury for all time the hatchet
of war. It seemed to me just the sort of gesture that would start the
new Government off on the right foot and I got several people like
Epp to undertake to support the idea. All that was needed was the
benevolent approval of Hitler. He thought it pointless, just another
trick on the part of a foreign correspondent—many of them had
treated him very roughly during the election campaign and he had
come to hate the sight of them.

I was given a set of offices in Hess's *Verbindungsstab,* diagonally
opposite the Chancellery. I was allowed to choose my own staff, and
although my deputy, Voigt, was a member of the Party, the others
were not. My secretary, Frau von Hausberger, had been brought up
in the United States and she and her daughter were Quakers. This
fact was known to Hess, who made no attempt to interfere with my
arrangements. I insisted that the superficial Nazi flummery should
form no part of our daily routine. No one was greeted with *Heil
Hitler* or the salute, and everybody greeted each other in normal
fashion with 'good morning' or 'good afternoon'. In due course we
became a civilian island in a sea of uniforms.

I continued to get the same expense allowance as before. In fact,
by the time they had deducted Party dues, tax and insurance, it was
down to about 850 marks a month – about £850 a year. This
remained my official income until the day I left Germany, so that
I was more or less working in an honorary capacity in the years that
followed. There was a certain amount of money coming in again
from my share in the Hanfstaengl firm, but I was always under
pressure to find the income to meet my expenses. Later in the year
I brought out a retrospective book of caricatures about Hitler, which
made a certain amount of money, and, in due course, wrote the
music for and helped to direct a couple of films. During the first
few weeks Goering invited me to stay with him in his *Reichstag*
President's palace. Of course it did not cost him a penny, but he
seemed to regard this as sufficient repayment for the sums he had
borrowed from me in less affluent days, which I had never seen back.

I then took an apartment for a short period in the Genthinerstrasse, and in the late autumn of 1933 moved into a charming house, almost a miniature *palais*, on the Pariser Platz, just by the Brandenburger Tor. That remained my Berlin home until the end.

I also found it expedient to appear in the Party uniform for the first time. I had always considered the dun-coloured affair the S.A. wore a monstrosity, so I took the liberty of designing my own. I sent for a superb length of chocolate-brown gaberdine from a London tailor and had it made up with a delicate little gold epaulette. Hitler had offered me a shirt and trousers out of the Party clothing-store, but if it was going to be tactically necessary to get out of my civilian clothes, I intended to do so on my own terms. My first appearance in it at a party given by Louis Lochner, the Associated Press correspondent, was, needless to state, the talk of the town.

If I interpose such minor details in a period of major revolution, it is not an attempt to dissociate myself from events. The Nazis had come to power with the declared intention of cleaning out the augean stables of economic disaster, unemployment, corruption, Communism, the futile and purposeless haggling of 32 parties in the *Reichstag* and restoring national dignity and honour. That is what I believed in as a member of the Party, and I will not attempt to justify in hindsight the fact that I went along with many of the draconian measures introduced. I will risk Anglo-Saxon prejudice by saying that I compared the process to the hacking out of underbrush so that trees could grow again. What I did, as one individual, within the measure of the possible, was to intervene to the best of my ability wherever the impetus of revolution produced unpleasant excesses. Many others did as much and more than I did, and I at least escaped in the end with my life. To do these things at all I had somehow to retain my place at Hitler's elbow.

My first brush came with Goering. I had been hearing from Lochner and people in the diplomatic round stories about unpleasant goings-on at the Columbia House, down near Tempelhof airfield. The S.A. were said to have taken this over as a private prison and interrogation centre for political enemies, whom they were alleged to be beating up. Then a Graf Schönborn, whom I knew, called on me at the *Reichstag* President's palace and confirmed the story with

specific details. I tackled Goering about it over breakfast. First of all
he denied the whole thing. Then I suggested that we satisfy ourselves
by a personal visit. Goering was evasive, then truculent, and finally
demanded to know who had told me the story. I was unwilling to
do so, but after extracting a promise that nothing would happen to
the informant, named Schönborn. I should have known better, but
then there was a lot I yet had to learn. Schönborn disappeared and
was detained for several weeks. He was naturally not exactly grateful
to me, but I had raised such hell that I had probably helped to get
him out as much as I had to put him in. It was my first taste of how
different things were to be from what many of us had hoped. Over
the next three years I voiced my protests whenever I could. But no
one should suppose that the rôle of King Canute is an easy one
to play.

It was necessary often to work by the most devious means. When
the Communist headquarters in the Liebknecht house was raided on
February 24, Goering, as Prussian Minister of the Interior, had
a flamboyant communiqué issued about the barrels of incriminating
material concerning plans for world revolution which had been discovered. Harried by the press, I could get no details out of him. The
next day I had lunch with Sir Horace Rumbold, the British ambassador. "If these suggestions are true, which I doubt," I told him,
"surely one way of getting at the facts would be for the British
Government to request details, especially as some of the territories
in their Empire are alleged to be affected." Whether he took my
advice or not I do not know as, two days later, the anti-Communist
campaign reached its most spectacular peak.

It must be remembered that we were in the middle of a last great
election campaign. On February 26 I accompanied Hitler on a wild
twelve-hour plane flight during which he spoke at three widely
separated cities. Late that evening we dined with Prince Viktor zu
Wied and his wife at their home in the Kurfürstenstrasse. I could
feel a cold coming on and before we left the Prince gave me a bottle
of aquavit, with the advice to drink myself into a fever. I was so
dog-tired that night that I did not start the cure, but the following
afternoon I felt so shivery that I decided to go to bed in my room
in Goering's palace and sample the remedy. The Goebbels had

invited me for later on, but I left a telephone message to excuse myself, put on a couple of old sweaters, piled the bed with blankets, ordered relays of hot lemonade to alternate with the medicine and settled down to sweat. We were all due to leave again for Breslau the next day, and I had to do something drastic.

After an hour or so of alternate draughts, with the bed-clothes up to my nose, I could feel the shivering lessening and a welcome warmth coursing through my limbs. I was nicely bathed in perspiration when the telephone in the adjacent sitting-room began to ring. It went on and on, no one came to answer it, so in the end I heaved myself out of bed, mopping my face with a towel, and went next door. It was Brückner, or one of the adjutants, I do not remember: "The Führer insists that you come this evening to the Goebbels. He wants you to play the piano for him." I explained rather tersely my position, said he had undone all the good work I had started, that I could not possibly come out with a feverish cold on me and that I was going back to my bed. I had just rearranged everything and was starting to warm up when the telephone shrilled again. This is too much, I thought, it can ring till it stops. It failed to do so, so I dragged myself next door again. This time it was Magda herself calling. I was ruining her whole party. I only had to wrap up and come along and sweat later, and so forth. I was suitably firm, took care to leave the ear-piece off its hook, and started my self-imposed régime all over again.

I tried to doze, and slowly realized that there was too much light to do so in comfort. I had left the door to the other room open. You idiot, I groaned to myself, you have left the reading-lamp on at the desk. I tried counting sheep but it was no good. Moreover there was a curious quality about the light. It seemed to flicker and was penetrating into my bedroom from some other source than the open door. Suddenly Frau Wanda, the housekeeper, burst in: "Herr Doktor! Herr Doktor!" she screamed in her falsetto, "the *Reichstag* is on fire!" This time I was up in a bound, ran to the window, which faced across the square, and there, in very truth, was the whole building enveloped in flames.

This time I did the telephoning and got Goebbels himself on the line: "I must talk to Herr Hitler," I said. What was it all about, the little gnome wanted know, was it nothing I could tell him to pass on? In the end I lost patience: "Tell him the *Reichstag* is on fire." "Hanfstaengl, is this one of your jokes?" Goebbels answered rather curtly. "If you think that, come down here and see for yourselves," and I hung up. I then called Sefton Delmer and Louis Lochner. No sooner had I put the receiver down when the bell shrilled again. It was Goebbels back: "I have just talked to the Führer and he wants to know what is really happening. No more of your jokes now." I lost my temper with him. "I tell you to come down here and see whether I am talking nonsense or not. The whole place is in flames and the fire-brigades are already here. I am going back to bed."

My room became like a railway station. Auwi came in, and then the Prince of Hesse. They were both staying in the palace. All I knew was that I was very annoyed at the ruin of my cure. "That's the end of that gas-works, anyway," I said. I suppose it was a callous remark, but I had always considered it an architectural abortion. The next day, of course, the Nazi newspapers came out with banner accusations that it was all the work of the Communists, and the notorious *affaire* was launched.

I am afraid this anecdote provides little new evidence of value. It was suggested later that I was one of the people who knew the whole story. Not only did the outbreak catch me in bed with a fever, but neither I, nor any of the other guests, nor any of the servants were aware of, or had noticed, any activity in the house to substantiate the theory that Ernst and his S.A. arsonists had entered the *Reichstag* through a tunnel from our cellars. On the other hand, it was a large building, they may have had a key to the coal-hole and worked completely unnoticed. What is not without interest, however, is the attitude of Goebbels and Hitler.

The little doctor was, of course, an accomplished liar, but if ever annoyance and suspicion were genuine in a man's voice, they were in his on the telephone that evening. For what the supposition is worth at this period of time, it would not surprise me in the least, on the strength of the evidence now available, that Goering planned the whole thing himself, necessarily with Hitler's knowledge, as a means of wresting a piece of initiative from his hated rival, Goebbels.

Whether Goering was in his palace that evening or not I have no idea. I did not see him.

My own suspicions did not grow until I read, much later in the year, the transcripts of the trial at Leipzig of Dimitroff and his associates. I had been named in a book published in London as one of those implicated in the *Reichstag* fire plot. I instituted proceedings for libel through a solicitor named Kenneth Brown, who later became my good friend. I was so appalled at the flimsy nature of the evidence produced at the trial that I flew to London to tell Brown to call off the action, but by that time the publishers had climbed down anyway.

The Leipzig trial injured Goering's prestige badly. He was furious. At lunch one day in the Chancellery he trumpeted: *"Mein Führer, it is an absolute disgrace the way these High Court judges are behaving. You would think we were on trial, not the Communists."* Hitler's answer was revealing: *"Mein lieber Goering,"* he said, "it is only a question of time. We shall soon have those old fellows talking our language. They are all ripe for retirement anyway, and we will put our own people in. But while *der Alte* [Hindenburg] is alive, there is not much we can do about it."

I claim a small share of the credit for the fact that Dimitroff was able to leave Germany alive after he had been found not guilty. In response to President Roosevelt's message, I kept in close touch with the American ambassador in Berlin, William E. Dodd. In many ways he was an unsatisfactory representative. He was a modest little Southern history professor, who ran his embassy on a shoe-string and was probably trying to save money out of his pay. At a time when it needed a robust millionaire to compete with the flamboyance of the Nazis, he teetered round self-effacingly as if he was still on his college campus. His mind and his prejudices were small. The fact that I was a former Harvard man made him regard even me as a Goddam-Yankee, but I did my best to help him exert what influence he had. On one occasion I even arranged for him to have a private interview with Hitler, without a member of the Foreign Office present, which was, of course, contrary to all protocol. Neurath, whose friendship I valued, was distinctly annoyed when he heard of it, and indeed I might have saved myself the trouble.

I forget the occasion, but it was some point I wished to drive home to Hitler. Dodd made no impression. Hitler was almost pitying: "*der gute* Dodd," he said, "he can hardly speak German and made no sense at all".

The best thing about Dodd was his attractive blonde daughter, Martha, whom I got to know very well. I used to sponsor her in Hitler's company in the hope that he would listen to my ideas through her. One day she and I were having lunch together and she told me that her father was very worried because he had heard that even if Dimitroff was released, he would never reach the border alive, and that Goering was behind some plan to kill him. This seemed to me the height of madness, so we concocted a counter-plot with Louis Lochner, who was also president of the foreign press association. On the pretence of introducing a new member of Reuter's staff, he invited Goering's press officer, a man named Sommerfeldt, to lunch. As a brash new-comer, who could get away with it, it was arranged that the young Reuter man should repeat Martha's story as a rumour and ask whether Goering had a statement to make. Faced by this he had, of course, to declare publicly that Dimitroff would most certainly be free to leave in safety, that he would make himself personally responsible, and so on. It worked, except that afterwards I am afraid the young Reuter man boasted of his part in the episode and the story got back to Goering. It would be an exaggeration to say that he expressed gratitude to me.

The March elections had brought Hitler, with his Nationalist allies, the majority he needed, but until he had obtained from the *Reichstag* the passage of the Enabling Bill which provided the legal basis for his dictatorship, he was markedly deferential to his nominal coalition partners. One experience of mine underlined this. Hugenberg, who, apart from holding three ministerial portfolios, still retained his interest in the Ruhr and the control of the Ufa film company, had sponsored a highly tendentious film called *Morgenrot*. Technically it was brilliant, but its subject was U-boat warfare, with distinct anti-British overtones in scenes concerning the camouflaged 'Q' ships of the Royal Navy. The première caused a furore, and several British correspondents, including Norman Ebbutt, *The Times* representative, demanded to know from me whether its tendency represented a deliberate statement of view on the part of the new Government. I was under pressure and Hitler was not available, so, with the apparent concurrence of Hess, I issued a statement saying that this was a private production with which the Nazis could not be associated. This was nothing less than the truth, but next morning I was called peremptorily to Hitler's presence to receive a dressing-down, on the grounds that the Nationalists were up in arms. I had to go and apologize to Hugenberg personally with an explanation that I had allowed myself to be misled.

The most significant political demonstration of this initial period of power was the ceremony in the Potsdam Garrison Church attended by President Hindenburg and all the representatives of pre- and post-Weimar Germany. It was, to my mind, perhaps the major turning-point in Hitler's ideological attitudes. Until then it was still possible to read anything into his intentions, with ample evidence from his own assurances, that he proposed in due course to restore the monarchy. Potsdam, with its menacing panoply of an Imperial Germany, provided the psychological parting of the ways. The *régisseur* was Dr. Joseph Goebbels.

The organization of the Potsdam ceremony was not an exclusive National-Socialist affair. The *Reichswehr*, the *Stahlhelm*, the monarchists, and religious and other traditional bodies managed to achieve equal representation. Goebbels resented this competition, and succeeded, in my presence, the evening before, in persuading Hitler not to take part in any of the preliminary rallies but only to appear at the Garrison Church itself. Instead, the little doctor arranged for ten o'clock in the morning an almost private visit of homage to a suburban cemetery where lay buried a number of the S.A. men who had been killed in the street brawls during the rise to power. I was a member of the official party.

It was a masterly piece of Thespian improvisation on the part of Goebbels. Clumping along between a guard of S.A. men, he laid a wreath at the foot of each grave, where Hitler and the rest of us stood each time for a minute or so in token of remembrance. From the direction of Potsdam came the booming of guns and maroons as the rival organizations gathered for the forthcoming ceremony. Goebbels kept up a sort of running funeral oration along the lines

of 'ah, young so-and-so. . . . I know his poor mother well'. I found
the *Horst Wessel Lied* running through my head: *'Kameraden, die
Rotfront und Reaktion erschossen . . ."* – the Red front had been
liquidated. The Minister of Propaganda was already conditioning
his master's mind for the coming fight with the 'forces of reaction'.

Hitler's mood on his arrival at the church had been determined
for him. I do not need to describe the scene in detail, the empty
Imperial throne, the Crown Prince, Hindenburg, old Field-Marshal
Mackensen in the uniform of the Death's Head Hussars. . . . This
was the 'reaction' in full regalia. Hitler paid lip-service to the fusion
of the old and the new, as for the time being he knew he must, but
for the connoisseur there was a fresh note in his speech. I was standing with Hess not twenty feet away from him. "Now it is the heroic
Weltanschauung which will illuminate the ideals of Germany's
future. . . ." I pulled myself together with a start. What was this?
Where had I read that before? This was not Schopenhauer, who had
been Hitler's philosophical god in the old Dietrich Eckart days. No,
this was new. It was Nietzsche.

I thought back only a few months earlier to a visit he had paid
during one of the election campaigns, while travelling from Weimar
to Berlin, to the Villa Silberblick, where Nietzsche had died and
where his widowed sister, aged 86, still lived. The rest of us had
waited outside, for nearly an hour and a half. Hitler had gone in
carrying his whip, but, to my astonishment, came tripping out with
a slim little turn-of-the-century cane dangling from his fingers:
"What a marvellous old lady," he said to me. "What vivacity and
intelligence. A real personality. Look, she has given me her brother's
last walking-stick as a souvenir, a great compliment. You should
have been there, Hanfstaengl" – which was his form of evasion when
he had excluded me from anything.

The episode had clearly caused a deeper impression than the
immediate involvement in the election campaign had permitted me
to appreciate. Hitler's mind was a deep-running river. You could
never tell when something it had absorbed would bob to the surface
again. From that day at Potsdam the Nietzschian catch-phrases
began to appear more frequently – *Wille zur Macht, Herrenvolk,
Sklavenmoral* – the fight for the heroic life, against formal dead-

weight education, Christian philosophy and ethics based on compassion. Schopenhauer, with his almost Buddhist gentleness, was buried for ever, and the Gauleiters started to take their inspiration from a savage bowdlerization of Nietzsche. The guillotine twist which Robespierre had given to the teachings of Jean-Jacques Rousseau was repeated by Goebbels, Hitler and the Gestapo in their political simplification of the contradictory theories of Nietzsche. Nor was that the only milestone reached at Potsdam. Until this formidable display by the representatives of the old régime, Hitler's historical hero had always been Frederick the Great. When, under Goebbels' prompting, he appreciated the risks and restrictions which a coalition with these traditional forces would entail, his allegiance subtly changed. From this time on, Napoleon emerged more and more as his model. The inspired sense of the art of the possible which had characterized the great Prussian king became submerged in the limitless lust for universal power of the Corsican.

No single man could halt the whirlwind of the revolution's progress. The political parties were banned, the trade unions sequestrated, pressure put on the *Stahlhelm*, but many pillars of the establishment remained, the Presidency, the *Reichswehr*, the Foreign Office, the Civil Service. Those of us on the conservative side of the fence had expected the agitation to diminish, not increase, but there still seemed ample safeguards left to provide a fire-brigade once the immediate conflagration had run its course. It should not be supposed that these measures were thrashed out in conference or in the cabinet, or that there was any real previous discussion in the party concerning them. Most of us literally read about them in the newspapers as they occurred. Hitler had his Enabling Law and was acting with the powers it granted him. The whole thing was run like the Grand National steeplechase. There was simply no occasion to hear what one jockey said to the other as they came to each hurdle.

In matters of policy the only field in which I dug in my heels was that of foreign affairs. I was an ally of Neurath and an opponent of Rosenberg and all he stood for. I also tried to maintain a measure of sanity in religious affairs. If I attempted to criticize Hitler's other coups to his face he would tell me it was none of my business and that he alone was responsible for his actions. One just had to niggle away at a minor level. On occasion I was able to get a Gauleiter reprimanded for talking some obstreperous nonsense about international affairs, but by and large my intervention was solicited at a more personal level. More and more stories penetrated of people being detained wilfully, without trial, not by the police, who still adhered to the law, but the S.A., who did not. The seed was being sown of the future concentration camps, but there was no coherence or comprehensive information and one heard of these things at second and third hand. Vengeful lawlessness it certainly was, but very few people detected in it as yet a system. People knew I had the ear of Hitler and I would, from time to time, be begged to draw particular cases to his attention.

One of my two most useful contacts was Rudolf Diels, who had been the anti-Communist security chief under Brüning and because of his administrative genius had been taken over as the first executive head of the Gestapo—still predominantly a police organization. The other was Heinrich Himmler. Diels was indefatigable. He was a trained security officer, of the type which in any country does not normally wear kid gloves. But what he did had to be done according to the book. Not only was he appalled by the liberties taken by the S.A. and the S.S., but he countered them wherever he could. He and I used to meet at receptions round Berlin and I passed on details of cases which had been brought to my notice. Quite frequently this produced the desired result. Our collaboration also attracted Goering's disapproval and he more than once warned Diels not to spend so much time in my company.

With Himmler the connexion was purely personal. With our mutual Bavarian background, he was prepared to listen to cogent arguments and act upon them. In this way I was able to secure the release of Ernst Reuter, who had been the Socialist mayor of Magdeburg and, after the Second World War, acquired a world reputation as the *Oberbürgermeister* of beleaguered Berlin. I knew nothing about him, but the Quakers had taken up his case, which was attracting considerable attention in England, and I was asked to intervene by one of their leaders, Miss Elizabeth Howard. After a dinner somewhere one evening I got hold of Himmler and told him it was clear that there would be a first-class international outcry unless the man was freed. Himmler gave me a name and number to ring, and it was fixed, just like that.

In another case, a Socialist deputy named Gerhart Seger had escaped to Scandinavia, but his English-born wife and child could not get an exit permit. Mrs. Mavis Tate, a British M.P., took up the case and even presented herself in my office. Again I settled the matter through Himmler. My only tangible reward, years later, when I was a British internee, was to learn that Mrs. Tate had stood up again in the House of Commons and opposed my release. There were scores of similar instances. One which Diels himself mentions, in his post-war memoirs, was State Secretary Pünder, the brother of a Cologne lawyer now prominent in the Bonn Federal Government. Other names which come to my mind are the family of Ganghofer, the Bavarian novelist, and Ludwig Wüllner, the *Lieder* singer.

Another man I was happy to help was Fritz Kreisler, the violinist. He was a Jew, but not in immediate danger. In fact Hitler was a great admirer of his playing. We were good friends and he had not only helped me with the orchestration of some of my marches, but worked up a melody of mine into one of the items in his repertoire, called *Canzonetta*. He read the shape of things to come and considered it prudent to emigrate to the United States. Through Schacht and Neurath, I was able to arrange for the transfer of his considerable fortune. Those of us who were in a position to help did what we could.

The pathetic thing was that many of us thought these embryo concentration camps were only a transitory manifestation. This was the version available even to those as near the inner circle of the Party as myself and information was so sparse it was difficult to disbelieve it. I took Philip Noel-Baker, a visiting British M.P., in to Hitler one day to broach the subject and myself brought up the suggestion that the agitation abroad might be stilled if one of the resident foreign consuls, in rotation, were permitted to report on the conditions under which such suspects were being held. Hitler took it quite calmly and said that it was a curious idea. He was not asking any of his consular personnel in England to visit British penitentiaries. The next time I was in the Chancellery, of course, I got hell.

Who did this Englishman think he was to make such an insulting request through me? He should look into his own gaols first, and so forth. Nor was this by any means the only sort of subject I introduced people to Hitler to talk about. When the German Government imposed the asinine regulation of charging a thousand marks for an exit visa to Austria, as part of the incipient campaign against their small southern neighbour, I took Luis Trenker, the Austrian film producer famous for his historical romances, to remonstrate with Hitler as a fellow-countryman. He got a dusty answer and I was snubbed for my pains. However, I derived a measure of exasperated amusement from the fact that Goebbels, who had heard of our visit, assumed I was trespassing on his theatrical preserves and hurried down next day to present Heinrich George, the actor, to Hitler as an antidote.

My worst set-back came from an attempt to transmit a solution to the rising wave of anti-Semitic agitation. Conditions had not remotely approached those after 1938, when the German diplomat von Rath was shot by a Jewish *émigré* in Paris. I had been the witness of an ugly, but by no means murderous, demonstration, tacitly furthered by Goebbels, as early as April 1, 1933, against Jewish shops in the Potsdamer Platz, and had remonstrated without effect with the instigator in the Chancellery. About the following August, word reached me through an American lady whom I knew, Mrs. Daisy Miles, who lived in the Hotel Continental in Munich, that an emissary from the United States would much appreciate an interview with me over the Swiss border at Lindau.

She drove me down and I found myself in conversation with Maxie Steuer, a leading Jewish lawyer from New York, who had been given my name by a number of American friends. His proposal, sponsored by such wealthy members of the American Jewish community as the Speyers, Warburgs and others, was that they were prepared to finance the emigration to the United States of all those German Jews, particularly recent arrivals from Central Europe, who wished to leave. The scheme took into account the proportion clause which the Nazis were proposing to apply to the professions and seemed an admirable solution to the prickly problem.

I flew back to Berlin and talked first to Neurath. He was

delighted. Then I saw Schacht. He was enthusiastic. With this backing I decided to approach Hitler. I caught him after lunch one day and we walked up and down diagonally across the terrace of the old Chancellery, where coffee used to be served on fine summer and autumn days. His response appalled me: *"Mein lieber* Hanfstaengl. The die is cast. Events are taking on quite a different shape." "But Herr Hitler," I protested, "this is our finest chance to deal with an insoluble problem." "Do not waste my time, Hanfstaengl," he answered sharply. "I need the Jews as hostages."

Trying to keep one's foot on the soft pedal had more of the quality of asking a pile-driver not to make a noise. Nevertheless, I sought allies wherever I could. One of these was General von Reichenau, whose reputation as a rabid Nazi was not entirely deserved. He had certainly been one of Hitler's most senior advocates in the *Reichswehr* and, although he had been called to a high post in the War Office, the excesses of the first year of power quickly disillusioned him. I had known him for the best part of ten years. We had first met with my young American military attaché friend, Truman-Smith, when Reichenau was still a major. Now I returned the compliment by persuading Reichenau to arrange for the return of Colonel Truman-Smith to Berlin as American military attaché. I felt every step to strengthen pro-American sentiments in Germany was justified.

Reichenau and the *Reichswehr* were not only shocked by the S.A.'s excesses, but increasingly perturbed at Roehm's pretensions to incorporate them in the Army with himself as Defence Minister. Nor was he impressed with the S.A.'s military potentialities. Someone had compared them with the freedom levies of 1813 against Napoleon, but Reichenau was scornful: "I can assure you that the Battles of Leipzig and Waterloo were won by the regular Prussian infantry," he snapped. I found this a very useful argument on which to play and was always giving Reichenau information from within the Party on which the Army was often able to act with some success. In return he passed on reports of his own in case I had the opportunity of working on Hitler. I was still closer to him than any of them, although Hitler was annoyed to discover that I knew the general so well: "The extraordinary thing about Hanfstaengl is that he seems to have friends and relations everywhere," he complained once in front of me. Having come from nowhere, it was something he could barely grasp. Another instance of the same sort of thing occurred when we all attended the inauguration of the Tannenberg memorial with Hindenburg in East Prussia. The old gentleman was very civil to me and talked in his deep bass voice about a cousin of mine of the same name whom he had known in Potsdam as an officer of the Guards Grenadier regiment. We stood tracing back genealogies for several minutes, to the utter fury and jealousy of Hitler's entourage.

Neurath was another prominent figure who responded to my confidences with his protection. He took me with him to the London economic conference in the summer of 1933, and helped me with currency through the Foreign Office on several other visits I made to England. These, I might say, were carried out entirely at my own expense. I wanted to give Hitler a true picture of opinion there and produce arguments which might at least induce caution in the field of foreign policy. I even tried to persuade him to arrange for an exchange of visits between the heads of State. Anything, I thought, to get him out, and try and normalize his viewpoint. The only immediate result was that Goering laid claim to the first invitation. If he was received by the King he thought he might get a British decoration to add to his collection.

I do not need to stress the point that important groups abroad, as well as within Germany, regarded Hitler at this time with distinct benevolence. Even Lloyd George, on whom I called, was no exception. He gave me a signed photograph to take back, on which he had inscribed: "To Chancellor Hitler, in admiration of his courage, determination and leadership." There were plenty of people prepared to acknowledge the new power which had arisen in Germany. During one visit to Berchtesgaden in the late summer I was detailed to help entertain Sir John Siddeley, the industrialist, and his wife. To this day I retain the memory of how he and Goering sat out on a balcony with great illustrations and blueprints of British military aircraft it was hoped Germany would buy. All, I might say, in flat contradiction to the terms of the Versailles Treaty.

It was during the same visit—I think it was when I went down to get Hitler's approval for my book of caricatures – that I was given another example of the pleasure which the Party leaders appeared to take in the brutality with which they wielded power. I had taken Egon down with me, by now an intelligent boy of twelve, and he was playing round in the bushes when he came up just behind Hitler and Goering: "*Mein Führer*," Hermann was saying, "I have just had to sign twenty-two death sentences for your approval." They were very satisfied with themselves, rubbing their hands, Egon reported to me. It had obviously become a matter of routine, and no clemency was exercised.

If I needed further indication of the way their minds were running, a conversation between Hitler and Goebbels, heard through the open door of the dining-room in the Chancellery, was all I needed: "As long as the old gentleman [Hindenburg] is alive," came Hitler's voice, "there are two things I cannot touch: the Army and the Foreign Office." Goebbels was quick to give a turn to the knife: "As far as that Potsdam bunch is concerned, *Mein Führer*, there is only one way to deal with them – line them up in rows against a wall and mow them down with machine-guns." So, of course, I went straight round to see Reichenau and told him the story.

It was the experience of power which turned Hitler into an irreconcilable fanatic. It took me most of 1933 to realize that the demon had entered into him. Even then many of us did not believe that the point of no return had been reached. We thought the impetus of the movement could be braked, the direction altered, even reserved. Whenever I saw Neurath, Schacht, Gürtner or General von Reichenau, which was frequently, we talked in the same tone. None of them had the *entrée* to Hitler which I still had, and in spite of my growing distaste, they begged me to remain where I was. Hitler had still not reached the point where he no longer talked over matters with those who enjoyed his confidence. The final decisions of a man in that position are often, in the last resort, taken in a matter of minutes, and if I happened to be there at that crucial moment there was always the possibility that the views I presented would prevail. The drawback was that the voice of reason was beginning to find less and less echo in his mind.

The final realization that Hitler and his movement had deceived not only me, but us all, came at the Nuremberg Party rally of the year of power. The preliminaries were somewhat enlivened by the presence for the first time in Germany of the Mitford sisters, Unity and her sister Diana, married to Sir Oswald Mosley. I had met them in London earlier in the year and they appeared at Nuremberg with letters of recommendation from, I think, young Otto von Bismarck. They were very attractive, but made-up to the eyebrows in a manner which conflicted directly with the newly proclaimed Nazi ideal of German womanhood. Their set purpose was to meet Hitler, and on our way to the Deutscher Hof Hotel, where he was staying, there were so many frank comments from passers-by that I had to duck behind a building with them. I pulled out my large, clean hand-kerchief and said: "My dears, it is no good, but to stand any hope of meeting him you will have to wipe some of that stuff off your faces," which they did.

I was quite happy to sponsor them, as it seemed to me that their English background and connexions might help to provide Hitler with glimpses of a world other than the introspective hot-house into which he appeared to be retreating. Hitler was in a private room and I sent in word, and various members of his party came out to walk, with ostentatious nonchalance, past our table for the purpose of returning with a report. The sisters clearly cannot have used my handkerchief industriously enough, as in the end we were fobbed off with Hess, who produced a few inconsequential remarks about how busy the Führer was, and there the attempt ended. Afterwards, Goering and Goebbels expressed mock horror at the idea of my trying to present two such painted hussies to Hitler, although their secret annoyance was the fact that I was the person called upon to effect the introduction. When the two girls returned to Germany later and paid the proper respects to the Hess and Rosenberg clique, they were, of course, welcomed as outstanding Nordic beauties. I am afraid they listened to my opponents in the Party far more than they did to me, although I subsequently saw quite a lot of Unity in Munich and even helped her to find the little villa near the English Garden, where she rented an apartment.

Nevertheless, I took them along with me to the rally. They were impressed, and doubtless I should have been pleased that the massed bands played, during the ceremony, in honour of the Party's martyrs, the Funeral March I had composed at the death of our little daughter Hertha. It really sounded very impressive, and Hitler congratulated me afterwards. I would have preferred to congratulate him on what many of us had believed would be the last Party rally. The so-called immutable twenty-five points of the N.S.D.A.P. had proclaimed for a dozen years that once power had been won and consolidated, the Party could be dissolved. Hitler clearly had not read them for some time. On the contrary, the theme of his speech was the 'State is the Party and the Party is the State'. We had been warned of the shape of things to come.

CHAPTER XII

CIRCUS AT THE CHANCELLERY

Metternichs in shirt-sleeves – Three lunches a day – Rings around a dictator – King Kong and Ludwig II – America from a chair – The schizopedic radical – The wine merchant who deserted – The loyalties of a Fouché – A flag without a pole – Intercession with Mussolini.

WHEN HITLER took up residence in the Reich Chancellery he installed as his boon companions the dreary crew who had made my life such a nightmare during the election trips which brought him to power – Brückner, Schaub, Schreck, Hoffmann and Sepp Dietrich. Too stupid to be anything but loyal and too unambitious to be a danger, they formed his innermost circle. They always reminded me of an old comedy by Gerhard Hauptmann called *Schluck und Jau*, which was a Hogarthian piece set in Saxony some time in the seventeenth century. The Elector or Duke is out hunting and his party finds a couple of tramps fast asleep and dead drunk. For fun they take them back to the Schloss, put them into the Elector's bed, and when they wake up befuddle their senses further by telling them they are the Grand Duke and his Chamberlain. The comedy lies in the fact that they come to believe it. To me this was the picture of the *Reichskanzlei*, not only of the Chauffeureska, as I called them, but all of them. Nobodies in their shirt-sleeves playing at being Metternich.

This inner clique felt they had a proprietory interest in Hitler. They were always around and acted half as gadflies and half like the blockers in an American football team. They could not bear to leave him alone with anyone and set themselves up as a sort of collective Party conscience to prevent him being subjected to influences which they thought deviated from the basic Nazi line. They were so constantly with him that they did not want to talk, they wanted to listen and by listening hinder anybody from talking to Hitler in an intelligent, constructive fashion. They were like the famous cavalry of Murat under Napoleon, which flew round the enemy like wasps without fighting. They would interrupt the middle of a conversation to show him a picture or bring him a piece of paper, or Hoffmann would intrude, taking his photographs.

It was the same with almost everybody, but particularly with anyone who was not a member of the old Party gang. It was the same in Berchtesgaden as it was in Berlin. Neurath complained to me one day: "I have just been down to the Berghof to try and get the Führer, but you know, Hanfstaengl, it is impossible to talk to him alone for more than two minutes on end. One of those louts is always barging in." Schacht said the same. And for me, who, in those first two years, was the only other person who was there almost every day, it was worse. Even Goering began again to call me the 'Questenberg in the camp', a phrase he had invented in 1923, which was a reference to the character in Schiller's *Wallenstein*, who is always recommending caution and delay and taking a long view of things. They had heard me complain time and time again about the S.A. and its excesses, about illegal goings-on which had been drawn to my attention and the necessity for discipline and consolidation. So they ganged up on me and in the end it became hopeless.

Hitler was as unpunctual and unpredictable as ever. There were no set hours. Sometimes he would appear at breakfast and sometimes he would not, filling himself up in his suite first with hot milk and gruel and digestive powders. Then he would come down for a few minutes, and if I had something on my mind this was often a good time to catch him. The day would start with reports from Lammers, who was head of the Chancellery, and Funk, who at that time was Goebbels' right-hand man in the Propaganda Ministry and gave him a review of the morning's news. Funk was committed after the war to the Allies' Spandau gaol, but he was a gifted fellow whom I never considered particularly dangerous. He had been a very good financial journalist in his time, and stood high in my estimation because he had a professional's contempt for Goebbels. He was quite influential because he knew a lot of the industrialists and had, in fact, found the funds which had paid the bills at the Kaiserhof. His weakness was drink. It ran in the family. An uncle of his, Alfred

Reisenauer – a favourite pupil of Liszt – had been a world-famous pianist and one of my boyhood idols, which constituted an additional link with Funk. Reisenauer's tour in America had to be cancelled – it was said – when he staggered dead drunk on to the platform during a concert tour in California. Funk himself would often appear with a shocking hangover. We always knew when he was in bad shape as his stock answer then, when Hitler asked for information about some new development, would be: *"Mein Führer, das ist wohl noch nicht spruchreif"* – "the matter is not yet ripe for discussion", which meant he had been too bleary-eyed to read the confidential information reports.

The high point of the day was lunch, and here the main sufferer was a little fat fellow named Kannenberg, the chef. He had run quite a decent restaurant in Berlin in the old days and then became cook at the Brown House. He never knew what time lunch was to be served. It would be ordered for one o'clock and Hitler would sometimes not turn up until three. I have known him cook lunch three times and throw away two of them, and he was still expected to keep proper accounts. It was a completely movable feast with a shifting population. Sometimes Goering would be there, sometimes the Goebbels, less often Hess, and Roehm as good as never. He had his own private court in the Standartenstrasse with his boy friends, in a house which I think had once been the town residence of Rathenau. The regulars would hang around and get hungrier and hungrier. Otto Dietrich, who usually joined us, was the wisest. His stomach could not stand the strain, so he always went over to the Kaiserhof at a quarter to one and had a snack, turning up at half past one prepared for all emergencies.

Even during the coalition period none of the Conservative Ministers ever appeared. The migrant guests were usually types like the Chauffeureska, old Party hacks, the occasional Gauleiter from the provinces, which, of course, suited Hitler excellently. There was hardly anyone to challenge what he said. There was no protocol about seats, it was first come first served, although the inner clique all sat at the far end, watching and listening and making a note of those with whom their interference play would be necessary.

It was impossible to know beforehand who was going to give the superficial varnish to the party. It became a constant strain to guess who was going to be there and what they were going to talk about. I used to wait for some dangerous piece of nonsense to get started and then try and put forward a more responsible point of view. But to achieve any result I had either to make a joke or play the *enfant terrible* with a mixture of flattery and insolence. One never knew when Hitler was going to break into some tirade. In the end I found it too difficult to keep up day after day. There were only two people I ever saw who could get Hitler aside alone. The first was Goering, who, if he had something on his mind when he came to lunch, would say, "*Mein Führer*, I simply must speak to you in private." The other one was Himmler, who used to saunter in, and the first thing we knew he had spent half an hour alone with Hitler in his downstairs reception-room.

The environment of power had its contributory effect on Hitler's character. He sat in the inner circle of authority, surrounded by three rings of guards. The adulation involved in the Führer principle would have turned steadier heads than his. His information was filtered and he was exposed the whole time to the influence of Goebbels and the congenital radicals. He lost whatever contact with the ordinary people he had ever had. His public speeches became fewer and farther between, and where he had once synthesized the feelings of his audience he now preached to the converted. He was denied even that outlet. He did not really know what was going on in the world and used to call for all the German newspapers, overlooking the fact that they all came out of the one sausage factory, and read them all through, looking for the one thing he could not find, which was reality.

People who have read the collection of his remarks at table assume that he kept up this running fire of comment and commentary the whole time. It is simply not so. During my years at the Chancellery he would rail against the enemies of the régime in his old propaganda style, or talk about past campaigns, but there was no discussion of the progress of his revolution. It was only after the war had started, when there were no more meetings to rant at, and he had a new audience of generals, that he produced for posterity, probably at the suggestion of Bormann, the pearls of wisdom by which he wished to be remembered. It was done for deliberate effect and came long after my time.

Hitler's reaction to the old Bismarckian Chancellery—it was not rebuilt to look like Grand Central Station until later—was to denigrate his great predecessor. "He had no idea about architecture and the proper use of space," Hitler used to complain. "Imagine having the kitchens put into the ground floor." He would try systematically to reduce the stature of the Iron Chancellor, and on the most extraordinary grounds: "Old Bismarck had simply no idea how to deal with the Jewish problem," he said at table once. The entourage had, of course, no feeling for tradition or their surroundings at all. Schaub and Sepp Dietrich were indulging in some piece of uncouth horse-play on one of the old brocade sofas when I lost patience with them: "Can't you realize that Bismarck probably sat there," I told them. "You might at least try and behave properly." Hitler was in the room, but he just looked away and bit his nails.

The intellectual level was nil. To give an example: Schaub one day had come across some nude pictures of Mathilde Ludendorff, taken when that eccentric lady was attending a nature cure of some sort, and these were handed round with appreciative guffaws. In the evening things were a little better, as even Hitler had to do a certain amount of official entertaining, and occasionally I was called upon to do my act at the piano. It was no longer as frequent as it used to be, or as often as people in Berlin assumed. This was probably due to the fact that I had been giving a party in my own house once when Rudolf Hess rang up from the *Reichskanzlei* saying that the Führer wanted me to come and play for him. So I left my guests and went. It was the sort of sacrifice you had to make to keep in with the man. They knew perfectly well I was having a party myself and I am sure they did it deliberately.

The evening company had not yet degenerated, as it did later, when Goebbels brought his actress friends, and no decent woman would go there. Nor were the guests fully *gleichgeschaltet*. There was a very characterful elderly lady named Frau von Dirksen, who was, I think, the stepmother of the ambassador to Tokyo, who said to Hitler once in my hearing: "You must realize that I am and remain a monarchist. For me Wilhelm II is still the Kaiser." It required quite a lot of courage to say that sort of thing, even in 1933. Hitler had annoyed her with a long philippic about the reactionaries and how the time was coming when he would clean out the augean stables of the foreign ministry.

The whole place was always a blaze of lights. It looked like a film set. I would sometimes go round trying to turn off some of the switches, but Hitler would have none of it. Shop-window lighting was his ideal. It may have had something to do with the fact that his sight was weaker than he ever admitted, as a result of being gassed in the war, but it was also true that he had no sense of colours and was completely insensitive to the effect of lights on them. For him a good photograph was better than a Leonardo da Vinci. What he really still liked in the evening was watching a film. He would have one shown almost every night in his private cinema. One of his favourites was *King Kong*, which he had run two or three times. It was, it may be remembered, the story of a gargantuan ape which developed a Freudian tenderness for a human female not much bigger than its hand, and then went beserk. A frightful story, but it had Hitler absolutely spellbound. He talked about it for days.

His taste in literature still reminded me of the bottom shelf of the bookcase in the Thierschstrasse. We were down in Munich again on some occasion when I walked into the Osteria Bavaria restaurant for lunch to find Hitler and the entourage installed at one of the tables. They were in the *patio* outside, so it must have been in the summer. Hitler was holding a letter in his hand on heavy parchment paper, and I immediately recognized the bold and unmistakable handwriting. "So Ludwig II has sent you a letter," I chaffed him. "How do you know who wrote it?" he asked, nonplussed. So I explained that the hand was known to any student of Bavarian history. Hoffmann had come across it at some antique dealer's and probably was suggesting that Hitler should buy it. It was a superbly written homosexual love-letter to a manservant, and Hitler was fascinated by it. He was reading it through and gloating over the phrases. He seemed to be deriving some vicarious satisfaction from the text.

My position was not easy. Hitler kept me around because he felt I was the one person of long acquaintance who could deal with the foreign press correspondents on terms of equality and keep them out

of his hair. He never understood their requirements or psychology
or why I could not discipline them as Goebbels and Dietrich disciplined the German press. He thought they had only to be threatened
with sanctions or expulsion to bring them to heel and somehow never
comprehended that they could work perfectly well in any other
country. I spent half my time protecting them, and in one case, with
the help of Funk, managed to thwart a serious attempt by Goebbels
to expel Knickerbocker. Hitler still listened to me from time to time,
but was always careful not to give the *camarilla* the impression that
he was taking my advice. He still regarded me in a way as his
American expert, although he never absorbed the things I kept
trying to tell him.

Once when there was a lunch for all the *Reichsstatthalter* at the
Chancellery he suddenly dredged up from the past my suggestion of
1925 about a world tour. He had been giving one of his interminable
résumés of the history of the Party, his favourite subject, and the
appalling difficulties he had met in rebuilding it after Landsberg.
"And what did our Mister Hanfstaengl suggest at the time, gentlemen? That I should abandon Germany and improve my mind
abroad." This, of course, brought a great salvo of mocking laughter,
so I expostulated and said what valuable experience it would have
been for the post in which he now found himself. "What is America
but millionaires, beauty queens, stupid records and Hollywood . . ."
he broke in. "I see America from where I sit much more clearly than
you have ever known it." The purest megalomania. Of all the guests,
only von Epp gave me a slight understanding shrug. It was no good;
Hitler never learnt. You could never get him alone, and as long as
Schaub, or a Gauleiter, or a *Reichsstatthalter* was there, he started to
bray as if he was at a public meeting. It was the only tone and milieu
in which he felt at home.

His intransigence concerning foreign countries was almost pathological. Some time during 1933 Neurath had proposed that a useful
service might be rendered by returning the famous head of Queen
Nefertiti to the Egyptians. It had been found by German archeo-
logists and its restoration had, in fact, been called for in the
Versailles Treaty. I supported the plan as a means of improving
relations between Germany and the Middle East. "There you are,

our Mister Hanfstaengl wants to give everything away," was Hitler's comment. I protested that the idea was to make the ceremony an excuse for friendly negotiations, but Hitler ended the discussion by saying that the fact that the Versailles Treaty demanded the return of the bust was sufficient reason for not doing so.

Another example of the workings of his mind came with the belated American diplomatic recognition of the Soviet Union, in November 1933 as I recall. We were travelling from Berlin to Hanover by train when he was given the news and had me brought from my compartment to tax me with it. "There you are, Hanfstaengl, your friends the Americans have teamed up with the Bolshevists," he greeted me. "That puts every other nation in the world in the same category," I told him. "We all recognized them years ago." Hitler was not to be put off. "The fact that America has now done so on her own is proof of what I say," he persisted. All he really wanted to do was find some means of making me look small before the other members of the entourage.

My activities as foreign press chief gave them endless opportunities to undermine my position. There was one occasion when an Arab professor who had written a biography of Hitler approached me to be presented to its subject. I will say that he looked like three characters out of the Old Testament all rolled into one, but I took him down to Bayreuth, where Hitler was staying, to be greeted by a barrage of scornful comments from Brückner and company about my companion. However, I was insistent. As we went through into the garden Hitler was just dismissing a group of beautiful, blonde young members of his youth organization, and when he saw my companion he almost sank into the ground with amazement. I doubt if he had ever seen an Arab before. I told him that the visitor was a distinguished author who had compared him in his biography to Mohammed. Fortunately the copy he handed over to sign was all in Arabic, so Hitler was no wiser than I was.

Needless to say, the visit was a sore subject with the Chauffeureska for weeks. I had to go through very much the same thing every time I arranged an interview for a foreign correspondent with any independence of mind, as full reports of their stories were always read and I was held to blame for anything short of fulsome praise. My other difficulty was pressure on Hitler from Goebbels, who wanted to take over the foreign press section himself. I had reached a *modus vivendi* with Otto Dietrich and had a friendly arrangement with Neurath's people in the Foreign Office. There were occasional forays from Rosenberg and, of course, from Bohle, who was building up his *Auslandsdeutsche* organization, but most of the trouble came from Goebbels. Of course, Hitler delighted in this sort of jockeying, which went on at all levels and enabled him to keep control.

The evil genius of the second half of Hitler's career was Goebbels. I always likened this mocking, jealous, vicious, satanically gifted dwarf to the pilot-fish of the Hitler shark. It was he who finally turned Hitler fanatically against all established institutions and forms of authority. He was insolent, intimate and infinitely pliable. He had those liquid eyes and a wonderful voice and a constant flow of malicious novelties. He was the incarnation of the suspended Socialist press, with a nationalistic varnish. He supplied Hitler with all the information he couldn't read in his own newspapers and nasty little stories about enemies and friends alike. His inferiority complex came, of course, from his crippled foot, and I am probably one of the few people alive today who have seen it without a shoe. It was in their Reichskanzlerplatz flat. We had come in out of the rain, I cannot remember the circumstances exactly, and were discussing something hurriedly when Magda called me into his dressing-room with them. There was his right foot with a sock over it, looking like a fist, awful, and that, of course, was Goebbels in a nutshell. With his right foot he gave the Communist salute and with his left the Nazi *Gruss*. He was not only schizophrenic but schizopedic, and that was what made him so sinister.

He was the other really great orator in the party, and his horizon, like Hitler's, was as wide as the Sportpalast. He saw only his audience and thought that if he could get them drunk with his words, the whole country would get drunk and that this drunkenness could be translated into English, French, or any other language, and be exported as a ready-made frenzy. I used to call him Goebbelspierre, which he later heard about and hated me for, because, I swear, many of the passages in his speeches came straight out of Robespierre.

Shakespeare's phrase in *Macbeth* is the best description of him: 'There's daggers in men's smiles.' Goebbels worked with an equipment of superficial smiles and false bonhomie, getting his enemy in a web of ridiculousness and then suddenly exposing him in some discreditable light. "He's such a nice fellow really, but you know he said something the other day rather silly, ha-ha!" was the line with which he used to tantalize Hitler. And Hitler would say, "Well, what was it, then?" with Goebbels playing the mock friend and going on, "I ought not really to tell you, but. . . ." Then, of course, Hitler would explode, and when Goebbels had him fairly crawling up the wall he would start defending the man against this outburst, knowing full well that this would add fuel to Hitler's flames. I saw him take over the press division of Gürtner's Ministry of Justice just that way.

Even Magda, whom he led a dog's life, was not spared his complexes. He had a private cinema-show in his house one time, and just as he was on his way out, up some highly polished wooden steps, to stand and greet his guests as they left, he slipped on his club foot and all but fell down. Magda managed to save him and pull him up beside her. After a moment to recover and before the whole company, he gripped her by the back of the neck and forced her right down to his knee and said, with that sort of mad laughter, "So, you saved my life that time. That seems to please you a lot." Anyone who did not witness the scene would never believe it, but those who did caught their breath at the depth of character depravity it revealed. I remember I had helped him once in similar circumstances at a public meeting when I was walking just behind him with Prince Auwi. You would have expected him to be grateful but, of course, it just fed his hatred.

With the rise of Goebbels, the importance of Rosenberg as a person waned, although there was little cause for consolation in that. He had set himself up in a sumptuous villa on the Tiergarten in charge of the foreign affairs section of the Party, ready to jump into Neurath's shoes. He paid a visit to London with great *réclame* and, praise be, made an awful fool of himself. After ostentatiously laying a wreath at the Cenotaph, someone threw it into the Thames for his pains. I only wish he had been thrown in after it. Hitler, who protected him to the end, but had, I think, less illusions about his usefulness, tried to pretend that his visit had been a success. I knew better and said so without compunction, which caused Hitler to turn on me in the *Reichskanzlei* and say, "Hanfstaengl, you carry your criticism of *Parteigenosse* Rosenberg much too far. If I hear any more of it, you'll be dismissed." My answer was to make something of a protégé of Ribbentrop, who was still on the fringes and relied largely on me as his channel to the court. Anyone, I thought, was better than Rosenberg. Ribbentrop certainly gave every appearance of agreeing enthusiastically with my thesis about the supreme importance of America and I had no reservations about supporting him. Hitler was not yet so impressed with him. *'Ach, das ist ja ein fader Patron'* was his almost untranslatable description – something between a dull fellow and a crashing bore. He later made the grade, but Hitler was right after all.

My close relationship with Neurath soon caused me to drop my sponsorship of Ribbentrop, and it was not long before a number of unpleasant facts concerning him came to light. Frau Meissner, the wife of Hindenburg's State Secretary, had known Ribbentrop as a boy when she lived in Metz before the First World War. His father was a regular officer stationed with a regiment at Wesel, on the Rhine. Young Joachim was known as the most stupid boy in his class at the gymnasium. His most marked early characteristics were those of ambition and vanity, which he never lost. Frau Meissner could hardly believe that the man who was rising in the Nazi Party hierarchy and becoming its specialist on foreign affairs was the same man.

The 'von' in his name had been acquired by purchase. One of the strange things about the Weimar Republic was that it did not abolish nobility and titles. It became legal to change one's bourgeois name if a childless aristocrat could be persuaded to adopt you. Ribbentrop, who in 1920 had married a rich heiress of the champagne firm of Henckel, found an elderly poor relation who agreed to serve this purpose. During the 'twenties he and his wife moved in smart Berlin society, in which a number of rich Jewish banking families were prominent. Ribbentrop obtained a loan from Herbert Gutmann, of the Dresdner Bank, which he used to found a firm specializing in the import and export of expensive wines and spirits. Either by accident or design, the trade name of the firm, made up of the initials of its full title, emerged in the unfortunate form of 'Impogroma'. During the winter of 1933, after Hitler had come to power, when Ribbentrop ran into the Gutmanns at a Furtwängler concert in Berlin he cut them dead.

Ribbentrop was the only man who became a leading member of the Party who had substantial private means. His first acquaintance in the movement was probably Count Helldorf, the Berlin S.A. leader. Being a vain and ambitious man, he had soon scraped an acquaintance with Goering, at whose instance the famous meeting took place in Ribbentrop's villa in the Berlin suburb of Dahlem between Hitler, Papen and Oskar von Hindenburg on January 22, 1933, which led directly to Hitler's assumption of power. Nevertheless, his full acceptance was only gradual. He was always to be found in the palace of the *Reichstag* President occupied by Goering, and he was for ever battening on to me in the foyer or up in my office in the Kaiserhof Hotel. His unsnubbable attempts to be included at Hitler's table were not always successful.

The weapon with which he wore down Hitler's lack of interest in him was his never-failing air of servility. Some memory of his father's modest military rank led him to behave in front of Hitler like an obsequious junior officer. Added to this was his own total lack of intellectual equipment. He took Hitler's phrases, embroidered on them and bounced them back, a quality which in the end endeared itself to the master he had chosen. But this alone would not explain his rise to the eventual post of Foreign Minister. He was, in fact, the beneficiary of the endless internecine warfare which went on between the senior Nazis. It took five years for Hitler to feel that he could dispense with the professional services of Neurath. During that time most of the Nazi leaders intrigued covetously for the succession. The most anxious candidate was probably Rosenberg, but then he had almost everyone against him and never had a real chance. Goering would have liked the post, but in the end had so many others that his insatiable appetite was more or less stilled. Goebbels, too, had ambitions in this direction, but even Hitler must have felt that his physical appearance was a drawback. The *deus ex machina* in the final appointment of Ribbentrop was probably Otto Dietrich, not that he had any particular love for Ribbentrop, but he conceived in the end such a ripe and savage hatred of Rosenberg that, for tactical reasons, he preferred to further the candidature of the relative new-comer. The fact that Ribbentrop was a late adherent to the Party was an advantage as he was not tainted by association with any of the warring factions within the Party. He had a certain superficial grace of manner, at least when occasion demanded it, but matched his obsequiousness in the presence of Hitler with an unbearable pomposity in the company of anyone else. Moreover, and this was probably determining, the other leading members of the Party correctly diagnosed him as a second-rater and did not see in him a serious rival in their competition for influence over Hitler.

Ribbentrop was permitted by Hitler to set up a bureau which competed on the one hand with the foreign policy section of the Party under Rosenberg and, on the other, with the Foreign Office proper under Neurath. With Party funds, contact was established with foreign diplomats and personalities and a rival information network was built up which often provided Hitler with a more colourful account of events abroad than appeared in the more sober and accurate reports of the Foreign Office. Ribbentrop finally destroyed Neurath's position by harping at every possible oppor-tunity on the necessity for Hitler to have someone at the head of the Foreign Office who was completely reliable and beholden to him and determined to impose National-Socialist standards on the tradi-tion-minded officials of the *Auswärtiges Amt.* "You will never get anywhere with the old team," he used to echo Hitler. "They will never understand your aims and will have to be got rid of."

It is probably by no means far-fetched to trace his final hatred of England, which had been the scene of his first diplomatic success in 1935 when he negotiated the Anglo-German Naval Treaty, to the refusal of the Fellows to admit his son at Eton. Ribbentrop was deeply embittered by what he considered to be a direct affront, which was in no way cancelled out when he was permitted to send the boy to Westminster School. In spite of his years in London as Ambassador, he never really understood the British, and his total misconception of the basic forces underlying British diplomacy were by no means the least factor in persuading Hitler that he might be able to get away with a cheap war.

Ribbentrop not only railed at the inefficiency of the German Foreign Office, but pleased his master with an equally derogatory attitude towards the German Army. But for this there was a more unpleasant reason. I learnt in due course from Neurath that there was a *Reichswehr* file on Ribbentrop with details of how, in September or October 1918, when the German Army was retreating eastwards, Ribbentrop absented himself without leave from his company. At that time he was a reserve lieutenant and in ordinary circumstances would have been tried as a deserter and shot. The revolution and the armistice saved his life. Goering and Hitler certainly came into possession of this knowledge and it may well have been used to keep Ribbentrop in line.

Goering, of course, flourished. He was in Hitler's good books, designed endless uniforms to go with the dozen hats he wore, and strutted round Berlin with epaulettes the size of a fruit-tart. He collected decorations the way other people collect stamps and used to blackmail his acquaintances among the old princely families to disgorge the grand cross of their ancestral order. Prince Windisch-grätz, who was very hard up, was one of them, and told me that this little pleasure had cost him £150. Goering was a complete child, no fool, and not a man to be trifled with, but conscious deep down that he was only a façade and could only maintain his position by bluff. He wallowed in the fat life he had organized for himself, and Hitler realized he would do anything to hold on to its fruits. When it came to rash and illegal action, Hitler knew where to find the man to carry it out for him. My own relations with Goering started to cool about this time. When I had been in London looking into the *Reichstag* fire libel I had remarked to someone: "Goering is not really a National-Socialist at all. He is a military-Socialist, a soldier of fortune." This had been reported back to him and cut him to the quick, as it was what many of the old Nazis held against him. "Don't let me ever hear of you saying that again, Hanfstaengl," he threatened, "or I'll know how to deal with you."

Most of the others were still background figures. Ley was a drunk. Himmler was still a bureaucrat, laying the foundations of his future power. Hitler felt he could rely on him: "He is one of those people who do their duty with icy determination," he commented to me once. Himmler's background as an agricultural student explains much. You will seldom find country-people looking at the landscapes in the Munich Pinakothek, but they will go in droves to spend hours at the German museum of technical inventions. Instead of gazing at gold-framed landscapes by van Gogh, they would rather finger through the pages of the newest International Harvester catalogue and look at illustrations of new threshing-machines. Heinrich Himmler was of that type. To him Germany was nothing but a big estate, with himself in charge of its safety precautions. If something was deteriorating it had to be improved or discontinued, if something was sick it had to be quarantined, if it spread contagion it had to be sterilized or liquidated. Suffering beasts do not perturb a farmer overmuch. As a rule they do not belong to the Society for the Prevention of Cruelty to Animals. Himmler inverted Darwin's theories as justification for turning human beings back into animals and saw himself as a sort of universal horse-doctor responsible for their selective breeding.

Himmler's prime virtue in Hitler's eyes was his unflinching loyalty. On some occasion I referred jokingly to him in his presence as 'our Fouché'. Himmler quite politely declined the allusion: "No, please, not that." He obviously felt that Fouché was too much the type of the political turncoat to be mentioned even jokingly in connexion with any man of honour.

Hess, in his ill-defined capacity as head of the Party liaison staff, tried to act as Hitler's middleman. His actions were disowned by Hitler so often that in the end he never took a decision, but put people off with vague promises of looking into the matter. Exasperated regional leaders coined a phrase to describe his attitude: 'Come unto me all ye that are weary and heavy laden, and I will do nothing.' Hess was already becoming highly peculiar and went in for vegetarianism, nature cures, and other weird beliefs. It got to the point where he would not go to bed without testing with a divining-rod whether there were any subterranean watercourses which conflicted with the direction of his couch. His wife used to complain: "I have as much experience out of our marriage as a candidate for confirmation." Bormann was still Hess's assistant. He was tidy, modest and thrifty, and, I thought, a good influence, as he and Hess waged a continuous campaign against corruption in the Party, and Bormann tried to keep orderly accounts. Hess gradually became a nobody, a flag without a pole. Even Hitler once said to me of his capacity as Party deputy: "I only hope he never has to take over from me. I would not know who to be more sorry for. Hess or the Party."

The only thing they all had in common were their petty rivalries and jealousies. Goering and Goebbels hated each other in their competition to make the biggest splash in Berlin; Goering and Roehm hated each other in their fight to curry favour with the Army. Even the personally mild Himmler had his knife into Goebbels, who had tried to turn Hitler's mind against the S.S. cavalry unit, which he described as smacking of class privilege. It was the apple of the old veterinary student's eye. Goering hated Hess, whom he called a *piesel* – a sort of half-gentleman, for having failed to turn up without excuse at a birthday party given by the Crown Prince. There was no end to it, like wild cats in a cage. I used to think of something Hitler had said to Anna Drexler in 1932: "If I come to power, I shall take good care to avoid what happened to Wilhelm II, who would tolerate no one near him who told him the truth. That I will never allow." With him it was even worse. None of them knew anything and he would not listen.

*   *   *

I had been stunned by the evidence at the 1933 Party rally in Nuremberg that the Nazi revolution, instead of having run its course and settling down into a renewed pattern of law and order was, on the contrary, only beginning. Instead of decreasing, radicalism was furtively increasing. Too many of us realized too late that the regeneration of the national life and economy was only part of the goal. Hitler and a majority of his followers really believed their anti-clerical, anti-Semitic, anti-Bolshevist, xenophobic catch-phrases and were prepared to keep the whole country in uproar in order to put them into practical effect.

I had formed a close friendship with the Italian ambassador, Cerruti, and his delightful wife Elisabetta. They kept the most civilized *salon* in Berlin. It must be realized that Mussolini was a relatively reputable figure at the time. His Fascist revolution enjoyed the approval of conservative circles in a number of countries and certainly his régime was still mercifully free of the anti-clerical, anti-Semitic radicalism I found so alarming in the Nazis. The two régimes, although similar in nature, were on opposite sides of the diplomatic fence. Italy was still one of the victorious allies, and Nazi intrigues in Austria, in an area which the Italians considered the nerve centre of their southern European sphere of influence, was a constant source of friction between the two countries. I determined to see whether the influence of Mussolini could not be invoked to restore more settled conditions in Germany.

The occasion was provided, curiously enough, by a first-class row I had with Goebbels. During 1933 I had tried to supplement my meagre income as foreign press chief by collaborating in a film about Horst Wessel. At some period after his death, a well-known German author named Hans Heinz Ewers, whom I had met in New York during the First World War, had conceived the idea of writing Wessel's biography and had asked me to introduce him to Hitler to obtain the necessary permission. Ewers' literary reputation at the time was somewhat doubtful. He had first made his name with novels of a distinctly erotic tinge, but he was an able writer and his book had glossed over the subject's more unpleasant characteristics and given the story an idealistic slant. Wessel, astonishingly enough, was the son of a pastor and the emphasis of the biography was on his patriotic idealism, which may have been stretching the facts somewhat, but was certainly not offensive.

Hitler had liked the book and when the Nazis came to power had made no difficulty about Ewers turning it into a film scenario. The author was in touch with me or had seen me again and proposed that I should write the music to it, which I did, using as the climax my not ineffective funeral march. In the end I more or less became assistant producer and was able to use my influence to highlight the patriotic message and respectable early background of Wessel, while omitting the more unpleasant aspects of Nazi ideology. We had an uproarious time during some of the location shots. One scene was to be a battle between the S.A. brigade to which Horst Wessel had belonged and the Communists, to be shot in the same Berlin suburb of Wedding where the original brawls had taken place.

It turned out to be too realistic for words. We had persuaded a number of members of the original Horst Wessel *Staffel* to take part, borrowed a number of authentic Communist banners from the Nazi Party museum in the Prinz Albrecht Palais for their film opponents and requisitioned a number of Berlin police in their uniforms as extras. The trouble was that most of the inhabitants of Wedding were as Communist as ever and when they heard a crowd of supers bawling their old battle cries really thought that the counter-revolution had started. They poured out of their houses, beat up our S.A. film heroes, threw flower-pots from their windows, assaulted the police and generally had a field day. The result of course was chaos but magnificent film material. It could not have been more realistic. There was blood everywhere, police helmets rolling in the gutters and confusion unbounded. It looked like something out of the French Revolution.

Proud of our realism, we worked on the other scenes with a will. We had a top flight actor, Paul Wegener, playing a Communist agitator, made up to look rather like Lenin and although some of the other parts were not so effectively done, there is no doubt it was good stirring stuff. I showed Hitler and Heinrich Hoffmann a rough cut and they seemed to like it well, but I had reckoned without Goebbels, and probably Hoffmann's tattle-taling. The première was arranged. The invitations had gone out. Everyone in Berlin society from the Crown Prince down was to be present and suddenly Goebbels forbade the film to be shown.

This was too much. A lot of money had been tied up in the production and now ruin stared us in the face. I stormed in to see Hitler and then Goebbels, but the little man had invented a thousand excuses why it was not to be shown, although his real reason was jealousy. It was too bourgeois in approach, emphasized Horst Wessel's Christian background too much, was not full of the National-Socialist revolutionary spirit, was trite—everything was wrong. Daluege, who had taken over the police under Hitler, had complained that showing his men rolling in the gutter was bad for discipline and so on. In the end a bowdlerized version was allowed to be shown with, I think, twenty-seven cuts and under the meaningless title of *The Hans Westmar Story*. It could never hope to return its outlay.

This led to my Italian visit. I will not pretend it was purely disinterested. I hoped that if we could get the film shown there we might see our money back. I talked to the Cerrutis, who thought that this would be an admirable reason for seeing Mussolini and would give me an opportunity of broaching wider subjects. They gave me a very nice letter of introduction and I set off for Rome.

I had told Neurath of my plans, which he regarded as an excellent idea. His son was a secretary at the Rome embassy, where our representative at the time was von Hassell, married to a daughter of Admiral von Tirpitz and even better known later as an opponent and victim of Hitler in the Putsch of July 20, 1944. Even at this early stage they had made it clear to Mussolini that there were influential groups in Germany who were very unhappy at the course of events. There was no difficulty in obtaining an interview with Il Duce.

Nevertheless, I got a distinctly cool and formal greeting when I marched into his huge room in the Palazzo Venezia. He was by no means sure that I had not come on Hitler's behalf to sound him out and that the Cerrutis had not exaggerated my independent attitude. He asked a few curt questions about Hitler and when I got on to the subject of the film, indicated rather brusquely that if I would care to leave a print with his staff he would have it shown and give me a decision. In desperation I made up a cock-and-bull story about the print being in bad shape owing to the cuts which had been made, some of which we had surreptitiously replaced and that only the German projectionist I had brought with me would be able to handle it.

Casting round for something to mollify his attitude, I produced feverishly from my brief-case the book of Hitler caricatures I had put together and even a copy of my own *From Marlborough to Mirabeau*. In the end he responded and named a time for me to show the film privately to him at the Villa Torlonia. Fortunately he liked it, complimented me on the music, and I plucked up courage to ask if I could have a further interview with him to discuss more serious matters. He agreed.

This second visit took place on February 17, 1934. Mussolini was in a much more affable and forthcoming mood. He stood up and offered me a seat on the other side of his huge desk, and as I sat down I noticed on a small side-table the flasks of yoghourt and rusks with which he fed his stomach-ulcer. For a moment he bent his head as he flipped idly at the pages of the Hitler caricature book and I saw on his *café au lait* coloured Imperial Roman skull the gross carbuncle which was always so carefully erased from his official photographs. He looked up: "There is something you wanted to say to me."

I pulled myself together. "Your Excellency, I would like to speak with you quite openly, as man to man. Relations between our two countries are bad. It seems to me entirely wrong that these difficulties should exist between our two Fascist States. I am very worried about developments and have had many talks on the subject with the Italian ambassador in Berlin. . . ." "I know, I know," Mussolini interrupted. "You must realize," I went on, "that I am seeing you without either Herr Hitler's knowledge or permission. When I say that there are disturbing tendencies within the Nazi Party, it is my private opinion. We have too many old members who have failed to realize that they now not only represent the Party but that they represent Germany as well. They think they can use the same cow-boy-and-Indian methods abroad as brought them to power at home. I have found it impossible, for instance, to impress Herr Hitler with the danger of the behaviour of the Nazi leader in Austria, Habicht——"

Mussolini's fist hit the table and he glared at me: "Habik! . . . Habik! . . . Do your people not understand what a dangerous and irresponsible policy that is?" I saw I was on difficult ground and returned to my original theme. "Your Excellency came to power within two years. Herr Hitler is encumbered with a movement which grew to $2\frac{1}{2}$ million members over the fourteen years of his campaign. The S.A. cannot be disbanded to swell the ranks of the unemployed and too many of our leaders have been conspirators for so long that they cannot adapt themselves to ordered circumstances."

Mussolini nodded. "That I understand. It is not easy. But Herr Hitler is a superb organizer and must tame his party zealots. You cannot allow *soldateska* to run a nation's foreign politics. A State means law and order and where there is a leader there must be discipline. There are always people who are useful in making a revolution, but when victory has been achieved they are dangerous and they have to be got rid of." I wondered if he was thinking of Roehm.

In his fluent but fascinatingly accented German, Mussolini was being very frank and saying just the things I wanted to hear. I decided to come to the point. "Your Excellency, it seems to me essential that you and Herr Hitler should meet. You are both admirers of Wagner and that will give a common starting-point. Think what it would mean if you invited him to the Palazzo Vendramin in Venice where Richard Wagner died. He would gain the benefit of your long experience and obtain much-needed insight into the problems of Europe as seen from outside Germany." To my delight Mussolini accepted the idea and I undertook to win Hitler over. I could hardly believe my good fortune. At last Hitler would hear from an equal some of the political facts of life he did not seem prepared to grasp. Moreover, he would hear them in his own language and they could meet alone. It would not even be necessary to have an interpreter.

As I got up to leave I asked Mussolini if he would sign a photograph, to which he agreed in high humour. Then I slid him a second one. He hesitated a moment, "Who is this one for?" he asked suspiciously. "It would help if I could take your greetings to Herr Hitler," I said. He bent over again and wrote: *"A Adolfo Hitler — Benito Mussolini, Roma, Febbraio* 1934." I slipped open my brief-case again and brought out a copy of a short memorandum I had written—no diplomat could have worked on this plan more carefully than I had—which contained suggested arrangements for the meeting. "I will give the other copy to Herr Hitler when I get to Berlin," I said. "When are you leaving?" Mussolini asked. "As soon as possible," I replied, eager to attack the other half of the problem. *"Va bene dottore,"* Mussolini saluted me, "give the Führer my best wishes."

I was still in a state of euphoria when I got back to Munich, only to be brought back to earth with a bump while I was still looking for a taxi to take me home from the station. Quite by chance I ran into two old friends who immediately seized me by the arm and said: "Thank heaven you're back, Putzi. The Party is trying to take over the German-American school out at Nymphenburg. They want to make a Hitler Youth leadership college out of it, or something. Poor Dr. Pfeiffer is at his wits' end. You have got to do something to help him." Oh! my God, I thought, here they are at it again worse than ever. I promised to do what I could, shook off my friends and found my taxi. In effect this seizure was something I was able to stop. I got hold of Neurath and told him what a deplorable effect this would have on German-American relations and the order was rescinded. The director was eternally grateful. In fact, of all the people I helped in these troubled times, I think he was the only one who not only did not forget but responded in kind when I was in trouble. On my return to Germany in 1947 I found that in spite of my break with Hitler and the years of exile, attempts were being made to seize the Uffing house under the de-Nazification laws. It was entirely thanks to Dr. Pfeiffer that the authorities were persuaded to see reason.

As soon as I got home I ascertained that Hitler was in Berlin and I left for the capital the next morning. Arriving at the *Reichskanzlei* the first person I saw, of course, was Schaub, ignorant and inquisitive as ever and on the look-out for a reason to block anything he did not like the sound of. He asked in his gross Bavarian way, what I had been up to, why I wanted to see Hitler, and maintained he was so booked up that it would be impossible for me to see him in private. Fortunately, at that point the door opened and Hitler himself came in. He seemed in a good mood: "Good morning, Hanfstaengl, where have you been all this time?" he asked. "I have good news for you, Herr Hitler. I am just back from Rome." His mental shutters narrowed perceptibly. "I have something very important to tell you." I could see the Chauffeureska getting ready to pounce. "Well, what is it, then?" Hitler asked. "Surely you can tell me here." "Herr Hitler, I really must ask to see you alone this time." "Very well, then, if it is so important," he said resignedly, and walked down the corridor with me to the music *salon*.

"Now what is it?" "Herr Hitler, I have just had an interview with Mussolini. . . ." He had been chewing a nail and looking out of the window, but he swung round: "What on earth do you mean, Hanfstaengl? You know how we stand with those people. . . ." "Herr Hitler, I assure you, I have seen him three times, twice in private audience. He has asked me to bring you his best wishes and to say that he will be pleased to invite you to Italy for a conference." I could hear feet shuffling outside in the corridor. The Chauffeureska were not going to miss this. The door was slightly ajar as Hitler had not let me shut it fully as we came in. "What is this nonsense, Hanfstaengl? What are you talking about? What were you doing in Rome, anyway?" I said that I had gone originally to arrange for the distribution of the *Hans Westmar* film in Italy, and this, of course, gave Hitler a splendid opportunity to back away from the main point of the conversation and slate the film again.

In desperation I took out of my brief-case the copy of the memorandum concerning suggested arrangements for the visit which I had given to Mussolini. Hitler looked at it suspiciously. "Is this supposed to be an invitation from the Italian Government?" Hitler asked. "It is nothing of the sort." It was time to produce my trump card. I had gone to Prantl, the former royal Bavarian purveyors of stationery in Munich, and bought a handsome silver frame for the Mussolini photograph, while being very careful to remove from the back the price (it had cost 72 marks) and the name of the maker. "What is more, Herr Hitler, Il Duce has dedicated this photograph to you," I said. "Just look at the superscription."

As I suspected, Hitler looked at the frame back and front, but this was a piece of evidence he could not get round. "Think what an opportunity this offers, Herr Hitler," I said, warming to my work. "It would make all the difference in the world to our position. Can I not have Mussolini informed that you accept the invitation in principle. You must grasp the opportunity while the iron is hot." But Hitler was not going to let any part of the triumph be mine. "This is not something we can enter into overnight, Hanfstaengl," he said crossly. "You see everything with the eyes of a journalist. I cannot possibly get away from Berlin as easily as that. We shall have to consider this matter very carefully."

"But this invitation is the one way out of our present situation," I went on feverishly. "I am convinced that if only you can have a private heart-to-heart talk with Mussolini. . . ." An adjutant knocked on the door and came in: "*Mein Führer,* the gentlemen are here." "You see, Hanfstaengl, how limited my time is," said Hitler, only too pleased at the interruption. Outside stood Generals Reichenau and Fritsch. "Look what Mussolini has just sent me," Hitler greeted them triumphantly, waving my picture-frame in the air. "*Aber mein Führer das ist fabelhaft. Kolossal,*" they chorused, and went happily off down the corridor with him. I was left alone. I had put the most superb trump into his hand and had not received a word of thanks. Whenever I tried to follow it up, he put me off or said that they were still studying the matter, that the time was not yet ripe, anything to keep me off the subject of my brain-child. How much longer can I stand this, I thought. Will nothing ever bring him to reason.

The European political barometer was set at stormy. The Disarmament Conference showed signs of collapse. Dr. Sauerbruch had examined the old President and was of the opinion that he had not many months to live. A few weeks later I was in Rome again, sitting at the side of the then Italian Minister for Propaganda, Count Ciano, at the première of the Italian version of our film, which was being shown under the title *Uno di Tanti* (One of Many). Mussolini was not there. He had received no answer, and relations between Germany and Italy continued to deteriorate.

CHAPTER XIII

A MURDERER'S WELCOME

Palm Court interlude – Disguised departure – Shock on the high seas – Harvard, class of '09 – The liquidation of Roehm – Assassin at bay – The mad hatter's lunch party – The Flying Dutchman.

IF HITLER did not want to tell you anything, wild horses would not drag it out of him. During the spring I tried several times to find out what his intentions were concerning the proposed trip to Italy, but he always found some airy circumlocution. I did not even know whether he had written a letter of thanks for the photograph. Not only was there no sign of any decrease in the hostility and suspicion in Germany's European neighbours, but there was a general, indefinable rise in the internal temperature. The jealousies and conflicts between the Party leaders grew more acrid and seemed to polarize round Roehm and Goebbels on the one hand, with their constant demands for greater rewards for the old Party fighters and S.A., and Goering and, to a certain extent, Himmler on the other, who represented the group more satisfied with their share of the spoils.

I was sitting in my office one afternoon when Otto Dietrich came on the line: "Hanfstaengl, you must come over to the Kaiserhof at once. There is no one to have tea with 'him'. Everyone else is away somewhere and I simply cannot make it." I groaned. It seemed that I had sunk to the position of Reichs stop-gap. I found Hitler sitting in his favourite palm court corner, not far from the pseudo-Hungarian orchestra. I assumed he wanted to be entertained, so we sat and talked about Wagner and Ludwig II, Strauss waltzes and what a pity it was he had never learned to dance, while Hitler beat time to some of the melodies. The lounge had in the meantime filled up. Word that Hitler was in the hotel always got around quickly and I believe more than one waiter even earned extra tips for spreading the news by telephone.

I cannot say that the public was of the best class. There would be a few provincial visitors, who doubtless carried a highly coloured tale home with them, but most of the clientele seemed to consist of over-dressed women, not entirely *demi-monde* and not entirely respect-able, either, who flounced in with furs and just that too much French perfume. You did not see any of the women, often of quite good family, who had identified themselves, from idealistic motives, with the Hitler movement during the last couple of years before it came to power. The Kaiserhof parade was made up of that fickle and feckless strata of society which always finds it convenient to associate itself with success. I thought back on his propaganda catch-words about the spartan life and how the true German woman was the home body who did not smoke, drink, or use cosmetics. The reality had proved otherwise. Hitler looked up at these women as they walked by with eyes that would have been lecherous if there had been any capacity to back them up.

"*Die blonde Front* is well represented today," I remarked rather sourly. The place looked like a metropolitan version of the Venus-berg. Hitler snapped back into his tragic Tannhäuser role: "*Mein lieber* Hanfstaengl, I have ceased to have a private life," he said. More is the pity, I thought. There was certainly no evidence that his tastes had become any less bizarre. It was around this time, or maybe somewhat later, that Party intimates were beginning to talk about two little ballet-girls, introduced by the egregious Goebbels, who from time to time were let out of a back gate of the *Reichskanzlei* in the early hours of the morning. They were sisters and always together, and the stories concerning them certainly did not indicate that Hitler was becoming normal, quite the contrary. Later, about the time I escaped, he developed a taste for watching the female cabaret artistes and acrobats at the Scala music-hall, and the less clothing they wore the better Hitler was pleased. I met one of them during my exile in London, of whom the best description would be that she was an experienced cynic: "You know, your Mr. Hitler is just an old *voyeur*," she said with a grimace.

My remark seemed to have brought him back to his public per-sonality again. It seemed a good opportunity to bring up the subject of Venice. I could get little response. "I don't see how anything can come out of the idea, Hanfstaengl. I have too much to do here and cannot possibly get away. The way things are building up. . . ." He broke off in mid-sentence. What has he got on his mind, I wondered. He gave no further sign and started to turn absent-mindedly the pages of one of the illustrated papers. I decided to broach another problem of my own: "If that is the case, Herr Hitler," I said, "you will not be needing me here. Have you any objection to my taking a short trip to the United States?" Hitler looked at me suspiciously: "What do you want to do there? Sell that film of yours?" "No," I answered, "this year is the twenty-fifth reunion of my Harvard class and it is more or less a point of honour to attend. It would be a good opportunity to talk to old friends; some of them are very influential by now. I may even see President Roosevelt." Hitler put on his mock sleepy act, rubbing his eyes with his knuckles: "Well, yes, as far as I am concerned. I have no objection." No messages, no instructions, nothing but a feigned disinterestedness.

My acceptance of the invitation leaked to the press in the States, and many of the newspapers conducted something of a campaign against my visit. I was sitting at home in Munich practising a Chopin *étude* which has always eluded me, when our dyed-in-the wool Bavarian cook knocked on the door of the studio and announced: "*Herr Dokta, Botsdam* is on the line." I was cross at being interrupted, the more so because I suspected the call was not even for me. We had had Prince Auwi staying with us for a few days and he had only just left, so I assumed that this was one of his contacts a bit behind the times. Instead, a female voice said through a cloud of atmospherics: "This is Boston. Is that Dr. Hanfstaengl?" She put me on to Elliott Cutler, our class president, who had very kindly rung me up to warn me about the press campaign. When I said that it would probably be better if I did not come after all, he would not hear of it, but suggested that it would be better if I came in a purely private capacity without too much fuss.

To camouflage my departure I held a garden-party at my Pariser Platz house in Berlin the day before I left. Everyone who was anyone in the capital was there, with the exception of Hitler, Goering and Goebbels, although the wives of the last two put in a formal appearance. The big Nazi trio cried off rather ostentatiously, with Hitler making up some cock-and-bull excuse about being afraid of compromising himself if cornered by one of the foreign diplomats, who would then probably send a totally false report of their conversation home. He was particularly afraid of Cerruti, which I took as a bad sign.

The next morning I rather melodramatically put on a pair of dark glasses, turned up the collar of my raincoat, and flew to Cologne, where I had arranged to join the German post office plane carrying the last batch of mail to the liner *Europa* at Cherbourg, its last European port of call on the outward journey. I might just as well have saved myself the trouble. Although I hurried up the gangway at the last moment, within a couple of hours everybody on board knew I was there. Lord Fermoy and his twin brother, Maurice Roach, Harvard room-mates, had seen me. Even the press had got hold of the fact.

That was relatively unimportant. Catastrophic was the news-flash the steward brought in with my breakfast in mid-Atlantic: "Venice, June 14. This morning Adolf Hitler's private plane landed at Venice airport. It was met by Mussolini, who conducted his guest, etc. etc." The swine, I thought, the double-crossing swine. He misleads me for weeks, waits until my back is turned, and then takes up my suggestion when he knows I cannot be there to guide the conversation along the right lines. Of course, Neurath and Hassell were there in their official capacities, but they were side-tracked, and there was no one to intervene in order to modify the Party line. Hitler had not even taken Goering with him, who might have introduced at least a measure of common sense. He just had his bosom cronies, Schaub, Brückner, Otto and Sepp Dietrich. We now know that he talked to Mussolini as if he was a public meeting and that this first contact was a near fiasco. Even if Mussolini did manage to say his piece about the necessity of removing the incurable revolutionaries, it was to have, before the month was out, a totally different effect to the one I had intended.

My arrival in New York was nothing if not colourful. The streets just beyond the dock area were filled with thousands of people shouting only barely discernible slogans. However, they left nothing to chance, as they were carrying banners and streamers with such phrases as: 'Oust Nazi Hanfstaengl' – 'Ship the Hitler agents back' – 'Free Ernst Thälmann'. It was a Left-Wing demonstration of considerable proportions.

The captain of the *Europa*, Commodore Scharf, called me up to the bridge, handed me his binoculars and said that there could be no question of me leaving by the main gate. I was in something of a dilemma. He was there to protect his ship, not me. The problem was, however, solved by the appearance of six extremely natty young gentlemen in brand-new Harvard blazers and ties, the senior of whom introduced himself: "Good morning, sir, my name is Benjamin Goodman, New York police department, and these are colleagues of mine." He showed me his pass and added: "President Roosevelt has sent a message to say that he hopes you will have a pleasant visit. We are here to ensure that there will be no incidents." I was obliged to leave the ship with them in a pinnace and was deposited far uptown at Grant's tomb.

It meant I had to curtail my programme somewhat and omit my promised visits to the museums and other old haunts, but I got to Boston without further trouble and the outcry somewhat died down. I stayed privately, saw old friends, and tried to put a bold face on what had happened in Germany. One morning the President of Harvard of my time, Professor Lawrence Lowell, called at the Cutler's house, where I was staying, and asked me to explain National-Socialism to him.

"You must realize how it started," I said. "We lost a war, had the Communists in control of the streets and had to try to build things up again. In the end, the Republic had thirty-two parties, all of them too weak to do anything of consequence, and finally it was necessary to roll them up into a State party, and that was Hitler. If a car gets stuck in the mud and begins to sink deeper and deeper and the engine stops, and then a man comes along and pours something into the works which starts it up again, you don't ask what it was he put in. You set to and get the damned thing out. It may only have been *Begeisterungsschnapps*, a mixture of mother's ruin and exaltation, but it is enough for the time being." And wise old Lowell looked at me and said: "This whatever-you-called-it, may be all right to start with, but what happens when the driver gets drunk on it?" That was it, of course he was right. I also received a rebuff from the current President of Harvard, Professor James Conant. I had offered to put up $1,000 towards founding a scholarship for American students coming to Germany. I had even arranged with several German mayors to subsidize them further when they got there. But Conant suspected that the money came from Hitler, which it did not, and turned down the offer.

The high point of these major reunions is the parade in the football stadium, which holds 80,000 people. The whole thing is an absolute circus, confetti, streamers, brass bands, and total confusion. We marched in straggling ranks, and there was a corpulent little fellow at my side whom, with the best will in the world, I could not for the life of me remember. He made himself very friendly and half-way towards the middle of the stadium, amidst the roar of applause that was going on, rather ostentatiously shook my hand. I only learnt later that his name was Max Pinansky, a judge from the State of Maine and a Jew. This gesture had the huge crowd in a frenzy and was caught by all the news-photographers, to appear on the front page of all the afternoon papers. I found myself, without having taken any initiative in the matter at all, more or less the hero of the hour. 'Hanfstaengl buries the hatchet' was the sense of the comments and, of course, it made marvellous pro-German propaganda, worth a hundred interviews with Hitler. At least it should have done. I was to pay for it later.

When I left Boston I spent a couple of days at Newport, Rhode Island, and attended the Astor-French wedding, the social event of the summer. The marriage took place in the Trinity Church on Saturday, June 30, 1934. I was sitting in the Astor pew, next to the aisle, enjoying the scene and thinking what an enviable life these really rich American families lived, when a rather scruffy fellow tapped me on the elbow. He had crept up the church on all fours. "Can you comment on this, Doctor?" he asked, handing me a crumpled Associated Press despatch: "This morning Captain Roehm and his followers were arrested by Adolf Hitler. They were taken from Wiessee to Stadelheim, where Captain Roehm, who, together with his followers, has been accused of plotting against the present régime, was executed. . . ." There followed a long list of names of people I knew, including even Count Helldorf, the Berlin chief of police, which proved to be an error. "Not here—later—outside," I managed to mutter, and then almost felt my knees give way. The orchids, rhododendrons and roses swam before my eyes. I dimly heard the priest saying, "Will you, John Jacob Astor. . . . Will you, Ellen Tuck French . . ." and the dull boom of the organ.

I racked my brains. For years my contact with Roehm had been minimum and formal, although he was always polite and even friendly and had seemed to regard me as a possible channel into the *Reichskanzlei*. He had even tried to persuade me that the accusations against him of homosexuality were invented by his enemies, although he must have been pretty desperate to try and bluff me. I had sensed the rising tension within the Party, knew of the aversion of Reichenau and the Army to the S.A. and was aware that Roehm and his brownshirts felt that they had been baulked of what they considered a fair share of the spoils of power. At the Nuremberg Party rally in the autumn of 1933 there had been a tremendous row between Streicher and Roehm when the latter refused to carry out Streicher's arrangements for the ceremony. "No one is going to dictate to the S.A.," Roehm had ranted, and had then drawn up separate plans of his own for the march past.

The night before I left for the States I had received an invitation to a social evening and cabaret show at his S.A. headquarters in Berlin's Standartenstrasse. I thought I would put in a brief appearance and arrived in the foyer very late to find the entertainment well under way. My intention was to excuse myself and disappear, so I sent word in to Roehm and waited. I stood looking at the opulent *décor*, Gobelin tapestries, valuable paintings, superb crystal mirrors, thick pile carpets and gleaming antique furniture. It looked like a millionaire's brothel. From the big hall inside came the clink of glasses and a roar of applause and conversation, with an unpleasant overtone of falsetto screeching.

The main door flew open and Roehm lurched out, his plump cheeks shining, a fat cigar in one hand and obviously drunk. Barely greeting me, he immediately launched into the most extraordinary tirade I have ever heard, cursing, shouting, threatening, and, as far as I could make out in the flood of words, concentrating his fury on

General von Reichenau: "Tell that friend of yours that he is a swine" was more or less the tenor of his remarks. "He has got Hitler on his side and does nothing but threaten me and the S.A." "Perhaps he is afraid of the effect of so many S.A. demonstrations on international and particularly French public opinion," I tried to interject. This brought another outburst. "But what does that matter? It is time the French learnt their place," he shouted. He was raving like a maniac. "For God's sake, Roehm, watch what you are saying," I implored, and in the end managed to extricate myself and take my leave. I could make neither head nor tail of what he had been saying and wondered what dark game was going on behind the scenes.

Now Roehm was dead. I managed to get rid of my newspaper acquaintance and his colleagues in some way by declaring in all honesty that I had not the faintest idea what had happened. The reports of an intended uprising made no sense at all, and made even less when further names were added: Schleicher, Strasser, Bose in Papen's office. The thing did not add up at all. I wondered for a moment whether I should return, but my family was still there, so I sent a guarded message to Neurath through the German Consul-General in New York and he indicated in reply that I should come back at all costs. The sailing dates so coincided that I found myself on board the *Europa* again.

In the English Channel we heard on the wireless Hitler's apologia before the *Reichstag* for the action he had taken. As probably the only man on board with real inner knowledge I was totally nonplussed and more angry than ever. The most extraordinary aspect was Hitler's claim to have been surprised and disgusted by the evidence of Roehm's homosexuality. This I knew to be a flat lie. As far back as the summer of 1932, in the middle of the *Reichstag* election campaign, a journalist named Bell, who had ingratiated himself with Roehm, had produced very precise details of the life the S.A. chief was leading, which had been splashed all over the opposition papers. I remember Hitler sitting on a folding chair in some beer-garden or other looking stonily at these reports and biting his small finger-nail, the sure sign of an impending storm.

We had all gone on to the Brown House, where Roehm was waiting, and the two of them disappeared into Hitler's office. The row that followed beggars description. It went on literally for hours, and some indication of the way that Hitler was shouting can be obtained from the fact that every window-frame in the building was buzzing with the noise. When I left for home in disgust he was still at it. It sounded like a continuous minor earthquake. The following day Roehm filed a libel action, which, of course, never reached court. Shortly after the Nazis came to power, Bell was found shot dead at the house to which he had retired in the Austrian Tyrol. The murderers were never found. An even more unbelievable passage in Hitler's speech was his suggestion that Roehm had been plotting with the representative of a foreign power—the clear inference being that it was François-Poncet, the French ambassador, an assertion so unlikely in view of Roehm's last conversation with me, that I almost commented aloud in the middle of the saloon. The moment I got back to Germany I besieged people for information. What appalled me was the fact that these people, however unpleasant the character of Roehm and some of his S.A. followers might have been, had been shot without trial, defence or process of law. I found my old friend General von Epp in despair. He had seriously considered cutting his roots and leaving the country and only the thought that his place as *Reichsstatthalter* would then be taken by the impossible Bavarian Gauleiter Wagner had determined him to remain. At Hess's liaison staff, where my offices were, the people behaved as if they were chloroformed. There was simply no information to be had. 'Thank your stars you were not there. It was a question of who fired first,' was the only reaction I could get.

Hitler, I discovered, was with the Goebbels in Heiligendamm, the very first and then still the most exclusive German Baltic sea-resort. I rang up and announced my arrival. I found a sort of cloud-cuckoo-land, hemmed in between the thick belt of pine-trees on the land side and the great bank of shingle protecting it from the sea. I got there to find the hotel where Hitler's party was staying almost deserted. "The Führer is not down yet," the adjutant told me, "but Herr and Frau Dr. Goebbels are on the beach with the children." It was like a scene out of some well-bred theatrical comedy of high society. I assured myself of a room for the night and wandered down to the line of spotless beach-huts. "Magda, look who has turned up," said the only too well-known voice, and there was the little cripple in flannels, for all the world like a rich paterfamilias greeting an old family friend. I must see Hitler, I thought, or I shall go mad.

"If you can come up now, Herr Doktor, the Führer can see you," the manager said on my return to the hotel. It was not a private interview. As usual, we were interrupted by the continuous to-and-fro of his ubiquitous immediate entourage. But for our greeting we were alone. He was sitting by the window, turning over mechanically the sheets of the daily press report that Goebbels now prepared for him. He looked up at me with a hostile glance and said – psychologists please note: *"Da sind Sie ja, Mister Hanfstaengl! Hat man Sie denn noch nicht totgeschlagen?"* – "So there you are. Haven't they done you in yet?" He pronounced my name in the High German fashion, with 's' like an English 's'. This was always a storm signal. If he used the normal German 'sh' sound I knew that things were more or less normal.

I really think I got black spots before the eyes. There was the 'Mister', too, a deliberately offensive reference to my Anglo-Saxon outlook. It was one of those moments when the impressions of a lifetime flash across one's inner mind like a speeded-up film. I suddenly saw a picture of his untidy little flat in the Thierschstrasse and the haggard-looking orator of genius who stood there in the hall, hungry for the beauties and success of life. The long years in between dissolved again into the livid face in front of me. I realized it was the contorted face of a murderer defiantly at bay, a pathological murderer who had tasted blood and acquired an appetite for more. Through the window came the vague and familiar sounds of a seaside resort. I pulled myself together with a shudder. What does one answer in such circumstances? I decided to put on a bold front.

"No, Herr Hitler, the Communists in New York did not get me after all," I answered, handing him over a bunch of press photographs and news clippings. Hitler seemed to take a moment to readjust himself. "Oh, that," he said. "I cannot believe that was so dangerous. We did away with that sort of demonstration in Germany some time ago." He flipped idly through the pictures and stopped at the one showing me with the Jewish judge at Harvard:

"Nice friends you have," he commented. "What sort of propaganda is that for the Party when the foreign press chief fraternizes with a Jew?" I tried to explain that the Jewish population in America was very large and that they were respected members of the community, but he cut me off short.

There was a moment's pause. "Hanfshtaengl [that started to sound a little better], you ought to have been there." What was he trying to say? He had used the more familiar pronunciation of my name, but what was he getting at? That I should have been on the June 30 list? "Have been where . . . ," I stammered. "In Venice, of course. Mussolini would have been pleased to see you again." His bad conscience has caused him to improvise a crass lie, although the old catch-phrase made it clear that the meeting had been a failure. "Well, that was hardly my fault," I answered heatedly. "I kept in touch with you about it right up until the moment I left. . . ." "I know, I know," he said, "but it was all arranged in a hurry at the last moment and by that time you had gone." Who on earth is he trying to fool, I thought.

It was quite clear he was not going to allow me to bring up the matter most on my mind. The door started to open and shut, his people came in and out, and soon we all moved in a body down to the dining-room. It was really like something out of Lewis Carroll, a mad hatter's luncheon party. With the whole of Germany groaning under this atmosphere of murder, fear and suspicion, there was Magda Goebbels doing the honours in an airy summer dress, with several other young women at the table, even one or two from the aristocratic families for whom Heiligendamm had always been the summer resort.

Hitler had undergone a sea-change. He was the jovial, light-hearted charmer, the man of affairs relaxing away from the cares of the world. I was still shaken to the roots by the greeting I had received and responded but dully to his chatter about 'here is our Hanfstaengl again', as if the years had rolled back and I was still the personal friend who had opened for him the doors to the world of art and society. I looked round at the other guests in the room and thought how they would be writing home: "Our table was quite near the Chancellor's. His guests were always in high spirits and all this talk about a crisis in the Party must be complete nonsense. Even Dr. Goebbels is enjoying himself and is out on the beach every day with his wife and children."

Goebbels sat across the table from me, and when someone brought up the subject of my trip to the States he was ready: "Yes, Hanfstaengl. You must tell us how bravely you avoided that Communist demonstration on the pier," he said with his mock gay laugh. I knew it, I said to myself; he has been at Hitler about this. I was in no mood for trifling. "Herr Doktor," I said, "how do you imagine I was to get through that mob alone? In any case, I was a guest in the country and had to conform to the security precautions the authorities had arranged for me." He was not to be put off so easily: "Well, no one can say that your arrival in the Jerusalem of the New World caused a very heroic impression," he went on. "You seem to have forgotten what great care you took during all the election campaigns to drive through back streets and avoid the Communists," I retorted tartly. Someone smoothed over the imminent quarrel. In any case, I was only wasting my breath. By now I was firmly classified as expendable, an unwelcome conscience against whom Hitler's mind was to be systematically poisoned. I learned that after the lunch he had returned to the subject with Hitler and described my arrival in New York as showing a lack of Party spirit and courage in front of the enemy. He even suggested that I should have accepted the challenge and tried to fight my way through. Hitler had just shrugged his shoulders. Such were the conceptions of international relations with which the Nazi leadership sought to impose themselves on the world.

During the afternoon I wandered round disconsolately. Clearly I had reached the point of no return. My last illusions were shattered. Instead of regenerating Germany, we had brought to power a bunch of dangerous gangsters who could now only survive by maintaining the momentum of their ceaseless radical agitation. What on earth were people like me to do? I was a German. My family and my whole thread of life was bound up in its future fate. Did the solution lie in exile or must I still stick with this thing and see if there was any way of applying the brakes? At this time the worst of Hitler's Germany still lay in the future: the concentration camps in

the sense in which we now talk about them, the systematic decima-
tion of the Jews and the plans for armed aggression. In the end
every restraining hand was swept aside by this criminal little inner
group of narrow-minded fanatics. It is given to no man to foresee
the future in its full dimensions, and I, who bore my small personal
share for what had happened, thought, erroneously, that there must
still be opportunities for edging the course of events into more
respectable channels.

Some time in the evening I came across Sepp Dietrich. Most of
the party had gone off on an excursion up the coast somewhere, but
he had returned earlier than the others. He was another Bavarian,
a rough-and-ready fellow, but not as personally hostile to me as the
others. "What in the name of God has been happening?" I asked
him. "I have only spent a day or two in Berlin, but the foreign
correspondents have been buzzing round me like hornets. Is there
not at least a complete list of the people who have been killed? Even
ignoring the question of trials and evidence, there must have been
some order and authority behind it. Who signed the warrants to
execute them? You give out a figure of a few score killed, but the
press people are putting their own lists together and it is starting to
look more like a thousand. Someone must have the correct information and this agitation abroad will never die down until it is given
in black and white." Dietrich as good as admitted that he had been
out at Wiessee with Hitler, but he was not talking. I really think that
even he was shattered by what he had taken part in. "You have no
idea," he muttered, "thank your lucky stars you were not around.
I got my orders signed, but I practically had to force him to put his
signature on them." I thought I saw a chance of breaking him down,
but before I could continue Schaub loomed up from somewhere in
the gloom and joined us, suspicious and surly as ever. The conspiracy
of silence descended again.

I was doing no good in Heiligendamm and the only thing seemed
to be to get back to Berlin. Hitler arrived back at the hotel in due
course, so I made up some excuse about having an early rendezvous
in the capital and took my leave. The picture had built up in my
mind of a man whose momentum had driven him into an extreme
position from which there was no escape, on whom normal arguments

no longer had any effect. His limited provincial mind had finally swallowed this twisted Nordic and Nazi myth *à la* Rosenberg and provided him with the one mental buttress in a dream world of infinite proportions. Beliefs and obsessions, however false, can foster superhuman energy while confusing the senses and destroying all judgement and appreciation of realities. Like an airman in a fog, who loses all contact with the earth and sense of direction, so Hitler, blinded by the cloud of Party and propaganda doctrine, lost progressively his contact with the realities of life.

That night a westerly storm blew up. The sky clouded over and the calm Baltic began to thrash on the shingle beach. Gusts of rain beat against the trees and rattled on the hotel windows. Sitting in my darkened room my thoughts turned to Richard Wagner, who, a hundred years before, sailing in just such weather from Riga to London, and only a few miles from this spot, had received the inspiration for his *Flying Dutchman*. The words of Senta's ballad coursed through my head:

> Have you met the ship upon the sea
> With blood-red sails and black mast?
> High on the deck the pallid man
> Master of the ship keeps unceasing watch.
> How the wind howls!
> How it whistles in the rigging!
> Like an arrow he flies, without aim,
> Without rest, without peace.

The parallel was too perfect. It was at that moment, deep down within me, that Adolf Hitler and I reached the parting of the ways.

CHAPTER XIV

THE LAST CHORD

Aftermath of a purge – What happened at Wiessee – Austrian misadventure – Short shrift at Neudeck – A wheel comes full circle – Funeral March farewell – Analysis of a medium – The prophet and the caliph – The militant revivalist – Pinchbeck Pericles – The tragedy of an orator.

THE NEXT morning, when I got up early, the storm had cleared and I wandered down to the beach for a breath of air before driving to catch the train. On the boat pier about a hundred yards from the hotel I found Princess Viktoria Luise of Brunswick, the daughter of the Kaiser and sister of Auwi. "Your Highness, I must talk to you," I said. So we walked to the end of the pier and sat there for nearly half an hour, while I told her of my complete disillusionment and my conviction that the only thing left was for people of our conservative temperament to dissociate ourselves from this bunch of assassins.

She by no means shared my preoccupations: "Things will calm down again," she answered. "This is probably a turn for the better. At least we have avoided civil war and got rid of those dangerous brownshirts." That, of course, is why Hitler got away with what he had done. A great many people came to believe his explanation that civil war had been avoided. The Army and Right-Wing elements were prepared to overlook the defiance of law and the peripheral deaths of Schleicher and other non-Nazis because the bulk of the victims had come from the feared and radical S.A.

The same atmosphere greeted me on my return to Berlin. 'It was high time – a house-cleaning was necessary – the whole S.A. leadership was corrupt' were the sort of remarks I heard, and not only from Nazis. I was convinced the régime would never recover the prestige and international standing it had lost through its complete disregard of legal processes, whatever the crimes ascribed to the

victims. I fully intended to resign my post, but was implored by
Schacht, Neurath, his State Secretary Bülow and others, to remain
and continue to try to use my position near Hitler as one of the
voices of reason. Politics is very much like a sailing-race, their argument ran. The wind can change from one moment to the next and
if you have jumped out of the boat, you are no longer there to give
a decisive touch to the helm. Even Gürtner, the Minister of Justice,
who had much to answer for in his attitude, hung on to office
because he was afraid that if he left, one of the wild men would take
over his Ministry and the whole judicial system would collapse. "It
is no good, Hanfstaengl, we have got to be patient," he said to me.
"Now this is over we must just try to put the pieces together again."

I made a thorough nuisance of myself everywhere, trying to
compile a proper list of the victims in an attempt to classify them
between those for whose death there had been some sort of authority
and those who had just been murdered out of personal spite or
revenge. I pestered the other people in Hess's liaison office, talked to
Körner, Goering's State Secretary, and tried to put my point over
to all the old Party members I knew. All I got was disinterested
shrugs or brazen effrontery. The survivors were not in the least
ashamed of what had been done. I heard Amann boasting at table
in the Chancellery: "Well, we cleaned that lot up all right," and
even suggesting that Hühnlein, head of the Nazi motor corps, had
been lucky to escape as he did. That was the atmosphere.

I even attempted to enlist the assistance of François-Poncet. We
found ourselves at lunch together with Sir Eric Phipps at the British
Embassy and I accompanied him on his afternoon constitutional to
the end of the Unter den Linden and back. "Your Excellency," I
said, "this matter has got to be cleared up. You are quite obviously
referred to in connexion with Roehm in Hitler's radio speech. Why
do you not get your Government to demand an explanation? Hitler
would then have to put his cards on the table and we would know
what is true and what isn't." He was far too old and wise a hand to
give me any immediate encouragement, but he must have done
something of the sort, although the only result was a statement by
the German Government that investigation had shown he was not,
in fact, implicated.

I had several talks with von Reichenau and his *Reichswehr* colleagues, under the impression that the death of Schleicher would produce on their part a demand for a full inquiry. But even they were prepared to be put off, or put me off, by assurances that all illegal acts during the purge would be brought before the courts. We waited for weeks and months and, of course, nothing ever materialized. I thought Helldorf might be a possible ally and pulled him into my office once out of the corridor to ask what he knew. I told him how in America I had read in the first reports that he was one of the victims. Helldorf was a good friend of mine and one of the more reasonable Party people, as his tragic rôle ten years later in the July 20 plot was to prove. At this earlier juncture he preferred discretion, and a warning, "Let me give you some advice, Hanf-staengl," he said. "Stop being so confoundedly inquisitive. People are beginning to resent it. I will tell you something more. I saw one of those lists they drew up. Your name was on it!"

As I recall, I only saw Hitler once in Berlin during July. He had gone straight from Heiligendamm to Berchtesgaden and was keeping well away from the capital until some of the dust had settled. He slipped in one evening and I managed to catch him the next day after lunch. "Well, Hanfstaengl," he said with a sort of mock joviality, "all this uproar in the foreign press seems to be dying down a bit." "That may be so," I replied, "but I can tell you that their correspondents are still in my hair day and night. Unless you let me give them the true facts and proper justification for all that has happened, the outcry will go on. You must not forget that many of them have been here for a long time. They knew many of the people involved and will continue to draw their own conclusions."

"I ought to send the whole bunch of them packing," Hitler exploded. "They have plenty of dung-heaps to rake over in their own countries and have to turn every mole-hill in Germany into a mountain. They are nothing but a danger to us." I was not going to let him off so lightly and returned to the attack: What was the truth about Roehm's foreign connexions? Who was the ambassador to whom he had referred? In the end he lost his temper. *"Die Akten über den Fall Roehm, mein lieber Hanfstaengl, sind längst geschlossen"* – "The files on the Roehm affair have long been closed," he shouted, and apart from vague accusations that Roehm and Strasser had been plotting with Schleicher and the Austrian Prince Starhemberg, that was all I ever got out of him.

*   *   *

There is still, twenty-odd years later, so much conjecture concerning the background to and details of the Roehm purge that a first-hand version I heard quite recently may not be without interest. As far as I know practically no documentary evidence has survived, but my account comes from Dr. Emil Ketterer, who was a *Gruppenführer* in charge of the S.A. medical services and Roehm's personal physician at the time. He had been a close associate since the Ludendorff Putsch days, when he had been a member of the *Reichskriegsflagge*.

During the period preceding his death Roehm was receiving treatment for a severe form of neuralgia from which he was suffering. This consisted of a course of injections and on the evening of June 29, 1934, Ketterer arrived at the Pension Hanslbauer in Wiessee, where Roehm was staying, to give him the last injection of the series. Ketterer, Roehm and S.S. *Gruppenführer* Bergmann had dinner together and then settled down until about 11 o'clock at night to play Tarok, the Bavarian three-handed card game. Roehm then went to bed, was given his injection and Ketterer was about to return to Munich when Bergmann suggested that he should stay the night.

There was, as Ketterer recalls, to be a meeting of S.A. leaders the following day, to be attended by Hitler, at which Roehm was to give an address on the subject of turning the brownshirt formations into a militia as a *Reichswehr* reserve. This plan had already been discussed at a previous meeting of the S.A. leaders in February 1934 at Friedrichsroda in Thuringia. However, at a conference shortly thereafter in the Propaganda Ministry with Goebbels and Roehm, Hitler had turned it down. He gave as his reason the undisputed right of the *Reichswehr* to organize the coming expansion in the German armed forces, and their military authority to do so was to remain unimpaired.

Roehm had been greatly incensed, had refused to drop the idea and told his brownshirt leaders that if Hitler refused to accept even a modified form he would resign his post and emigrate to Bolivia again. The plan was one which he had discussed with Hitler in outline over a number of years and he attributed Hitler's unexpected opposition to the influence of Blomberg, Reichenau and the *Reichswehr* officers. The meeting planned for June 30 was designed as an attempt to oblige Hitler to change his mind under the combined influence of all the senior members of the S.A. If this had failed, and Roehm had resigned, the bulk of them, led by *Gruppenführer* Willy Schmidt, who had formerly been the chief of the personnel division, were prepared to resort to force and obtain their demands by means of a second Putsch. They wanted the S.A. to be divorced from the Party and, with their formidable strength in the country, could probably have carried the day, forcing Hitler's resignation if necessary. How far the action was intended to be imminent is, of course, not clear, but both Roehm's state of health and his declared intention to resign hardly suggest that he was preparing an immediate coup.

Ketterer was found a bed in the adjutants' room on the first floor, but he remained in the lounge until about one o'clock in the morning. Half an hour earlier *Obergruppenführer* Heines arrived from Breslau and wanted to see Roehm, but Ketterer prevented him by saying that he should be allowed to sleep off his injection. Ketterer also flatly contradicts the stories that the Hanslbauer was the scene that night of a homosexual orgy. Count Spreti, who was Roehm's acknowledged boy friend was staying in the *pension*, but apart from Heines, Bergmann and the two adjutants and two drivers, there was no one else in the place.

About five o'clock in the morning, Ketterer was awakened by general shouting and uproar and shortly afterwards found two civilians by his bed whom he describes as plain-clothes detectives. A little later S.S. *Standartenführer* Höflich, the adjutant of Gauleiter Wagner of Bavaria, an opponent of Roehm, came in to tell the two detectives that they could leave, as, by the order of Hitler, Ketterer was not to be arrested. He got up, put on his uniform, went down the stairs in some agitation and at the bottom saw Hitler and Lutze, who succeeded Roehm after the purge. Ketterer was about to go and speak to Hitler when Lutze took him by the arm on one side, told him that Roehm was being arrested, at which Ketterer protested vigorously, and then accompanied him in a car back to Munich. He never saw his patient again.

*   *   *

The Roehm business was by no means the only scandal of that summer. On July 25 came the shocking news of the murder of the Austrian Chancellor, Dollfuss, unmistakably the handiwork of the local Nazis. Hitler was at Bayreuth. A message came through the teleprinter in the liaison office: "Hanfstaengl to report to the Führer immediately. Special plane waiting at Tempelhof." "There they go again," I said to myself. "I am ignored and snubbed and threatened and then when they organize some new *Schweinerei* I have to go and show my decent face and act as camouflage."

I was caught up in the usual whirl of a Hitler crisis. A car standing with engine running at the little Bayreuth airport and shouted exhortations to hurry, as if a display of energy alone solved all difficulties. We tore through the town to his villa and in the hall I saw Otto Dietrich, who was dictating directives into the phone for the German press: "The Führer is in Bayreuth in a purely private capacity. The news has taken him as much by surprise as anyone else. . . ." You certainly need a controlled press to believe that, I thought. Out on the lawn there was a sort of frieze of senior Nazis; Habicht and Proksch, the two Party leaders from Austria, over on the left, and at the far end, striding up and down agitatedly, Hitler, Goering and the very rumpled-looking German Minister in Vienna, Rieth.

I had known Proksch for years, as far back as 1923. He was by no means one of the wild men. As soon as he saw me emerge he came over and said in his fruity Austrian accent: "Thank God you're here, *Herr Doktor,* what a dirty business. Our strength was growing every day and time was on our side and" – looking over his shoulder – "they have to send down this fellow Habicht to take over with full powers from Hitler. The man used to be a Communist, they must have known that." (Habicht was a member of the German *Reichstag*.) "*Mein lieber* Proksch," I said, "it is the same thing everywhere. Nothing but hot-headed louts badgering Hitler that the time for action has come. They think that is the way to run a foreign policy."

I could see that this conversation with a man known to be a moderate was being noted, so I walked over to Habicht. "Well, that is a fine mess you have organized," I greeted him.

"What do you mean?"

"You break up the china shop and what is the result? Complete fiasco. Why didn't you wait and come to power by legal means like Hitler did in Berlin?"

"What makes you say things have gone wrong? The operation was worth it."

"Now for God's sake what are you talking about?" I said aghast.

"Well, that *Schwein* Dollfuss is dead, isn't he?"

I exploded. "You think that is the end of the matter. You will probably get civil war and the Italians marching in over the Brenner." I was so furious I turned on my heel and walked away from him.

By this time Hitler had come over. "Well, what are the foreign papers saying about us now?" he tried to joke, but I could see from their eyes that he and Goering were really worried. We walked up the steps on to the veranda and into the library. Goering was booming away about Italian divisions mobilizing on the Austrian frontier: "*Mein Führer*, we must reckon with the possibility of Italian military intervention. We have had reports since yesterday that there are several Bersaglieri divisions taking up position at the Brenner and on the Carinthian frontier. It looks like a partial mobilization." Hitler blustered: "I will soon deal with that pack. Three German divisions would sweep them all into the Adriatic." Goering calmed him down and he came to the point: "Hanfstaengl, we want you to go down to Vienna and report on the situation," Hitler said. "Talk to the British and American Ministers. You know all these old women in striped trousers, anyway." – "What am I to say to them, Herr Hitler?" I asked. "I must have some formal instructions." Hitler was in the clouds. He was in a tight spot and knew it, and was falling back on his last resource, a barrage of words: "This Herr Dollfuss had been putting our *Parteigenossen* in concentration camps for months. People must realize that this tiny Catholic minority at the top had no right to exert such a tyranny when most of the population want union with Germany. Dollfuss was the dictator, not me. I have 90 per cent of the German nation behind me and he had less than a tenth of his."

I could see all this was pointless. "Herr Hitler, some of the foreign correspondents in Berlin have gone to Vienna. Let me ring up and find out what the situation is and then let us decide what is to be done." – "Yes, yes, Hanfstaengl, do that," said Hitler, satisfied with any sort of initiative. I knew how to get hold of Louis Lochner, the very sober and experienced Associated Press correspondent. He had been on the phone just before I left Berlin. I managed to get him on the line, and he had not wasted his time. He had seen everyone of importance and the burden of his information was that the crisis was over and barring any provocative moves from Germany, there was no likelihood of physical intervention from the Italians.

This I reported back to Hitler and Goering and it was just the straw at which they needed to grasp. They were reassured, and, what seemed more important to me, calmed down. There was no more bombastic talk about sweeping the Italian divisions into the Adriatic. When I came back into the room I had found them pontificating about an occupation of Italian South Tyrol as a counter-measure, although even Hitler was expressing doubts about the danger of stripping his western and eastern frontier forces to do so. They were quoting Frederick the Great and Clausewitz to each other, as if a dozen years had taught them nothing. They never did learn, but at least my information, although they had again got away with murder, stopped this nonsense. All is not yet lost I thought. Which goes to prove how gullible I had become or how desperately a man clings to false hopes.

We all sat down to lunch. In the middle of the meal an S.S. orderly came in and announced: "State Secretary Meissner on the telephone." Brückner went out to answer it. Meissner was Hindenburg's *chef de cabinet* and I wondered how bad was the news of his old chief's health. Everything seemed to be happening at once. The

President's death would cause another crisis, with the monarchists, probably led by von Papen, making a last effort to stake their claims. The same thoughts may have been running through Hitler's mind: "Of course there is no question of Rieth returning to Vienna as Minister," he was musing and then, in a sudden flash: "I have it! Papen is the man. What was it you called him two years ago, Hanfstaengl? – *Ein Luftikus* – And Catholic into the bargain. He would talk his way round those priests and nuns in Vienna until they didn't know whether they were going or coming." – "A fine idea," Goering chimed in. "It would get him out of Berlin too. He has only been in the way since the Roehm business." – And let no one imagine that I have invented that conversation.

Meissner's news was that the President's health had taken a final turn for the worse. Leaving the Austrian situation to take care of itself, Hitler and his staff flew to East Prussia. Within a week Hindenburg was dead. This was to be the last major political event with which I was associated as Hitler's foreign press chief, but I have little to add in the way of new evidence. I do not know to what extent Hitler's mind was clear as to the steps he should take to meet this eventuality. If he had any plans they were not discussed in my presence, and I strongly suspect that the final consolidation of his power that followed was the result of purely pragmatic decisions. The question of the succession was taboo in his inner circle. Some of the Nazis were talking in terms of General von Epp as President, and conservative and monarchist circles were advocating the election of one of the royal princes. It was only on our return to Berlin that I first heard bruited the idea that the offices of Chancellor and President should be combined.

Our first reception at Neudeck, the President's estate, in the last days of July, was chilling. Only Hitler and Brückner, as his adjutant, were invited into the house and I can remember Otto Dietrich and myself sitting on a bench near the outbuildings without the slightest suggestion of hospitality being offered to us or indeed to anyone else. This, on an East Prussian estate with a feudal tradition of at least formal welcome and refreshment to travellers and visitors, was an indication of the mood in the President's entourage. Hitler was tight-lipped and uninformative as he came out and gave no hint later of what had passed. We went to stay the night at the Finckenstein estate of Count Dohna, where Napoleon had spent part of his romance with Countess Walewska, and his bedroom remained intact; but Hitler abruptly declined the offer to sleep in it.

The inevitable was announced the next morning by a Meissner dissolved in tears. His devotion to the old man was genuine. "The President lost consciousness shortly after you had left," he sobbed. "His heart can give out at any moment." Nevertheless Hitler flew back to Bayreuth and it was there that news of the President's end reached us. Back we flew to Neudeck, to be greeted at the estate by silent, distrustful crowds from the neighbourhood, with a triple ring of S.S. men guarding the house. My chief memory is of the regrettable behaviour of Heinrich Hoffmann who, grasping and unseemly to the last, used his influence to keep all other photographers out and then tried to sell his own pictures to the foreign press at black market prices. It caused the most frightful scandal and for once I even had Goebbels on my side, although in his usual manner he soon welshed when the complaints died down and he was able to score a point at my expense with Hitler for backing the demands of the foreign press too zealously.

My next problem was the insistent rumours in the world press concerning the existence of, and Hitler's alleged intention to suppress, Hindenburg's political testament. I brought up the subject before Hitler, Goering and Goebbels at tea-time, in the garden of the Chancellery. Hitler was nettled. "Tell your foreign friends to wait until the document is published officially," he said. "They are suggesting that the wording is going to be doctored," I replied. "I don't care what that pack of liars thinks," Hitler shouted. "The only way to satisfy them," I interposed, "would be to have the testament photographed and copies distributed. Let me have it for half an hour and I can get the branch of our family firm in Berlin to do the work." Hitler looked at me pityingly. "You have the strangest ideas, Mister Hanfstaengl." – I caught the tone and knew there was something wrong. I can swear there was a smirk on the faces of both Goebbels and Goering. A day or two later at dinner in the Chancellery, the subject of the testament came up for discussion again. I had the feeling that their plans were by no means proceeding smoothly, but my objections were brusquely brushed aside by Hitler, who turned to me and said sharply: "My dear Hanfstaengl, this is no laughing matter. If anything goes wrong here not only will they string us up but you as well." They wanted time and of course they used it. The usable part of the testament was produced triumphantly just before the referendum which confirmed Hitler's' assumption of supreme power and Oskar von Hindenburg was put on the radio to say that this represented his father's wishes. With Goebbels at the head of his Ministry of Permanent Revolution nothing now stood in the way of the realization of Hitler's paranoiac nightmares.

I still continued glumly to attend the midday sessions at the Chancellery, but the point had been reached when Hitler often failed to greet me. That our final row was trivial in nature did not hide the fact that it was fundamental in character. Its roots lay back in the very first evening I had seen him, when I had taken an instant dislike to a member of his entourage. This was a man of dubious personal character who had subsequently filled a number of minor posts on the fringes of the movement. Our paths had crossed a number of times, but when, after Hitler's accession to power, he had tried to obtain for himself a position of greater influence, I had gained access to his police dossier and shown it to Goering, who not only vetoed the appointment but had him arrested. In the end the man escaped abroad and the subject of his activities came up for discussion at lunch in the Chancellery.

Hitler was sitting two places away from me. By this time my cup was full: "There you are, Herr Hitler," I said, "I have warned you for the past eleven years against having people of his type around." Then I went into some of the details of the police dossier which I knew only too well. "The whole movement has been tainted by allowing such people too much freedom. Can you wonder that we get a bad name?" Hitler was livid with fury. "It is all your fault, Hanfstaengl," he retorted. "You should have handled him much more diplomatically." I was beside myself. "How do you expect anyone to handle a man like that diplomatically?" I answered. The atmosphere was becoming very awkward and unpleasant. Hitler tried to cover himself by pretending that the police records were a case of mistaken identity. "I will get them together again and show them to you," I rejoined hotly. "These facts concern him alone and everybody else knows it." The lunch party broke up with everybody wondering what the next move would be. I busied myself getting the material together again, and in the meantime the subject was not raised. Two or three days later I was in the Chancellery for lunch and as we sat around Hitler suddenly said: "Hanfstaengl, *spielen Sie das Ding da von Ihnen*" – play that thing of yours. "Which one?" I asked confused. "Your funeral march," he said. The massed bands had played it not so long before at the Nuremberg Party rally. This was odd, I thought, with a sense of foreboding. So I thumped it out and he acknowledged it rather grudgingly. Melodramatic as this may sound, it was the last time I ever saw him.

A day or two later I brought in the police files and laid them on Brückner's desk. He cleared his throat and looked embarrassed: "The matter is under investigation," he said. "The Führer would prefer you not to come here for the next two weeks until a decision has been reached." I heard later that the files had been put on Hitler's desk and that as soon as he heard what they were, he swept them on the floor in a rage and shouted: "I never want to hear about the matter again." Those two weeks became two years, and then I had to run for my life.

*   *   *

If Hitler had succeeded in finding compensation in the humiliation of the few women he was able to persuade to consort with him, he might never have swum within our ken, or ended in a criminal lunatic asylum or gaol, which would have come to the same thing. As it was he had additional mental qualities of a transcendent order. His brain was a sort of primaeval jelly or ectoplasm which quivered in response to every impulse from its surroundings.

What most people forget in their judgement of Hitler's character is that his simply did not fit into the four classifications of personality laid down by Albrecht Dürer: the sanguine, the melancholy, the choleric and the phlegmatic. His characteristics were those of a medium, who absorbed and gave expression, by induction and osmosis, to the fears, ambitions and emotions of the whole German nation. No single aspect of his temperament was so firmly developed that it was possible in the long run to use it as a channel to influence his mind. He could sprawl for hours like a crocodile dozing in the Nile mud or a spider immobile in the centre of its web. He would chew his nails, look boredly into space and sometimes whistle. As soon as some person of interest – and there was no one he did not find interesting for a time – joined his company, you could almost see him mobilizing his internal machinery. The asdic pings of inquiry would go out and within a short time he had a clear image of the wavelength and secret yearnings and emotions of his partner. The pendulum of conversation would start to beat faster, and the person would be hypnotized into believing that there lay in Hitler immense depths of sympathy and understanding. He had the most formidable powers of persuasion of any man or woman I have ever met, and it was almost impossible to avoid being enveloped by him.

It is popularly supposed that Hitler addressed everyone as if they were a mass meeting. This is only partly true. It is predominantly true of the period after 1932, when he started to use a microphone for his speeches. He became drunk with the metallic boom of his own voice, which of course was not his own voice. The loud-speaker amplifies the human organ of speech, but it completely denaturalizes it into the tones of a bull-frog. Then, when he came to power, the final deification of the Führer cult fed his paranoia to the point where he was incapable of carrying on a conversation as between equals. None of this was true of his early years, when he still retained the capacity to harness people as individuals and awaken in them the conviction that he was appealing to their best instincts.

Even so his power was the power of speech. He thought that if you talked long enough and vehemently enough, repeated your arguments a dozen times in a dozen forms, there was no obstacle, human or technical, which could not be overcome. The Nazi movement was a movement of orators, except for essential administrators like Himmler and Bormann, and people were useful to Hitler in direct proportion to their ability to move a mass audience to hysteria. No one without this gift ever played more than a secondary part in his régime. He thought the whole world was a slightly larger Hofbräuhaus or Sportpalast and could in the end be moved by the same methods. He had this chameleon-like gift of reflecting the wishes of the masses, and somehow their message was transmitted to him on a wavelength which was not that of speech, but some other set of vibrations into which he could tune himself. This may have been one of the reasons for his complete contempt for foreign languages and the necessity of learning and understanding of them. He would talk to a foreigner, using an interpreter for the words, but his mediumistic gifts seemed to work just as well with a Hottentot or a Hindu.

Back in 1923, when I probably stood at my nearest to Hitler, he once outlined the appeal he was trying to make, the appeal which brought him to power, only for the ideals to be corrupted by the power which destroyed him: "When I talk to people," he said, "especially those who are not yet Party members, or who are about to break away again for some reason or other, I always talk as if the fate of the nation was bound up in their decision. That they are in a position to give an example for the many to follow. Certainly it means appealing to their vanity and ambition, but once I have got them to that point, the rest is easy.

"Every individual, whether rich or poor, has in his inner being a feeling of unfulfilment. Life is full of depressing disappointments, which people cannot master. Slumbering somewhere is the readiness to risk some final sacrifice, some adventure, in order to give a new shape to their lives. They will spend their last money on a lottery ticket. It is my business to canalize that urge for political purposes. In essence, every political movement is based on the desire of its supporters, men or women, to better things not only for themselves but for their children and others. It is not only a question of money. Of course every working man wants to raise his standard of living, and the Marxists have cashed in on this, without being able to proceed beyond a given point. In addition, the Germans have a feeling for history. Millions of their countrymen died in the war, and when I appeal for an equal sense of sacrifice, the first spark is struck. The humbler people are, the greater the craving to identify themselves with a cause bigger than themselves, and if I can persuade them that the fate of the German nation is at stake, then they will become part of an irresistible movement, embracing all classes. Give them a national and social ideal, and their daily worries will to a large extent disappear. It was Count Moltke who said that one must demand the impossible in order to achieve the possible. Any ideal must appear to a certain extent unrealizable, if it is not to be profaned by the trivia of reality."

The contrast between the Hitler of the early 'twenties and the Hitler in power was that between a prophet and a priest, between Mohammed and a Caliph. In his early years he was the articulate unknown soldier who spoke for the millions of his dead comrades and tried to revive the nation for which they had fought. There was a revivalist quality about his movement; I write revivalist, because it might be blasphemous to say religious, but anyone who studies the organization of his movement will find many parallels to the Catholic Church militant. The Nazi hierarchy was organized after the fashion of Ignatius de Loyola – in which one can see again the influence of Goebbels, who had been educated by the Jesuits. Blind obedience to one's superior was the tenet of both organizations and, with the magnetism and fanaticism of Hitler at the centre, a direct comparison led through Goebbels, as general of the order, to the provincial Gauleiters who provided the next link in the chain.

To this must be added the incredible powers as an orator which gave Hitler his initial control over the masses. He knew that in a drawing-room or in ordinary society he was a relatively insignificant figure. The cross that he had to bear in life was that he was not a normal man. His fundamental shyness when confronted by individuals, particularly women, to whom he knew he had nothing to offer, was compensated by this titanic urge to win the approval of the masses, who were the substitute for the female partner he never found. His reaction to an audience was the counterpart of sexual excitement. He became suffused like a cock's comb or the wattles of a turkey, and it was only in this condition that he became formidable and irresistible. When he came to power he thought the same approach would dominate a country, and for many years it did, only for the edifice to collapse because the outside world was not subject to the same spell. He found relaxation only in the atmosphere which corresponded to his own psyche, in the erotic crescendos of Wagner's music. He could immerse himself in this torrent of sound and become what he could allow himself to be in no other circumstances – nothing, a neuter.

People often ask if Hitler was nothing but a demagogue. I have tried to show how much more there was to him than that, but he did possess to a remarkable degree the gift of all great demagogues, that of reducing complicated issues to fiery catch-phrases. He was a great admirer of British propaganda methods in the war, which the Germans with their long statements signed by fifty professors had never remotely matched. The danger of course lay in the fact that in the end he did not realize he was indulging in over-simplification. The shades of grey in an argument or situation naturally seeped into him, but what came out was always jet black or pure white. To him there was only ever one side of a question. Rosenberg, his most dangerous mentor, had developed the dilettantist theory of the superiority of the Nordic race to the point of caricature. Nevertheless, its directness appealed to Hitler and he swallowed it whole. My fight with him over the years was basically an attempt to prove that things were not simple but complicated. I used one simile, when I first started playing the piano for him, that it would be hopeless to try and play his beloved *Liebestod* using only the white keys. He looked at me half-amused and half-disconcerted, but the phrase stuck, and I used it from time to time over the years, when my advice became less and less welcome.

Hitler was not so much a distiller as a bar-tender of genius. He took all the ingredients the German people offered him and mixed them through his private alchemy into a cocktail they wanted to drink. If I can mix my metaphors he was a tight-rope walker as well, maintaining until he had beaten down all possible sources of opposition, a precarious balance between their conflicting demands. His so-called intuition was nothing but a camouflage for awkward decisions which might offend one or the other faction. His greatest strength lay in his one-track mind. A lot of us could become famous or illustrious or powerful if we only did what Hitler did. On Tuesday he did what he had made up his mind to do on Monday, and the same on Wednesday, all through the week and through the months and years. He got there, with all the mistakes and drawbacks such an attitude embodies. The rest of us form a resolution over the week-end, wake up on Monday undecided, next day change our mind again and more or less undo what we did yesterday by a little incon-sistency tomorrow or the day afterwards. Hitler kept to his course like a skyrocket, and got there.

It may be a source of astonishment, but Hitler's secret idol was Pericles. One of Hitler's many frustrations was his failure to become an architect, and the great Greek architect-politician was a sort of adolescent hero to him. I knew most of the books Hitler had read in his early days and one of them was a hundred-year-old tome called *Historische Charakterbilder* by A. W. Grube. It used to lie in the jumble of his Thierschstrasse flat, and he knew many of the details of this potted history by heart. To Hitler the council of the elders on the Areopagus hill, which Pericles had stormed, represented the corrupt bourgeois forces the Nazis had sworn to liquidate. In his blind devotion to symbols, Hitler could not even see that the parallels became pathetic. I suppose Anaxagoras, Pericles' mentor, was funny little Professor Poetsch, who had given Hitler instruction in Linz. If Phidias was Heinrich Hoffmann, then Zeno, the dialectitian, was presumably Rosenberg. And there of course you ran out of names, for Hitler the Pinchbeck Pericles had no Aspasia.

Because Pericles carried thunder on his tongue, and the goddess of persuasion resided on his lips, Hitler thought words were all that Pericles had ever used and saw in himself the reincarnation of the rebellious agitator-soldier. But in his case the tragedy of an orator became the tragedy of his hearers.

CHAPTER XV

WILDERNESS AND FLIGHT

Unacknowledged banishment – The warning of Rosalind
von Schirach – No bed of my own – The Chancellery on the
telephone – A mission to Spain – The intrusive cameraman –
Goering's plot frustrated – A race with the Gestapo – Fiftieth
birthday of a fugitive – Unity Mitford repeats a remark – No
joke on a parachute.

I CARRIED ON. It was neither heroic nor imaginative but sheer
inertia. In due course my office was moved from the liaison staff to
another building farther up the Wilhelmstrasse on the corner of
Unter den Linden, opposite the Adlon Hotel. My old rooms were
taken over by Ribbentrop, now emerging as the rival of Rosenberg
in the foreign affairs field. Hitler never admitted that I had been
banished, and word that I was no longer in his confidence did not
penetrate outside the inner circle. I could still see Hess and Goering
and, occasionally, Goebbels and could always talk to Neurath. The
foreign press office kept going of its own momentum. I arranged
interviews through Lammers and Funk, passed on information and
did my best to keep my foreign diplomat friends apprised of what
was going on, always in the hope, in spite of everything, that the
situation would at long last settle down.

The unrealities and shifts to which one was put in such an
anomalous situation were legion. Everyone was pretending that
nothing had changed. When Edda Ciano came to Berlin and said:
"Where is our old friend Hanfstaengl?" Goebbels of course had to
invite me to the luncheon he gave her at a country club near his
home at Schwanenwerder. I, in my turn, had to pretend that I was
still a member of the inner circle in case Mussolini should want to
use me as a channel for some communication to Hitler. With Goering
some remnant of old cordiality remained, until I criticized him to his
face one day in 1935 for raiding German museums to provide paintings
and *objets d'art* for his sumptuous residences. At the last birthday

party of his I attended, which was a double-decker affair, with his family and intimate friends on the first floor and the Party hierarchy in the downstairs lounge, I found myself relegated to the second division.

The pretence could not be kept up completely. When my old friend William Randolph Hearst, whom I had accompanied in an interview with Hitler in the autumn of 1934, sent his London correspondent Bill Hillman to see Hitler I had to back down. The occasion was the Saar plebiscite at the beginning of 1935, when Hitler had announced that Jews in the disputed territory would be exempt from regulations then current in the rest of Germany. Hearst's idea had been to see if the occasion could be used to obtain from Hitler an assurance that this was the prelude to a general relaxation in Germany as a whole. I had to tell Hillman that I was no longer *persona grata*, and we went through the pantomime of handing in a sealed letter from Hearst to Hitler through Brückner, who gave us his word of honour that it would be put straight into Hitler's hand and that he would make himself responsible for an answer. After we had waited for an hour, the ineffable Schaub lumbered out with the open envelope in his hand to say that Hitler had no statement to make.

My mood was not improved by a story I heard from Rolf Hoffmann, who was the representative of my foreign press department at the Brown House in Munich. Round about this time I had had a new studio portrait made which showed only too clearly the defiant frame of mind I was in. I had sent a copy of this to Hoffmann, who had hung it in a frame on the wall of his office. One day he was on the telephone when Hitler came in. Hitler made a sign that he was to continue with his conversation and then stood for at least two or three minutes glowering at my photograph from not more than a foot away. His concentration was so intense and the expression on his face so threatening that Hoffmann became distinctly uncomfortable. When he put the telephone down it was a moment or two before Hitler broke away, but then he made no comment on his thoughts and delivered only some banal message. Hoffmann was so disturbed at Hitler's mood that when I was in Munich the following week he took me on one side and warned me of his conviction that something unpleasant was afoot.

The campaign to neutralize me was not without its ludicrous aspects. I had gone down to Nuremberg for the 1935 Party rally and tried to get the foreign press away from the prevailing atmosphere by holding a reception for them at the Germanisches Museum. I had put together a speech with which I was rather pleased. After all, it was my own subject. "Gentlemen," I said, "I am delighted to greet you in the city of that great painter Albrecht Dürer. . . ." What happened by the time Goebbels' ministry finished truncating its report? The passage read: "Dr. Hanfstaengl, the foreign press chief, yesterday welcomed journalists to the city of the Führer. . . ."

Out of sheer cussedness I renewed contact with some of the old Party stalwarts of the early years. Anton Drexler, disregarded and forgotten, was almost a cripple. His whole ambition was centred on a little invalid-car, which the grateful Party never saw fit to give him. He was in despair at the turn events had taken, but was wholly without influence. Hermann Esser had at last managed to find a sinecure as a Bavarian State minister, and I used to see him whenever I was in Munich. It was he who brought me up to date on the Eva Braun situation. She had gone to school with his second wife and they saw a lot of each other. It was clear that Eva was no more than a piece of domestic decoration in the dream world in which Hitler now lived. She could hardly leave Munich without Hitler's or Bormann's permission and one day appeared in tears at the Essers' to complain of her serf-like existence: "I am nothing but a prisoner," she blubbered, and then volunteered the telling information, *"Als Mann habe ich von ihm überhaupt nichts"* – "As it is I have nothing from him as a man."

Nevertheless, Hitler repaid her presence with his protection. She turned up unobtrusively at the Nuremberg Party rally in 1935 in a very expensive fur coat. Magda Goebbels, who thought she was the one woman to whom Hitler ought to pay attention, was ill-advised enough to make some disparaging remark, which aroused Hitler to a fury. Magda was forbidden to enter the Chancellery for months and went round imploring people to put in a good word for her, instigated doubtless by her husband, who could not bear to think of his hold over Hitler being diminished in any way. In the end she was received again, but there was always a rivalry between the two women. One would not have to be a very good playwright to dramatize the emotions which led each of them to stay until the last in the besieged Führer-bunker as long as the other was there.

In 1936 I lost another early link with Hitler. My wife divorced me. Her distaste for Hitler and his followers had long preceded mine, although he continued to send her flowers on her birthday until she left Germany for the United States, where she spent the war years. Long absences and increasing incompatibility made our break inevitable.

My position in Berlin became more and more insecure. My staff at the office were being spied on and questioned about my general attitude to events. The Party organization challenged me to produce a genealogical tree to prove that with a grandfather named Heine I was not partly Jewish—yet another example of their purblind obsessions. Friends would try and warn me that my uninhibited comments were running me into trouble. I remember Martha Dodd telling me as early as 1934: "Putzi, your crowd doesn't trust you any more." A more direct warning now came from Rosalind von Schirach, Baldur's sister. She and her father were increasingly opposed to the brother's behaviour and she took her courage in both hands to come and see me. She recounted how Baldur had drunk a little too much at their home in Bavaria one evening and had told her to keep away from me as I was on the black list and would not be around very much longer. I began to see the writing on the wall and, at the suggestion of another friend, started to smuggle out gold and platinum objects to London to be ready for all eventualities.

I continued to intervene with Himmler when I could on behalf of individuals who had fallen foul of the Nazi system, and, at the instance of her American mother, managed to get a girl named von Pfister out of a concentration camp in Saxony, where she had been confined for making disparaging remarks about the régime. I railed against the turn of events to everyone who would listen, and one of my friends at the time, Edgar von Schmidt-Pauli, author of the book *Men Around Hitler*, testified for me in 1948 that it was more than anyone's life was worth to walk along the street with me and listen to my comments. It is a compliment I am happy to accept.

Everything I had believed in had been betrayed, but at least I was not alone. Frau Bechstein, a fellow-sponsor of Hitler a dozen years before, who had received from him a miserable bunch of flowers on her birthday, went up to him at a reception and called him 'a shabby sort of Chancellor' to his face. I take my hat off to her. I grew progressively more unguarded in my condemnation. At the beginning of 1937 I remember a party at the Swiss Legation in Berlin where I talked for a long time to General Joachim von Stülpnagel, who was at that time head of the Army personnel division and in 1939 became commander-in-chief of the reserve Army. Several members of his family were senior officers and among the most determined opponents of Hitler's military policies, although in the early days of power Goering had boasted of his friendship with them. We talked, probably with misguided frankness, about the gathering war-clouds. Hitler had marched into the Rhineland and the Spanish Civil War had broken out, with active German intervention on the side of Franco. "This can only lead to disaster," I said. "Only the *Reichswehr* can now step in and call a halt."

This sort of behaviour got bruited around, and the anti-Hanfstaengl mood in the Party hierarchy reached a dangerous pitch. During the year I had written the music and helped in the production of another film to be called *Volk ohne Raum*. I had been in London again at the end of 1935 and had seen Sir Robert Vansittart, the permanent head of the Foreign Office. The burden of my conversation with him had been that providing affairs in Germany showed signs of settling down the British Government would have no objection to discussing the problem of the former German colonies. It had seemed to me that if this possibility could be put over to my countrymen in a reasonable fashion it might divert their minds from more dangerous ventures and serve to relieve the internal tension.

The film was an attempt to achieve this, and the story was written by Hans Grimm, the poet. Some of the financial backing came from Schacht. I should have known better than to leave out of account the accumulated venom of the Minister of Propaganda. This time Goebbels banned the film without even seeing it and, in a final effort to discredit me, persuaded Hitler that I had drawn too large a sum in expenses during its making. The Hitler comment that was reported to me was that if I was allowed to earn too much money they would have seen the last of me and that it was much better to keep me dependent on them. At the last moment I managed to borrow enough money to stave off a charge of misappropriation of funds, but the net was now closing.

I never went anywhere without carrying in my pocket a valid passport with visas for Switzerland, France, Holland and England. As 1936 became 1937, I took to sleeping at the houses of friends such as Voigt, my assistant, and Thorak, the sculptor, rather than risk a dreaded early-morning call at my own apartment. The final bizarre *dénouement* was at hand.

*   *   *

My connexion with Hitler started with a telephone call, when I was asked to meet the American military attaché, who drew him to my attention. The last act had the same prelude. I was sitting in the study of my Munich home when Berlin came on the line. It was half past four in the afternoon of February 8, 1937, and I was preparing the speech I was going to give on the 205th anniversary of George Washington's birth a fortnight later. *"Hier Reichskanzlei,"* came the voice. "Dr. Hanfstaengl? – you are requested to report urgently in Berlin. Captain Bauer has been instructed to bring you by special plane from Munich airport." It was only one of the adjutants. There was no point in asking for details. What is all this suddenly about? I asked myself. I had had practically no contact with the inner circle in the Chancellery for two years, but this air of military secrecy was nothing new. The fact that Hitler's personal pilot had been sent for me was vaguely reassuring. Hitler must know about it, I thought. Perhaps, after all, he finds he needs a cooler head around. Hope springs eternal.

After this flying start, the usual hiatus ensued. Bauer never did turn up, but orders were orders, so I took the first Lufthansa plane the next morning and was in Berlin by midday. I found at my office that Fritz Wiedemann, Hitler's A.D.C., had been inquiring if I had arrived, and asking me to report at the Chancellery at four o'clock. The instructions he had for me were the last I expected: "Herr Hanfstaengl, the Führer wishes you to fly immediately to Spain to protect the interests of our press correspondents there. Apparently they are having a lot of trouble and it needs someone like you to set matters right." I deflated like a balloon. "Then why on earth all this hurry?" I asked. "The day after tomorrow is my fiftieth birthday and I have a family party down in Uffing. Surely this business can wait until after that. In any case, why have they picked on me for the job?"

"I understand the matter is urgent and you are to leave tomorrow," answered Wiedemann. "Don't you know General Faupel, our ambassador there, very well?" That was quite true, I did. My orders started to make rough sense. Wiedemann was still talking: "Why don't you keep to the arrangements, Hanfstaengl?" he said in a friendly tone. "Some of us miss you badly around here. If you make a success of this mission, I have no doubt the Führer will have you here again, and your influence would be very valuable."

In retrospect I can only assume that Wiedemann was speaking honestly. He was a cut above the other members of Hitler's immediate staff, a decent, slightly provincial regular officer who had commanded the infantry company during the war in which Hitler was a messenger. He and I had always got on very well together. If only what he says is true, I thought. Perhaps this can still be put on the right rails. "*Ministerialrat* Berndt, in the Propaganda Ministry, will fill you in on all the details," Wiedemann went on. "I should go over and see him right away."

I knew Berndt. He was the head of Goebbels' press division, and was the man who kept an iron hand on the *gleichgeschaltete* German press. His job was to see that the newspapers never wavered from the narrow line laid down by his chief. He received me affably enough. "Our people are not getting the assistance they should from the Franco authorities. There is a Captain Bolin who seems to be the cause of the trouble. You must get him to change his attitude. You will fly to Salamanca and put up at the Grand Hotel, which we have taken over entirely as the headquarters of a dummy commercial organization called 'Hisma', to which you will be attached."

This all seemed perfectly straightforward. Then Berndt went, with what seemed undue relish, into a lot of unnecessary detail about how dangerous conditions in Spain were, with no defined front lines, enemy patrols appearing at the most unexpected places, and so on. I do not know whether he was trying to frighten me, but he had been in Spain himself a few months earlier and may have thought me a sympathetic audience. "We shall have to give you a false passport," he continued. "Please send us over a couple of photographs as soon as you can." This request was accompanied by further details of the dangers of being shot down over Communist Spain and the necessity, for security reasons, of not telling anyone, not even my own office staff, of my mission. "How long can I expect to be away?" I asked. "About five or six weeks." "Now look here, Berndt, I know your people. That means anything up to three or four months. I can't leave for that length of time at this notice. Even if I abandon my birthday-party, I still have domestic arrangements to make. Besides, most of my clothes are in Munich. I can't travel in striped trousers and a Homburg to a war area." "Get your things sent up from Munich by plane," Berndt answered. "We have had a lot of trouble to arrange this flight and you must leave at four o'clock tomorrow afternoon. We will send a car to pick you up at three to take you out to the airfield. I will have your papers and all the formalities fixed by then."

Back in the office I hurriedly made my own arrangements, told my staff and as many of my friends and family as I could reach that I would be away for some time, left word that if anyone inquired after me that evening I was having dinner at the Finnish Legation, and went home to my apartment to change. It was a stag party and over coffee an additional guest turned up, Colonel Bodenschatz, Goering's personal adjutant, who was also to play a part in the events that followed. He greeted me with effusive friendliness, repeated again the argument about what a splendid opportunity this was to rehabilitate myself with Hitler, and said that Goering himself would like to see me the following morning before I left.

I found the fat fellow in his most jovial mood, just as if the hostility between me and the Nazi triumvirate had never existed. He said he wanted me to report direct to him about the situation I found and let him have a completely unbiased appreciation of the political scene in Spain. Then, in his coarse way, with loud guffaws, he told me to be careful of women when I got there, and how half his air-force personnel already had venereal disease. But that was Goering, completely in character.

By the time the car arrived at my flat I was still annoyed at being hustled around in this fashion, but more or less reassured about the nature of my mission, and, perhaps rather foolishly, hopeful that all this might lead to my getting my hand on that brake again up in the Chancellery. There had certainly been no public signs of any change in Hitler's policies, but it seemed not impossible that he felt he had overreached himself, especially over the German intervention in Spain, and that the point had arrived where my Cassandra voice would not be unwelcome. This was to prove quite the most fatuous piece of wishful thinking in which I have ever indulged.

There were two people in the car, one a Propaganda Ministry functionary and the other a rather untidy and sloppy young fellow in a camel-hair coat, who introduced himself as Jaworsky, and said he had been attached to me as photographer and knew Spain like the palm of his hand. His camera was dangling round his neck, but as far as I was concerned that was the only qualification he had. I had always chosen my own staff and did not like the way he had been foisted on to me. On the way out to the airfield he and the other fellow – I think his name was Neumann – kept up a loud conversation about the horrors and brutalities of the Spanish Civil War, with gory details and even pictures of mutilated female bodies. My opinion of Jaworsky sank even lower.

To my surprise I noticed that the car was not running south to Tempelhof aerodrome, but along the western highway that led out of the city. However, it was explained to me that we were going to Staaken airfield as I was, in fact, due to travel in a military plane. Then, at a corner in the Adolf Hitler Platz, on the outskirts, we picked up Berndt, who climbed in the front seat, leant over and handed me a German passport. "We are calling you August Lehmann," he said, "and your profession is given as painter and interior decorator." What a damn silly idea, I thought, and looked at him sharply. There was, I swear, a smirk at the corner of his lips. When we got to the airfield entrance we stopped and Berndt disappeared through the gates for twenty minutes or so. When he came back we drove through and eventually stopped near a group of aircraft. Bodenschatz was there waiting for us with the station commandant, Colonel Kastner.

From the moment we left the Pariser Platz, Jaworsky had been recording every detail of this journey with his camera, although I told him sharply a couple of times not to waste his film. From now on the thing was buzzing the whole time. The pilot came up and introduced himself as Captain Frodel. Then Kastner produced a parachute which he said I should try on. Now I am not exactly built for all this fiddle-faddle with straps and webbing and had never worn such a thing in my life, so I was doubtless pretty awkward about it, especially with Jaworsky recording the whole process. I was given detailed instructions how to use the parachute, counting up to eight if I had to jump and then pulling the ring, and so on. The plot then thickened with the arrival of a sinister-looking individual, a real Gestapo type, whose only introduction was the remark from Kastner: "The name doesn't matter." We were certainly an oddly assorted crew, and I began to wonder what was going on.

"Machine in order?" called Bodenschatz to the pilot. "Absolutely 100 per cent, sir," he answered, although I thought there was a tense and worried look about him. I climbed aboard. It was a light bomber, or so I imagined. I have no eye for such things. The whole interior seemed festooned with hand-grenades and I found my seat was made of bare metal. This is a fine way to spend nine hours, I said to myself. The engines were running, but Jaworsky and A. N. Other lingered outside talking to Bodenschatz and the commandant. Finally, when my patience had reached its limit, they climbed up, the door was bolted, and we took off.

We can hardly have been in the air for ten minutes when Jaworsky came aft and said: "The pilot wants to talk to you." I hunched my way forward and was motioned into the co-pilot's seat. We started to talk about this and that over the roar of the motors, and I noticed that he seemed to cut the conversation short whenever our anonymous companion loomed up behind us. However, when the fellow was away for a few minutes, Frodel looked straight at me and said: "Aren't you Dr. Hanfstaengl?" "Of course," I answered, astonished, "who do you think I am?"

"I know you only as August Lehmann, but I recognized you from newspaper photographs. What instructions do you have?"

"Nothing in detail," I replied. "I am to go to the Grand Hotel in Salamanca and report to General Faupel."

It was Frodel's turn to be astonished. "Who said you were going to Salamanca?" he asked.

"Of course I'm going to Salamanca," I said brusquely. "The whole thing was arranged yesterday on orders from the Führer. There is some trouble with the German correspondents there."

Frodel's voice took on a new urgency: "Herr Hanfstaengl, I have no orders to take you to Salamanca. My instructions are to drop you over the Red lines between Barcelona and Madrid."

I suddenly realized what an arrant fool I had been. I had walked straight into a trap. "You must be mad, Frodel," I shouted distractedly. "That is a death sentence. Who gave you such orders?"

"They were given me in a sealed envelope two minutes before I got into the plane. They are signed by Goering in person. There is nothing I can do. Orders are orders."

"This is fantastic," I shouted. "If they want to get rid of me there are simpler ways than this. Why waste petrol. Why all this paraphernalia of photographers, planes and pilots? And why bring in so many people in the plot – Wiedemann, Berndt, Bodenschatz, Goering – it is too incredible. . . ."

"I don't understand, *Herr Doktor,*" Frodel was saying. "I was told that you had volunteered for this mission."

"Volunteered?" I spluttered. "I was called to the Chancellery forty-eight hours ago and told to join Faupel in Salamanca. It was the first I had heard of it. I speak no Spanish and not enough French to get by. They'll pick me up straight away. Frodel, there must be some misunderstanding. Put down somewhere and call Berlin so we can sort this out." Frodel shrugged: "It is no good, *Herr Doktor,* my orders are imperative. Try and keep calm; we'll see what turns up. I have seen this sort of thing before. Nothing but *Schweinereien* whichever way you look."

What a way to kill a man. I could see how their minds had worked. Everything covered up and the pestilential Hanfstaengl out of the way. I could almost see the *Völkische Beobachter* headline:

'Foreign Press Chief Hanfstaengl loses his life on secret mission,' and then probably a laudatory obituary. Everything nice and neat and regretful – and final. The third man turned up again in the cabin and Frodel asked me to go aft.

Suddenly, after flying for about half an hour there was a clatter from one of the engines. Frodel throttled it right down. We stumbled forward. "There's something wrong," Frodel shouted with a meaning look at me. "I shall have to put down and have it seen to." I blessed the man under my breath. There was still a chance. We landed on a little airfield surrounded by pine-trees. It turned out to be Waldpolenz, not far from Leipzig.

The place seemed almost deserted. There was no sign of any mechanics. They had probably packed up for the day, and Frodel went off to find the commandant. My companions seemed completely nonplussed at the turn events had taken, uncertain what to do next. In this I saw my opportunity. It was very much the way in the Third Reich. Orders were orders, and allowed no latitude. If they could not be carried out you had to wait for a fresh set. They had probably been given only the simplest instructions and even the Gestapo type may have been left with the impression that he was only there to assist in the carrying out of a risky but perfectly straightforward operation. We found the canteen and I ordered a round of drinks in the hope of gaining time. Frodel joined us, said that there was no hope of repairing the machine until the next day and that the commandant would have a car ready in twenty minutes to take us into Leipzig to stay the night. I thought of the thick woods I had seen and looked at the Gestapo type. At all costs I must get away.

Making some excuse about feeling airsick, I left them. I felt I must inform someone of the plight I was in and took the risk, in the general confusion of the situation, of going into the telephone-booth and calling my office in Berlin. Fortunately we kept late hours because of press inquiries, and my secretary, Frau von Hausberger, was still there. I told the horrified woman that I had fallen into a trap, but that I would be obliged to play along for the time being and would try and call her up again as soon as I could. She managed to tell me that several foreign correspondents had been asking where I would be spending my fiftieth birthday and, not knowing what to answer, she had rung up Wiedemann. He had suggested that she should state that I would be 'in the bosom of my family at Uffing' for the occasion.

As soon as I came out of the telephone-booth I bumped into Frodel. I told him that I had just been on to Berlin and had received orders from the Führer to return to Uffing. This seemed to satisfy him and, when I started to complain about the trick which had just been played on me, he put his hand on my arm and said: "Say nothing more, there are the others. I want no part of this business." I ordered another round of drinks to keep up appearances, but, pleading my upset stomach, left them again. By now it was pitch dark outside. I walked straight out of the building and in no time was outside the airfield on a road. Before long I caught up with a peasant woman and her cart and obtained from her, in a broad Saxon accent, the information that there was a railway station not much more than a mile away. In a quarter of an hour, striding my fastest, I was there. There would be a train to Leipzig in ten minutes.

If this story appears to lack coherence and rational motivation, I can only say that I am not writing a cut-and-dried thriller, but an actual account of events as they happened. The local train chugged in and I climbed aboard. As my compartment drew abreast the closed barrier I saw, to my horror, Frodel's face above it. "We were looking everywhere for you," he shouted. "Join us in the Hotel Hauffe in Leipzig. . . ." His voice trailed away. Was it a friendly warning? Where were the other two? Would I be picked up at one of the intermediate stations? I had no clothes but those I stood up in and was in the geographical centre of Germany. One thing only I knew. I must get out of the country without delay. I banked on the fact that all the offices in Berlin would be closed and that whatever the instructions of my Gestapo friend had been, the German bureaucratic hierarchy would not provide new ones until the following morning.

I tried to ask my fellow-passengers what was the name of the last station before Leipzig, but before they could make up their minds we had passed it and were arriving in the city. I lagged behind the crowd streaming off the platform, walked through the compartment of a train on the other side, and made my way out through another barrier. There was no sign of a reception committee, so I jumped in a taxi to the Hotel Astoria. There I found that there was a night express leaving for Munich in a couple of hours. I decided to try and get hold of my secretary again. The good woman had had the sense to stay in the office. "Are you all right?" she asked agitatedly. "Yes, I am in Leipzig – alone. If anyone asks if you have heard from me, tell them I rang to say that I am returning to my mother's house at Uffing for my birthday-party."

I went out, got another taxi, and drove towards the Hotel Hauffe, telling the driver to wait at the corner with the engine running. Approaching gingerly, I looked through the plate-glass doors. There was no one in the entrance-hall, but there, by the porter's lodge, stood, of all things, my luggage. I walked in. "Heil Hitler, Herr Doktor," said the porter, who knew me from my many visits to Leipzig with Hitler. "The gentlemen said you were coming and I have been waiting for you. Your room is all ready. Shall I send your bags up?" "I've just met a friend and am staying at the Astoria. Put my bags out in the taxi straight way, will you?" I said, handing him a fat tip. Then I wrote a note to Frodel: "Have rung up the Chancellery and received new instructions. Spending night at the Astoria. See you tomorrow."

The next morning I was in Munich. I found that there was a train for Zürich leaving in little more than an hour. I dashed over to the Hotel Regina, which is near the main station, and rang up my sister Erna at her villa in the suburb of Solln. I implored her to come over immediately to the hotel, in her nightdress if necessary, as I had something desperately urgent to tell her. I waited until the last moment, but she did not turn up. Three hours later I was over the Swiss border at Lindau. It was my fiftieth birthday and the last sight of my homeland for a decade.

*   *   *

Over the course of the years I have been able to put together most of the pieces of this macabre jigsaw puzzle. It seems that a remark by Unity Mitford started the chain of events. We had continued to see a lot of her in Munich, and she became a close friend of Erna.

She was always gadding in and out of the Brown House, was sponsored by Goering, Rosenberg and Streicher, but for my taste spent far too much time with the wrong people in the Party. She was infatuated with Hitler. It was the Führer this and the Führer that. I suppose she had some idea that, with her sister married to Sir Oswald Mosley, she might always go one better and end up as Hitler's wife. Because she was so much *persona grata* I made a point of keeping in with her, and tried to put over my own ideas in the hope that she would repeat them. Probably all she reported were my angry criticisms of Goebbels and Rosenberg and the Chauffeureska and my complaints of the way Hitler was misled by them.

I may have gone too far one day. We were out on the Starnberg Lake with Egon in my yawl, and I must have been railing away in my usual fashion when she turned on me and said: "If you think this way you have no right to go on being his foreign press chief." "Certainly I have a right," I retorted. "If he only tolerates yes-men around him it will only make things worse." After we had tied up at the Royal Bavarian Yacht Club, Egon, who was fifteen at the time and already very observant, said: "Father, that woman hates you. I saw it in her eyes."

The fatal remark of mine she repeated was one I had made criticizing the crazy militarization and soldier-cult in the Party. "With all due respect to those who were killed," I had said, "if there is another war I would sooner be in the trenches than sticking it out in New York the way I had to. In the front line the danger is direct, and you are with your own people. As an enemy alien in a hostile country you are all alone and every day is an intolerable strain. I used to get my windows broken, my staff and I were threatened and insulted. There is no respite."

Fritz Wiedemann himself, in his memoirs published in 1950, described Hitler's fury when this story was repeated to him. Wiedemann was instructed to call me to Berlin the next day and states that the whole aircraft episode was a savage joke to scare me stiff and bring me to heel. Jaworsky's film sequences were shown in the Chancellery to sarcastic laughter. The story kept them all in high spirits until, Wiedemann writes, they discovered that I had fled to Switzerland. Then they became worried. I knew too much.

The only footnote I can provide comes from quite a recent meeting with the pilot. Some years after my return from exile I tracked him down in Augsburg and took him out to a particularly liquid lunch. He admitted that as far as the story of a flight to Spain was concerned he had played a part, that he did not know I was to be his passenger until he saw me, and that he had faked the engine defect. What he claims were his real orders sounded even more sinister. He was to fly a circular course and then cruise up and down above Bork airport, near Potsdam, and await further radio instructions. He had been given to understand that Goering was entertaining high officials from abroad and that, as a climax to an exhibition of air manœuvres, a dummy on a parachute was to be shot down. . . .

It still does not sound like a joke to me.

CHAPTER XVI

THE CATOCTIN CONVERSATION

*Bodenschatz as emissary – Egon abstracted – Bribes, blandish-
ments and threats – The warning of Reichenau – The non-
enemy alien – Eels in a bathing hut – Cramped quarters in
Canada – Haushofer triunfans – An offer to Roosevelt – State
prisoner at Bush Hill – Reports for a President – No inducement to revolt – A black-list ignored – Return to the ruins –
No world for Hitlers.*

No EXILE has a particularly pleasant story to tell, and mine is no
exception. I remained in Zürich under cover for some time, engaged
chiefly in frenzied efforts to get Egon out of Germany secretly to join
me before the Nazi authorities learnt my whereabouts and started
to watch for the movements of my family over the frontier. He was
still at school in Starnberg, and at one point I was engaged in a
nightmare exchange of guarded telephone messages with his head-
master to obtain the issue of a passport, at the same time as the
police at Uffing, not twenty miles away, had issued an order for my
arrest.

I had signed myself in at the Hotel Baur au Lac as Dr. Franzen
and spent most of my time hidden away in a room on the top floor.
However, I could not stay there the whole day and apparently one
of the naval attachés at the American embassy in Berlin had seen me
in the foyer. Shortly thereafter – it must have been about the middle
of March – he was at a party with his ambassador and heard Mr.
Dodd and Louis Lochner commenting on the fact that they had not
seen me around for three or four weeks and asking each other if
they knew where I was. He immediately vouchsafed the information
that he had seen me in Zürich, and this news soon filtered through
to the Chancellery.

The result was a barrage of overtures, continued spasmodically
over a couple of years, to induce me to return. The arguments

progressed from protestations that the whole episode had been nothing but a practical joke, through peremptory orders to bribery and threats. The vehicle chosen for the immediate approaches was Bodenschatz, whose name, to my astonishment, was announced to me by the porter of the Hotel Baur au Lac above five weeks after my arrival. He brought a letter from Goering, couched in hearty 'thou' terms, trying to persuade me that the whole affair had been nothing but a piece of horse-play 'intended to make me reconsider certain over-audacious remarks I had made', and assuring me on his word of honour that I could return to Germany in perfect safety and freedom under his protection. There was even a hand-written postscript at the bottom, saying, 'I expect you to accept my word.' I was not going to be taken in so easily, and was soon having high words with Bodenschatz. My chief preoccupations were to win time until I had got the boy out and to say nothing which might implicate Frodel, if he had in fact given me an opportunity to escape. I fulminated that the whole thing was an absolute scandal, that I had been treated in the most disgraceful fashion and that I would need time to think the matter over. Bodenschatz proposed to go up to Arosa for a couple of days and come back for an answer.

Two days later there was still no sign of Egon, so I sought to confuse the issue by railing at Bodenschatz about Goebbels, whom I suspected of concocting the whole plot. Did Goering's guarantee guard me against future vengefulness on the part of the little doctor, I wanted to know? Bodenschatz obviously had reserve instructions to get tough if necessary. "We cannot keep this thing quiet for ever," he said. "The foreign press people in Berlin are already starting to ask all sorts of awkward questions. If you won't see reason things might become very unpleasant for your family. . . ." I had thought out my answer to that one. "Tell your boss to get any idea of hostages out of his mind," I answered sharply. "If I hear that one of them has been as much as threatened I shall publish everything I know about the whole Nazi régime. All my records have been in places of safety for some time and I can tell you even Goebbels wouldn't get his trousers on again for a fortnight." That silenced Bodenschatz, who had by that time reached the end of his arguments. I even felt a certain grim sympathy for him in his unpleasant task. "Very well," he said resignedly, "I will report back to Goering and ring you from Berlin. There must be some way of settling this."

Within three days he was announcing another visit with fresh assurances. What he had to offer when he arrived was clumsy bribery. It was true, he said, that my offices in Berlin had been closed, but only as part of the reorganization of the information services. I was offered an important post under Goering in connexion with the four-year plan – and was at liberty to name my own salary. Goering had seen Heydrich and the warrant for my arrest had been withdrawn. I was to make up my mind by Easter whether to accept the offer. Otherwise I must take all the consequences of my deliberate emigration. That was all I needed to be told. The same evening at long last I went to collect Egon at the station. The last umbilical cord was cut.

From Zürich we went to London, where I got Egon into St. Paul's School on the recommendation of Oliver Onions, the author. I had some money in England, the proceeds of a libel case I had won against the *Express* Newspapers in 1935, and any more I needed I borrowed from English friends. It has all been paid back. The cat-and-mouse game with Berlin continued. I heard that Hitler had even brought Hermann Esser up to Berlin and tried to persuade him to travel to London and use his influence to get me to return. "Give him my word of honour it is safe for him to return. The whole thing was a joke and there was no need for him to run away," Hitler was reported to me as saying. Esser took the precaution of inquiring of one or two friends of mine in the German foreign office whether they thought his journey would bear any fruit. "Don't waste your time," he was told. "What sort of guarantee do you think you could offer? Hanfstaengl won't come back, you may be sure of that."

The triumvirate must have been really worried about what I might publish because they even alternated further blandishments with the threats and sent Bodenschatz to London to say that Goering's guarantee was still valid and that I could reconstitute my office with my old staff. By now the international situation was deteriorating fast. The talk of war was already in the air, a possibility I dreaded. "You can tell Herr Hitler," I said to Bodenschatz, "that if I get a personal letter of apology from him and the offer of an effective post as his personal adviser on foreign affairs, I would consider returning." Of course, no such letter ever arrived, although Hitler told Winifred Wagner that he had actually sent one. I even wrote, through the diplomatic bag, to my old friend Truman-Smith in Berlin, asking if he would make guarded inquiries among our mutual acquaintances as to whether my life would be in danger if I returned. He immediately got in touch with General von Reichenau, who replied after a couple of weeks that 'it would not be safe for our mutual friend to come back'. The next information I received was that my property had been seized and subjected, in the first instance, to a fine of 42,000 marks as 'tax on flight from the Reich'.

Even then their efforts to get me back in their power did not cease. Martin Bormann wrote to say that all these punitive measures would be cancelled and the cost of my stay in London refunded if I returned. Bodenschatz came again and even brought the husband of my former secretary, who worked in Goebbels' office, with a lulling message from the little demon himself. When I proved obstinate Bodenschatz turned tough. "If you do not come back, there are other methods of silencing you," he threatened. I told him that my memoirs were all written and in my solicitor's safe. If I died a natural death, they were to be destroyed. If anything else happened to me, they were to be published.

Even Unity Mitford attempted to act as a final go-between. I did not know then that she had been the probably unwitting author of my misfortune. Europe had rocked under the impact of the Anschluss, Munich and Prague. With the advent of the Polish crisis I realized my worst fears were about to crystallize. Hitler's mania to dominate his surroundings had become madness. The day after his armies marched into Poland I sent Egon to America. After a last lunch together at a little Italian restaurant in Soho, I saw him off on the boat-train. I intended to follow him as soon as I could. Then I returned feeling helpless, bewildered and miserable, back to my little flat in Kensington. That evening a peremptory ring came on the bell. Two plain-clothes men stood at the door: "Mr. Hanf-staengl? We have orders to take you into custody as an enemy alien!"

Internment is not a desirable condition. The British authorities had spread their net wide. There were political and Jewish refugees, Nazi functionaries from Bohle's organization of Germans abroad, the staff of the German hospital, the crews from ships seized at the ports. I could not feel I belonged to any of these categories. After a couple of nights at London's Olympia we were removed to a compound at Clacton-on-Sea and the leaden hand of camp discipline started to descend on us. Could the British not realize how I had fought against what had come to pass? What further use was I in a hut stuck behind barbed wire? I was allowed to get in touch with Kenneth Brown, my solicitor, who had helped in my London libel cases, and prepared a petition to the Crown for my release. My letters of recommendation should have been enough. They came from Sir Robert Vansittart, Sir Horace Rumbold and Sir Eric Phipps, the British ambassadors I had tried to help in Berlin, the Earl of Munster, Lord Fermoy, Vernon Bartlett. . . .

'Ministerial case' stood on my dossier when I came up for hearing before the advisory committee under the chairmanship of Sir Norman Birkett. The application was refused. "The reason", wrote Kenneth Brown later, "was your willingness to return to Germany if you received the requisite assurances from Hitler." The idiots, I thought, don't they realize I only wanted to go back to try to stop this thing. To destroy Hitler, they were going to destroy Germany. The only place they had for me was one I was not yet prepared to fill. "Dr. Hanfstaengl," said one of my interrogators, "if you were to help us with our propaganda you could write yourself free." It was not a pretty proposition, but then war is war. "Don't you realize that Dr. Goebbels would be able to claim that anything I wrote was done under pressure and therefore untrue," I said. "There are other ways I could help, but not as your prisoner."

I do not think my British friends have any reason to be proud of the conditions in which we were kept. From Clacton we were moved to Seaton-on-the-Sea, where we were housed in bathing-huts. The food was a scandal. We had weak tea and biscuits and biscuits and weak tea. The ground was a swamp. There was a hole in the wooden floor of the hut through which, lying in my bed, I could catch eels. I do not regard them as a delicacy myself, but those who did were prepared to polish my shoes for me in return. The next stop was the race-course at Lingfield, in concrete cubicles under the grandstand. At least they were dry. Here some of the internees built an escape-tunnel, which was discovered. They were then confined in a walled paddock under the open sky on bread and water. Some of us used to walk past and throw in some of our rations. I was caught at this and moved to the punishment camp at Swanwick for my trouble.

This was completely in the hands of militant Nazis, who carried on a terror campaign against anyone they suspected of not being of their turn of mind. The guards seemed to wash their hands of the whole proceedings, and only pure good fortune enabled me to smuggle out a message to Kenneth Brown, who managed to get questions asked in the House of Commons by a group of Liberal Members of Parliament. I was transferred back to Lingfield, and conditions improved. The only thing that kept me going under the grandstand was the blessed presence of a piano, where I was able to practise to my heart's content and make up a chamber quartet with three of the other prisoners. This did not improve my popularity. The war was going well for Germany and few of the internees wanted to risk having anything to do with anyone who had broken so ostentatiously with Hitler. The Battle of Dunkirk brought new orders for us. We were evacuated hurriedly to Liverpool, where several thousand of us from the various camps were crammed on board two ships for transportation to Canada. I found myself in the *Duchess of York*. The other was the *Arandora Star*.

We were very roughly handled at our destination, a barrack camp at Red Rock, near the Lake of Ontario. The few stoves gave practically no protection against the bitter winter cold, even though we kept up a day and night watch to keep them alight. A spilt cup of coffee froze on the ground where it fell. There were quite a number of deaths. By October of 1941 it was clear we would not survive another winter there, and we were moved into the casemates of Fort Henry, near Kingston. The vaults were easier to keep warm but dark and damp, and the only exercise place for 800 internees was the central courtyard, 35 paces long and 17 wide. Sanitary installations were non-existent, and our lavatory-cans had to be carted away every morning for disposal. The guards were so afraid of an epidemic that the whole place was liberally sprinkled with chlorate of lime. I used to call it our most chlorious year, but it was not a laughing matter. We got inflamed eyes, our teeth and nails worked loose and the soles of our shoes parted from the uppers. Conditions were about as bad as they could be.

It was in these circumstances that I experienced the culmination of the fearful obsession of twenty years. Germany and America were at war. Haushofer *triunfans*. I did not doubt that Hitler and his crew were toasting the accession of the 'Prussians of Asia' to their cause with the attack on Pearl Harbour. Now I knew for certain that Germany would be defeated. If there was to be anything left of my homeland I must make some attempt to place my knowledge at the disposal of the Allies before they pulverized the good and the bad alike. One day a correspondent of the Hearst Press named Keyhoe obtained permission to visit Fort Henry. I managed to have a few words with him in a corner. "I know your boss well," I told him. "Will you do me a small service?" Fortunately he recognized my name. I gave him a letter, which he slipped into his pocket. It was addressed to the American Secretary of State, Cordell Hull. A few days later it was on the desk of my Harvard Club friend, Franklin Delano Roosevelt. In it I offered to act as a political and psychological warfare adviser in the war against Germany.

The response was immediate. A large black limousine drew up at the gates of Fort Henry. With authority obtained through the American ambassador in Canada, Pierpont Moffat, from the Premier, Mr. Mackenzie King, the occupants asked to see prisoner No. 3026. My visitors were John Franklin Carter, an adviser to the President whom I had known in Germany, and his wife. "The President accepts your offer," he told me. "But first tell me how things are with you here." Although I spared them most of the details, I am afraid poor Mrs. Carter was reduced to tears. I told them it would be impossible to work from my present place of detention, which Carter fully appreciated, although he warned me that there would be a number of difficulties to overcome before the final details could be arranged.

It was several months before anything further happened, but one day an American agent called and took me away with him. It was

June 30, 1942, the anniversary of the Roehm Putsch. "I have a disappointment for you, Dr. Hanfstaengl," he said. "We cannot allow
you full freedom. We have, so to speak, borrowed you from the
British and they have insisted that you remain in custody." I was
so delighted to be getting away from Fort Henry that I raised no
objection. "I understand," I remarked, "I am the first piece of
reverse Lend-Lease." We drove to Carter's villa in Washington,
where my host's warm and friendly welcome wiped out the misery
of nearly three years. "Before we have lunch, Dr. Hanfstaengl," he
said, "I must introduce you to the guard the President has selected
in accordance with our arrangement with the British Government."
It was something of a cold douche, but I thought the sooner I met
the fellow the better. Carter ushered me into the next room, and
there stood Sergeant Egon Hanfstaengl of the United States Army.
We gave each other a bear-hug and I burst unashamedly into
tears.

My first interview almost brought the mission to an end there and
then. I was to be accommodated in an officer's bungalow in Fort
Belvoir. I was introduced to the commanding general and we talked
about this and that and the course of the war. During this conversation I got up and walked over to the big wall-map of the Atlantic.
"There is only one place for you to start the invasion of Europe,
General, and that is here," I said, putting my finger on Casablanca.
"It is the nearest point for your depots and you will be able to take
possession of North Africa and roll up Italy in no time." Now I
know nothing about military strategy and was just making what
I hoped was an intelligent comment. If I had let off a bomb the
general could not have been more appalled. He broke off the conversation without comment, left the bungalow, where the guards
were quietly tripled and Egon promptly removed. I heard afterwards that the general had thundered that I was a spy and obviously
knew all about Operation Torch. The matter went right up to the
President, who, I am told, laughed heartily, but suggested that it
might be better if I was accommodated elsewhere.

The pith of what follows has been told with great skill in
fictionalized form by John Franklin Carter himself in his book *The
Catoctin Conversation*, which he wrote under the name of Jay

Franklin. In it he puts into my mouth, as my contribution to an imaginary conversation with Roosevelt and Churchill during the height of the war, at a hunting-lodge in the Catoctin Mountains, the substance of the reports I wrote over the next two years.

I was, in fact, the first prisoner of State in the history of the United States. My actual hideout was an old-fashioned villa at Bush Hill, about twenty-five miles out of Washington, beyond Alexandria and on the way to the Civil War battlefield of Bull Run. Formerly a handsome brick house surrounded by a wide veranda, with the decaying remains of stables and slave quarters, I doubt if it had received any running repairs since the boom of 1850. It lay some way off the main road in 150 acres of oak, maple and beech forest. It had been selected by a Dr. Henry Field, one of my principal inter-locutors, who had driven out to find the two spinster ladies who owned it cowering behind a bush in order to escape the violence of a drunken butler. They were delighted to lease it to the Government for the duration of the requirement. In the main living-room, worn, rotted brocade peeled from the walls, drooping over the portraits of early American ancestors.

The rest of the household consisted of George Baer, a Jewish painter whom I had met once in the Munich artists' suburb of Schwabing before he fled the Nazis, and his American wife, the daughter of the well-known tenor, Putnam Griswold. The only drawback was that they considered the duties round the house some-what beneath their dignity. There were various domestic crises, and although we developed a complicated roster for doing the washing-up in turn, in the end they left. Our catering arrangements thereafter varied between the chaos and near-starvation caused by a drunken cook and periods of gluttony when order was restored. Certainly life was not dull. The best part of it was that Egon had been allowed to rejoin me.

I had a comfortable study and a huge and powerful radio, on which I used to listen to all the German broadcasts to help me with my reports. Every week six or seven typewritten sheets on the subject of current developments were on the President's desk. A constant stream of visitors from the Armed Forces and the State Department came to listen to my explanations of the internal stresses and strains of the Nazi régime. The only fly in the ointment was Dr. Field, with whom, I am afraid, I did not get on very well. He used to drive out at least twice a week and, quite apart from being one of those people who always thinks that they know better, took an undue pleasure in causing me minor annoyances. He took exception to the continued presence of Egon, and I heard from Carter that Lord Halifax had even voiced to the President his doubts concerning the effectiveness of my guard. Roosevelt was reported to me as retorting: "He may be Hanfstaengl's son, but he is also my sergeant." The President was also gracious enough to order a Steinway grand to be installed in the villa. It took Field nine months to arrange for a tuner to call, by which time it was found that the unfortunate gentleman in question was tuning angels' harps in heaven.

My reports covered a wide field. I was able to give the whole background of the Nazi hierarchy and intimate biographical details of its members. By reading between the lines of Hitler's or Goebbels' speeches I could deduce what criticisms were current in Germany for allied propaganda to exploit. My personal knowledge of the internal stresses of Hitler's Reich enabled me to counter a number of the wilder Allied suppositions. For example, in February 1943, when there had been no public reports of Hitler's activities for some time, the fact that it was Hermann Esser who had read a proclamation to the Old Guard of the Nazi Party on the twenty-third anniversary of its foundation, caused a widespread rumour that Hitler had been liquidated. I pointed out that he must still be alive, as I knew that his demise would be the signal for a revolution in Germany led by the *Reichswehr*, and of this there had been no sign. In May of the same year I must have been one of the first people to realize that there was truth in the German claim that the massacre of Polish officers in the Katyn forest had been carried out by the Russians, but, of course, this was an unwelcome warning at the time.

One of my suggestions on the psychological warfare front—it must be realized that I am speaking from memory and that I have been able to retain practically none of the documentation—concerned relations between Germany and Italy. I knew, from the correspondence of Francesco Crispi with Bismarck, that one of the tenets which this founder of Italian independence had laid down was that

Italy should never be brought into a situation involving conflict with England. Crispi was still a national hero even to the Fascists, and his dictum could be used to undermine the policy which was ruining his country. Towards the end of 1943 I predicted correctly that there was no sign of German internal political weakness and therefore it must be assumed that the military front would continue to hold. Goebbels had devised some skilful pro-Christian propaganda – the man's resource was infinite – to counter the announcements of the presence of Vishinsky as Russian representative at Algiers and allied support for Tito in Yugoslavia.

I soon sensed the real danger in the situation. Hitler was reaping the whirlwind he had sown. No one could deny the Allies their mood of righteous anger. What made me fear for the future of Europe was the mood of hate and revenge with which they seemed to be planning the total destruction of Germany. To me in 1943 and 1944 the formula of unconditional surrender meant the destruction of the last European bastions against Communism. And that seemed to me a fate even worse than Hitler. "You are playing Goebbels' game," I used to tell my visitors. "You seem to prefer razing Germany to the ground to giving her a chance to capitulate. If you think your carpets of bombs are going to make the Germans surrender unconditionally, it shows you know nothing of the people or their present leaders."

In September 1943 I wrote, in one of my appreciations to the President: ". . . To prolong this war means to lose it. Total military victory will mean nothing if it ends in a political fiasco. . . . There are only two possibilities. A union of the Christian Democratic forces, or a Communist Germany, with Stalin in Strasbourg. If a Christian Democratic Germany is preferred, then every day lost is a risk. Unless the Allies provide the Germans with the possibility of making a revolt against Hitler worth while, then the war will only lead to the exhaustion of both sides and a Soviet Republic will be set up in Berlin. The transition from swastika to hammer and sickle is only a short step. There is only one group in Germany capable of carrying out what Badoglio has done in Italy, and that is the group which, since 1933, has tried to restrain Hitler and wrest his power. They have already provided enough victims in the fight against the atheistic philosophy of the Nazis. The old Prussian *Reichswehr* represented by Hindenburg, Groener and Seeckt never accepted this Austrian corporal. Hitler has never trusted his generals and has dismissed all those who counselled caution. It is a completely false diagnosis to assume that they are his supporters. The precise opposite is true. . . . It is essential, therefore, to convince them of the fact that they are not all to be tarred with the same brush. . . ."

There is no satisfaction in being a prophet without honour. "If you insist on beating Germany before dealing with the Japanese," I used to tell my visitors, "you will see how Stalin will blackmail you in Europe. You must look beyond the enemies of today to the enemy of tomorrow. Get in touch with Raeder, Rundstedt or Kesselring. They are not Nazis. Make a Badoglio coup possible if you want to keep Europe intact. Schacht could be made Chancellor as a prelude to the introduction of a constitutional monarchy. Princess Viktoria Luise would be acceptable as regent." It was no good. My advice was suspect. I got very much the impression that the British, who saw my reports, countered my arguments. I did not give up. As late as the end of August 1944, after the invasion of France, I was still pressing the same views. "Germany will be defended to the last inch," I wrote to Roosevelt again, "as long as the demand for total surrender is maintained. The July 20 plot failed because there was no encouragement to possible supporters to seek an alternative to the fate that awaits them. Germany will not make peace this year. Unconditional surrender is the last life-belt Hitler and Goebbels have. . . ."

My self-appointed mission had failed, had been a failure for many months. In September 1944 Carter came out to see me with the inevitable news: "The presidential election is only six weeks ahead. His opponents in Washington are threatening that if you are not returned to the British authorities they will disclose your presence and mission here. You know what that would mean. It would give the press just the weapon they needed to tip the balance." That evening I was deeply depressed. Egon had requested overseas duty and was now in New Guinea, and if one of his charming letters had not arrived quite fortuitously, I think I would have ended things there and then. As it was, the suicidal mood passed. I put my papers in order and was ready for the guard when they came to take me away. My next stop was the Isle of Man.

A year later, after the war had ended in the way I had so despairingly predicted, the London *Daily Mail* published on its front page on September 14, 1945, a list one of its correspondents had found at Gestapo headquarters, of all those to be immediately liquidated if the invasion of Britain in 1940 succeeded. There were many illustrious names in the roster, but figuring modestly half-way down was that of Dr. Ernst Hanfstaengl. By this time I had been transferred to a camp at Stanmore, near London. My attention was drawn to the newspaper by some German-Jewish fellow-prisoners, who congratulated me and said that it could not be long now before I was released. I showed the copy to the head of the intelligence staff at the camp and managed to get a letter out to my solicitor, Kenneth Brown, drawing his attention to it. He tried to get some action, but my captors were apparently still not prepared to appreciate the inference.

In the spring of 1946 I was transported to Germany and kept for another six months in an internment camp at Recklinghausen. My resistance to the frustrations and miseries of the previous dozen years was almost at an end. My blood pressure dropped from 160 to 45. My big bones weighed just under ten stone. On September 3, 1946, I was released, with 15.40 marks in my pocket for a third-class ticket to Munich and five marks subsistence money. Germany was a mass of ruins, the currency hopelessly inflated. Since then we have experienced the sort of feverish economic recovery I remember from the Weimar Republic in the late 'twenties. I hope with all my heart this is not where I came in. My one desire is to live long enough to see a Germany, and indeed a world, where Hitlers are no longer possible.

AFTERWORD

ERNST FRANZ SEDGWICK HANFSTAENGL
(February 11, 1887–November 6, 1975)
My father as I see him now – nearly twenty years after his death.

When I was a toddler I was struck by my father's voice. My mother later told me, "Whenever you heard him coming home, you flinched, looked apprehensive, and whispered: 'Papa is coming.' "

When I was a boy I was fairly frequently struck by his hand and his leather belt for not obeying his injunctions precisely enough. But I was also struck, and increasingly so, by his immense charm and warmth – and, as I grew older, by his vast knowledge, which he delighted in imparting: "Boy, who knows how long I shall live. Drain me, suck me dry as though you were a sponge!" Thus he was one of my two greatest teachers, and certainly the one who had the most profound psychological effect on me.

Then there was his piano playing, which was literally extraordinary. One of his teachers, August Schmid-Lindner, said that in his long career as a pedagogue he had "never known anyone as *naturally* at home on the keyboard as this Ernst Hanfstaengl." Indeed, my father would readily and flawlessly play short pieces in any key, and in any style. One of his pièces de résistance was doing "Hänschen Klein" à la Bach, Mozart, Beethoven, Schumann, and Wagner, and he once fooled a knowledgeable audience with this trick in his grand apartment at Pariserplatz No. 3 in Berlin. He announced that a student of musicology in Vienna had discovered a totally unknown waltz by Josef Lanner, had sent him the manuscript copy, and that now he had the pleasure of playing this long-lost little gem. It was a delight. When he had finished playing, people crowded around the piano to look at the "Lanner waltz manuscript." What they saw was: J. S. BACH, PRAELUDIUM XII.

I recall how my father had practised Praeludium XII and suddenly said: "If Bach had been born a hundred years later, he'd have composed it like this. . . ." (Wilhelm Backhaus once said to my father: "Some things you play better than any of us: Schubert songs, Strauss waltzes, and military marches.")

Inevitably, we must come to the politically and historically significant aspects. My father *loved* his father, who was a Bavarian Bismarckian and a *Kulturkämpfer*. And despite the grievous disappointments dealt him by the House of Wittelsbach, my father remained at heart a monarchist. He had hoped to see Hitler as *Reichsverweser*, doing for Germany what Francisco Franco did in fact do for Spain: reintroducing the monarchy, albeit a constitutional one. My father favoured the English model. This accounts for his cultivating a relationship with the House of Hohenzollern: we not only had Prince August Wilhelm (the son of the kaiser who espoused the brownshirt) as a houseguest many times, but also the present head of the House of Hohenzollern, grandson of the last kaiser, Prince Louis Ferdinand of Prussia, was a paying guest in "Villa Tiefland" for six or eight weeks. (The young prince was, at that time, a bit of a hellion. My mother, with her calm, natural authority, told him: "Imperial Highness, please take at least one proper meal with us every day and do not come home after midnight. You need some sleep." Prince Louis Ferdinand conformed, and his mother phoned mine after his stay and said: "I have not seen my son looking so well in years. However did you do it? Bless you!")

My father spent all of World War One in New York, which meant that he lacked the *Fronterlebnis* and was therefore never fully accepted by the Nazis, most of whom had in common that "experience of fighting at the front." Two of his three brothers died: the youngest of typhus in Paris in 1914, the middle – his favourite – killed in action in 1915. His eldest brother had only a daughter, and my father suddenly realized that it was now up to him to produce a son to carry on the name. This drove him rather precipitously into marriage, an institution for which, with all his polygamous impulses, he was eminently unsuited.

Upon his return to Germany, my father found his beloved homeland impoverished, hungering (the British blockade after the armistice still had its effect), and, above all, *humiliated*. The candid brutality of Brennus' *Vae victis* would have been much less psychologically humiliating and infuriating to the Germans than was the sanctimonious and hypocritical war-guilt clause of the Versailles Treaty, which placed the *moral* responsibility for starting World War One entirely on the Central Powers, Germany, and Austria. One might say, without being guilty of terrible simplification, that without the untenable Versailles Treaty there would have been no Hitler.

We now reach my father's first experience of Hitler, which he describes in these memoirs. All I can add is that my father, having heard

Hitler speak, was convinced that this man would be the future leader of Germany. His eldest brother, Edgar, with whom he disagreed about virtually everything, scoffed at the idea that "this mountebank, this ridiculous charlatan" could ever amount to anything. (Thus our family, like many others in Germany, was politically split: my parents were Nazis, while my uncle Edgar was a founding member of the German Democratic Party in Munich in 1919, and a candidate for the *Staatspartei* – successor to the Democratic Party – against Hitler as late as 1932.)

The ensuing period – Hitler's slow and tortuous rise to power and the early years of the Third Reich – is described by my father in this book. I would therefore like to leap ahead to a chapter that he, for reasons I hope to make clear, rather skimped on: World War Two.

I, the boy who had romped on the floor with "Uncle Dolf" and had loved him as the most imaginative and histrionically potent playmate one could wish for – I, the ex–Hitler Youth, who had now become "an Englishman by aspiration," was shipped off to the U.S., the land of my birth, on September 2, 1939, aboard the Canadian Pacific liner *Empress of Britain*. That same evening, my father was arrested by two agents from Scotland Yard "on His Majesty's prerogative" as an enemy alien.

My father had arranged for me to enter Harvard, his old alma mater. My career there was, to put it kindly, checkered and incomplete. On my twentieth birthday, February 3, 1941, I enlisted in the U.S. Army Air Corps. But that's *my* story, relevant here only in that my enlistment, widely reported in the press, endangered my father in his internment camps, dominated as they were by Nazis who regarded him as a traitor anyway.

Eventually John Franklin Carter, one of FDR's brain-trusters, arranged for my father's transfer from British custody in Canada to U.S. custody. (I call it the first and possibly only piece of reverse lend-lease during World War Two.) This was the beginning of the so-called S-Project, so named because my father was then known as Doctor Sedgwick. It was certainly one of the most fascinating, albeit largely ineffectual, enterprises of World War Two. Having been assigned to it myself for a period of nine months as a staff sergeant U.S.A. and my father's prison chaser, bodyguard, and private secretary, I can furnish a few significant glimpses.

Even before his flight from Germany my father had warned: "The way we're going there will be war. . . . America will again be against us – and we shall lose again!" Once the war had started, he was convinced that Germany would be defeated; if he ever had any doubts at all, they were dispelled when Hitler attacked the Soviet Union. Consequently he reasoned that the best service he could render his beloved fatherland was to hasten the inevitable defeat. Thus he agreed to furnish the U.S. government with information on the characters and inner workings of the Nazi ruling clique and to act as adviser on psychological warfare and on basic geopolitical questions. Like Admiral King, though for somewhat different reasons, my father consistently urged that the war in the Pacific be given priority: "If the war in Europe ends and you're still stuck with your war against Japan, your allies will arrange matters as suits *them* and not necessarily *you*."

As a result of my father's contributions and his clear advocacy of specifically American interests, U.S. representatives at the various allied conferences were often better informed and no longer so readily deferred to British Imperial experience. The British did not like that and, during 1943, had Ambassador Lord Halifax twice request the return of my father to their own custody. President Roosevelt denied the request both times on the grounds that Dr. S. was being useful, ultimately to *all* the Allies, and that moving him would impair this usefulness. When FDR's second refusal was about to be given to Lord Halifax, we three guards at the S-Project were instructed to stand twenty-four-hour watches until further notice, because it was considered possible that the British might try to kidnap their prisoner! (I could hardly believe that such suspicion could exist between the best of allies!)

Katyn. Within twenty-four hours of the first news of this heinous massacre, Dr. S. knew that it had been perpetrated by the Soviets: "The Nazis would never dare offer safe conduct to anyone willing to come and look at the evidence if they didn't have the goods. And look at the reaction of the Polish Exile Government in London!" His advice: "Of course you can't allow Goebbels to drive a wedge between you and your Russian ally. But put this in your desk drawers, and when the Germans are defeated, open those drawers and show the American people that the Soviets are no better than the Nazis." (This advice, which was aimed at what Grand Admiral Dönitz eventually offered to the Western Allies [give us gasoline etc. and we'll drive the Russians back to where they belong], shows that, despite his vast knowledge and startling perspicacity, my father never really understood the workings of a democracy: such abrupt reversal of policy is possible only under authoritarian regimes. Nevertheless it would have been in the interest of the U.S. to have been less euphoric and trusting with regard to "Uncle Joe" Stalin.)

The Badoglio coup against Mussolini. When my father heard the *annuncio di grave importanza* on our superb radio at Bush Hill and noted that they were playing not "Giovinezza" but the "Marcia reale," and that the *Reichsrundfunk* made no mention of the events in Italy, he concluded, within twenty-four hours, that this had caught the Germans totally unprepared. He now bombarded Washington with memos: "Here is your chance! Get from Sicily [where the U.S. had military positions] into Southern Italy! Establish an unopposed beachhead!" The memos went on for ten days. Then we heard a short, impressive speech by Hitler, and my father wrote a final memo: "Now you can forget about it. The Germans have reacted." The result was Salerno, Rapido River, Anzio, which might all have been avoided.

My father took all this extremely seriously. He was almost more concerned about the GIs than about the German soldiers. One of the other guards and I habitually tried to calm my father with phrases like "Relax," "Don't take it so hard," "Things aren't all that bad." One day he exploded at us in German: "*Ihr tut Euch leicht! Versteht Ihr denn nicht, dass ich hier* Hochverrat *begehe!*" ("It's all very easy for you! Don't you understand that I am committing *high treason* here!") This was an important revelation for me. I suddenly realized just how inwardly torn my father was.

After the war, when I returned from two years of useful but unheroic service in the Southwest Pacific, I tried to locate my father, who had been rather unceremoniously dumped by the U.S. government in 1944 – like the proverbial squeezed orange – and returned to British custody. I had cocktails with a lieutenant colonel at the Mayflower Hotel in Washington and asked him his opinion of my father's contribution. He began by saying he was only a major at the time, fit for little more than "emptying wastebaskets." He had read my father's memos and found them convincing, but he found the counterarguments of the generals equally convincing. The Pentagon rather expected German resistance to collapse as soon as the Rhine was crossed and the war reached the German heartland. My father, specifically asked about this, warned: "Beware of a false analogy with 1914–18! This is a truly revolutionary setup and you must be prepared for some tough, last-ditch, counterattacking resistance even after you've reached German soil." The colonel ended by saying that "if your father's advice had been taken, fifty thousand American casualties could have been avoided."

Eventually my father was repatriated and "de-Nazified." He was even considered by some of the Free Democrats for further political work in Germany. But nothing came of this, and my father spent the rest of his life enjoying the present and suffering from the past: endlessly lacerating himself about what went wrong and what he might have done to avert the disaster triggered by his erstwhile friend Adolf Hitler.

EGON HANFSTAENGL
Munich
March 1994